Choice-Centered R

Choice-Centered

Relating

and the Tarot

Gail Fairfield

With a
Foreword by James Wanless

SAMUEL WEISER, INC.
York Beach, Maine

Dedication

For Deb, without whom . . .

First published in 2000 by
Samuel Weiser, Inc.
P. O. Box 612
York Beach, ME 03910-0612
www.weiserbooks.com

Library of Congress Cataloging-in-Publication Data

Fairfield, Gail.
    Choice-centered relating and the tarot / Gair Fairfield.
      p. cm.
    Includes bibliographical references and index.
    ISBN 1-57863-143-2 (pbk. : alk. paper)
    1. Tarot. 2. Interpersonal relations—Miscellanea.
    3. Choice (Psychology)—Miscellanea. I. Title.
    BF1879.T2 F34 2000
    133.3'2424—dc21   00–029006

EB
Typeset in 10.5/13 Sabon
Cover design by Ed Stevens
Cover art is The Lovers card from various tarot decks. *The Universal Waite Tarot, Tarot of
Marseilles, Tarot of the Spirit,* and *Ukiyoe Tarot* decks reproduced by permission of U. S.
Games Systems, Inc., Stamford, CT. 06902. Copyrights © 1990, 1996, 1993 respectively by
U. S. Games Systems, Inc., Stamford, CT. Further reproduction prohibited; *Tarot of
Marseilles* © 1996 reproduced by permission of U. S. Games Systems/Carta Mundi; *The
Voyager Tarot* copyright © 1984 James Wanless and Ken Knutson, used by kind permission
of Merrill-West Publishing, Carmel, CA; *Motherpeace Round Tarot* deck is copyright ©
1981, 1983 Motherpeace, used by kind permission of Karen Vogel and Vicki Noble;
Medicine Woman Tarot by Carol Bridges copyright © 1989 Earth Nation, used by kind permission; further reproduction of any of these decks is prohibited.

PRINTED IN THE UNITED STATES OF AMERICA

07 06 05 04 03 02 01 00
8 7 6 5 4 3 2 1

The paper used in this publication meets the minimum requirements of the American
National Standard for Information Sciences—Permanence of Paper
for Printed Library Materials Z39.48-1992 (R1997).

Contents

PART TWO: ISSUES AND EXAMPLES

PART THREE: TAROT INTERPRETATIONS

Foreword

by James Wanless, Ph.D.

Above the portal to Delphi in Greece, the greatest oracle of the ancient world, it was inscribed, "Know Thyself." That is, in fact, what oracles like tarot are meant to do—give us insight into ourselves and our lives. Unfortunately, oracles have become debased into fortune-telling. Perhaps, in the medieval world, it was somewhat possible to make predictions, for change was not so prevalent. This is not true in today's world, where we change domiciles, partners, jobs, lifestyles, and identities with frequent regularity. How can we predict anything in this changing 21st-century world? We can't, nor should we. As Gail Fairfield shows in this book, tarot is truly a tool for revealing options and possibilities about ourselves. In so doing, we are empowered, and not enslaved by the cards. We are freed and not fated. The Choice-Centered Tarot approach evolves tarot into its rightful position as a "fortune creation" process.

The modern world is all about choice. In fact, a newly emergent human dilemma is the multiplying variety of choices we face. How do we make our choices? Often we make decisions for ourselves according to how we see others choose to live their lives. We follow these models of behavior, almost unconsciously. *Choice-Centered Relating and the Tarot* starts out by having us look at how we determine our choices in life by our models. In this enlightened tarot process of reading the cards, we must first clarify the model we want to follow. Right away, we get to the source for making better decisions.

In this revolutionary tarot practice, the cards only assist us in our choices by giving us insight, which is information. Tarot is an information resource. With that knowledge, we are better prepared to make better decisions. If the cards reveal things that we don't want to see, then we are prepared to prevent and preempt them, which we have the power to do. If we like what we see, then we are inspired to fulfill their promise. We have the choice to either say yes or no to the cards. Information is power, so tarot is ultimately an empowerment tool.

And since it is information that comes to us through the mystery and surprise of selecting facedown cards, we break through our habitual ways of thinking about ourselves and life. It's truly an "aha!" game that frees our mind to explore a whole menu of possibilities. The cards show us a new way of thinking about ourselves that unlocks the box of our own perceptual limitations and narrowness.

Choice-Centered Relating and the Tarot thus places us in responsibility for ourselves. We choose how we respond to the cards. This is so different from the old world way of doing tarot, where we place the power over our lives in the hands of the cards or a card "reader." Tarot is not a magic bullet that solves our issues for us. In fact, when we consult the tarot, we are choosing a process for taking more responsibility for ourselves.

Central to our quests are the questions we ask. What we are given in this book is a complete set of questions to ask about ourselves and our relationships, and a methodology for asking questions. Without good questions, there are no good answers. As Albert Einstein once said, "The formulation of the question is far more important than the answer." Choice-Centered Tarot and choice-centered living is question based. Tarot becomes, in this approach, a means for developing our curiosity, the cardinal principle of Choice-Centered Tarot for successful living and relating. From questing for answers through our curiosity, we gain experience, all leading to deeper wisdom.

In this book, you will find the organizational structure of a tarot deck and a wealth of interpretations for each card. We are given, in a very real sense, a road map for how to live the complete life. Very few such personal maps exist, and tarot may be the most exquisite, and appropriate for the 21st century. In our world today of change, uncertainty, speed, complexity, diversity, and even chaos, how do we make correct decisions to govern our lives? The only way is through our intuition, an immediate and comprehensive little feeling that points the way. Tarot is an intuition tool for tapping our natural intuitive genius, so although the cards give a general map of life, each of us must intuit what the card means to us personally. By following our own intuition catalyzed by the cards, we are living authentically. In our authenticity we find our way to the ultimately fulfilling life.

Picture-symbols, as in the tarot, have always been triggers for intuition, new ideas, and powerful perspectives. As Aristotle wrote, "The soul never thinks without a picture." The power of the tarot's Magician archetype, representing our ability to manifest and materialize anything, is in the power of the image, which strikes our imagination. Picture or metaphoric thinking through tarot is, thus, a tried and true way for innovation, particularly for creating our own life.

As we see in *Choice-Centered Relating and the Tarot,* the various relationship readings provide us a map for what we must do in order to create the conditions for successful partnering. But the map, itself, does not get us there. We must walk the talk and take action on the suggested journey. As it is said, "A vision without action is a hallucination." Enlightened tarot is about acting upon the wisdom of the cards. We must meet the universe halfway by our own steps to co-create what we really want in life.

It has been said that "success is an inside job." So true, and that is what tarot gives us, an innerself formula for doing our best. There are no guarantees in life about succeeding, but at least we can give it all we have. In the Choice-Centered way, all the readings are designed to tap the gifts we have within us. And I bet that if each of us truly expressed our inner resources, we would live a rich life, full of love, friendship, and synergy.

The beauty of the tarot is that the images have the power to inspire. They move us into action if we have them before our eyes. I always keep the cards out that appear in my readings to be reminded of what needs to be done. In fact, I will never repeat the same reading over again unless I have acted on the previous reading.

And the so-called "negative" cards are to be seen as positive catalysts in this approach. Such cards are wake-up calls, they alert us to a lesson that must be learned. I always say that these "caca" cards are fertilizer for growth, so compost them. Use the negatives to positively move through your obstacles and challenges. In such a way, tarot is again a wondrous teacher and growth path.

As the cards we select are always changing, they mirror back to us our own changing consciousness and life circumstances. The cards keep us on our toes, constantly reminding us to keep up, stay flex-able, be change-able, and response-able. As we change and adapt, we grow. As we change, we survive. As we change, we keep alive. The map of tarot is fluid, ever-changing, as we must be.

This highly conscious approach to tarot transforms it from gypsy-like hocus-pocus into a real spiritual and personal growth practice. It opens our minds and hearts, and confers responsibility and power into our own hands. High level tarot is about helping us be all that we are meant to be and can be. Tarot is a rich psychology that says through its 78 cards that we have at least 78 different aspects of ourselves that we need to consciously live out in order to be whole—happy, healthy, holy, and wealthy. The purpose of tarot is for us to see and then become all of ourselves through its symbolic and archetypal picture story of our human journey.

Life is about growing, and relationships are the growing grounds. There is no greater path than working through relationships to discover the divine. Through the divination process of tarot, we do just that, providing we play with it as originally intended. *Choice-Centered Relating and the Tarot* restores this venerable oracular art to a way of knowing ourselves, guiding ourselves, and realizing ourselves through the mirror and magic of relationships.

Preface

I wrote this book because I love the tarot and its applications, and because I am continually intrigued and amazed by human interactions. Reading the book will be useful to you if are curious about relating, or if you are interested in the tarot. If you're fascinated by both, so much the better!

You can experience the information in *Choice-Centered Relating and the Tarot* from two different perspectives. If you are a big-picture person, you will probably want to read the book straight through to gain an understanding of the larger concepts and philosophy, and then utilize the specific sections and techniques that are meaningful to you. If, on the other hand, you prefer to consider the details first, you might want to jump right in to the chapters and topics that immediately catch your attention. If you use this approach, the overall structure of the book will emerge for you over time. There is no "right" way to absorb this material. It's your choice.

Having said that, let me invite you into a world of ideas that I've been developing for nearly thirty years. During that time, I've studied the tarot, taught classes about the tarot, and consulted with clients using the tarot. I've written books and articles about the tarot and presented lectures at conferences. I've used the tarot on the radio and TV. Through it all, I've sought ways to help people understand that the tarot is a useful tool, not a spooky mystery, and that they can utilize it to uncover insights about their lives and choices. My focus has never been "fate is out to get you or bless you." Instead, I've worked with myself and others to help us all remember that we do have the ultimate freedom and responsibility to create the futures that we want for ourselves.

In all this time, I've found that people ask more about relating than about any other topic. It doesn't seem to matter whether the relationships in question are romantic, family, or business connections. It doesn't even seem to matter whether the initial topic of concern is money or career or health or spirituality. Somehow, when all is said and done, the quality of our relationships significantly influences the quality of our lives.

This book is my best effort at passing on the tool of the tarot as it applies to the life theme of relating. Thanks for joining me.

—GAIL FAIRFIELD

Acknowledgments

Everyone I know has, in some way, contributed to this book because everyone I know has, in some way, related to me. I thank you all.

Specifically, I appreciate Deb Clark, Kay Ries, and John Hoslett who have been important teachers for me. I'm grateful to my parents, John and Betty Fairfield, to my sisters, Linda Smith, Gwen Vitzthum, and Janet Figge, and to my daughter, Sara Clark, for their forbearance and support. Additionally, I value Susie, Susan, Nan, Annette, Shana, Pat, Kris, Cassie, and Jane who have been especially giving of their time and energy when my learning curve about relating has been steep.

PART ONE

Core Concepts

I was born with a deep curiosity about people and about Universal Truth. As a result, I've spent most of this life exploring the frameworks of human behavior, philosophy, and religion that might give me some insight into the "nature of things." My quest took me into Psychology and Education, into two decades of experimentation with everything from the Ouija board to astrology to Jane Roberts' Seth material to the tarot, into two years of intense training in Neuro-Linguistic Programming (NLP) and into my own therapy and personal growth. It's been exciting and frustrating, profound and fun, stimulating and confusing, and ultimately rewarding, just like life.

For a long time, I thought that I would find the one system or way of thinking that would integrate everything into one neat package called the truth. What I've discovered is, indeed, a package, but it isn't very tidy; instead, the "nature of things" seems to be quite organic, ever evolving and changing. In fact, it seems that the only constant in the universe is change.

1

Choice-Centered Living:
Truth as Change

C hange is constant. Or is it? Take a moment and think about things that never change—despite the influences of time, nature, or human intervention. Write down or mentally name everything that comes to mind. Now, ask yourself: "Do these things really always stay the same? Is there any force that will affect them?"

When you answer that question, you'll probably end up with the same short list that most of the people in my workshops generate:

- Love;

- Death;

- Spirit;

- The life-force;

- The natural laws on Earth.

As you read this short list, I can almost hear you saying: "Even these things change—at least our understanding of them does." I agree. It does seem to me that, although love, death, or spirit may exist as eternal truths, every person, generation, and culture experiences and describes them in unique ways. And, over time, every person, generation, and culture gains new perceptions of the truth.

Just for a minute, imagine that the truth is in a room surrounded by doors, windows, and audio equipment. At a given time, depending on the doors you open, the windows you look through, and the sounds you hear, your experience of the truth is structured in a unique way. You form a model of it in your mind and heart. Your model is a perfectly valid representation of the truth in that moment. So are the models of anyone else who might be peeking into the "truth room." Ultimately there are an infinite number of models or representations of the truth.

Now, imagine further that any time anyone forms such a representation, it has an impact on the possible models that anyone else might consider. If someone forms a really exciting model and is charismatic about describing it, a whole religion or philosophy can be born. This worldview is, in turn, another valid representation of the truth.

If you really want to stretch your mind, imagine that every time someone interacts with the truth, it changes! If we (you and I, plants, animals, rocks, stars) are all part of the living plasma or ooze of the universe, by growing and maintaining, expanding and contracting, questioning and answering we not only participate in creating models of the truth, we participate in creating and changing the truth itself.

So what's real? What's reliable? If the universe is flexible and evolving, if our understanding of it can change with the creation of each new model, if *the truth* itself is constantly changing, how can we guide ourselves through the seemingly sloppy chaos of living? How do we find a grounding or a center in the middle of it all? How can we experience the constancy of change as enchanting instead of terrifying? Well, given human frailty, we align ourselves with our favorite models of the inexplicable.

The following stories about four ordinary people illustrate two contrasting models of the truth: the models of fate and of choice. It won't take you long to discover my preference. If you agree with me, the rest of this book will make sense to you.

The Model of Fate

Sam is a realtor who recently visited a psychic to find out what fate had in store for him. As it turned out, she was incredibly accurate. She told him about his past and predicted several things about his future. Her historical information was on the mark and one of her prophecies has already come true. Sam is excited about some of her projections and nervously worried about others. He's waiting to discover whether the rest of her divinations will unfold as she's described them. Since some of her forecasts extend out for two or three years, he has a while to wait. When the waiting is over, he'll know one thing for sure. He'll know whether she's a reliable psychic. He'll either be amazed by her talent or disappointed in her abilities. What he may not know is what he could have done to change the course of his life. He may not know anything new about himself or his potential. He may not feel empowered when considering his options. If he believes that the future is locked in and that his biggest challenge is to find an accurate oracle, Sam is living by a model of the truth called "fate."

Maria manages a shoe store that is part of a chain. Every month, she receives computer printouts from her district manager about her past month's performance. She also receives bulletins that set her goals for the upcoming month. She posts these forecasts so that she and her employees can work hard to make the computer predictions come true. If road construction, a nearby festival, or freakish weather affect their ability to live up to the computer's expectations, Maria feels nervous and insecure. On the other hand, if her figures match the projections precisely, she's elated. Month after month, she wonders whether her sales will fulfill the quota. Month by month, she strives to make sure they do. In Maria's case, the oracle comes from logic and science instead of intuition. However, the effect is no less devastating. Maria is not adapting the computer's goals to fit her own situation. She's not asking why they are struggling to meet external expectations instead of adapting to local circumstances. She's not curious about how they can improve service or satisfy customers. She just wants to make the future unfold as planned. As long as she's locked in to this future, she is also living by fate.

When we operate from the point of view of fate, we're always waiting to find out what will happen. As we wait, we can consult oracles of the intuitive sort in an attempt to predict the future. We can also make logical projections, supported by computers or intellectual reasoning, about what will happen. In both cases, we are trying to find out what will unfold so that we can be prepared for it. In some instances, we even create self-fulfilling prophecies. And in all cases, if we operate from a fate-filled perspective, we're powerless. Even if the psychic or computer fortune-tellers are accurate, we are still trapped by their predictions and may go through our lives looking for better and better forecasters, while personally making fewer and fewer choices.

The Model of Choice

Susan, a secretary at a small manufacturing company, has been offered a position in the sales department. In considering the change of work and the move to commission-based pay, she's concerned about its impact on her life. Her existing job demands about 40 to 45 hours a week and she knows that, in the new job, she would be expected to work up to 50 or even 60 hours weekly. Her parents and friends are impressed with the offer and are encouraging her to take the new job. She isn't sure that she wants to sacrifice any of her other priorities. In addition to her job, she's considering these factors of her existing lifestyle:

> *Fun and hobbies*: movies and coffee bars, sailing, travel;
> *Personal growth*: church activities, occasional workshops;
> *Contributions*: volunteer work at library
> *Relationships*: several close friends, parents and one sister,
>   Tom (currently dating), future partner, children some day;
> *Health and fitness*: exercise at gym.

Susan realizes that she has a choice. Just because an opportunity exists, it doesn't mean that she must take it. What she wants is more important than what her parents or friends want for her. If she takes the job, she'll have to cut back on her volunteer work and begin to exercise at home (instead of at the gym) in order to make more time for work. If she takes it, she'll know it's because she wants the increased money and the excitement of learning something new— not just because she wants to please her parents! If she doesn't take the job, however, she can maintain her current priorities and avoid upsetting her lifestyle. In that case, she'll also be deciding for herself. She is making her decision from a model of the truth called "choice."

Joe is a therapist who just got some devastating news. He has found out that David, someone with whom he is beginning to fall in love, has AIDS. He's nearly overwhelmed by his feelings: fear, confusion, uncertainty . . . and love. David wants to continue their relationship, but he understands that the new information is upsetting to Joe. Joe is not quite certain what to do, but he is sure that he can decide how he wants to respond to the situation. He knows that he can break up with David and retreat from the pain. He can also back out of the romance and try to become "just friends" with David. Or, he can continue to practice safe sex while exploring the relationship. He knows that it's up to him. He can work from the model of truth called "choice."

Switching Between the Models of Fate and Choice

Sam, Maria, Susan, and Joe have already indicated their orientations with regard to fate and choice. What would happen if they switched models?

If Sam opts to live by choice, he can still visit his psychic to find out the probable direction of his future. He can see her insights as a description of what will happen if he continues on his present path. If he likes that future, he can continue with current behavior, confident that he's creating it. However, if he's not pleased when he glimpses parts of the future, he can choose to change something in his own behavior or attitudes. Instead of being at the mercy of the prediction, he can choose actions and reactions that will create alternatives.

When Maria receives her computer printouts, she can use them as guideposts that let her know where she and her business are probably headed. If the results look good and seem reasonable to her, she can continue on with her current procedures. If she knows that the road construction or the street fair are coming up, she can personally adjust her expectations. When the weather changes, she can adapt her plans. On the other hand, if she doesn't agree with the computer projections, she can decide what to change and how to give feedback to her district manager. Instead of being ruled by the projections, she can use them as guidelines that can help her make appropriate choices.

If Susan decides to live by fate, she can see the job offer as something that she "should" pursue. She can think that, because it's arrived, it's "meant to be." Later, if the job becomes too stressful and parts of her life start to fall apart, she can rage at the fates for assigning her the impossible task of "doing it all." Without questioning her options or changing any of her other priorities, she may end up sick or completely exhausted—and cursing her luck!

Joe can decide that the fates are out to get him. He can think that, just when he finally finds someone to love, AIDS is destroying his happiness. He can struggle with the unfairness of it all, rage at David, and throw temper tantrums. Or he can decide that, because David is in his life, he's "supposed" to take care of him, that somehow rescuing David is his personal mission. Ultimately, Joe can take on the burden of relating to David with a sense of noble self-sacrifice and acceptance of his fate.

These examples may seem obvious—and my bias toward the model of choice is also obvious, to say the least! But it's amazingly easy to fall into the trap of fate-oriented thinking. It's incredibly seductive to think that we can have solid predictions about the future—even negative ones. For most of us, it's easier to celebrate or bemoan our fate than it is to take responsibility for our choices. This is probably because, when we think we know what's going to happen, we feel more in control of the chaos—even if we don't like it. However, I think it's actually much more empowering to live by choice than it is to succumb to fate.

As humans, we can choose how we want to act and react as we open doors, look through windows, and listen to the sounds of the truth. We can choose to reshape or heal the experiences of the past, to enhance or deepen the present, and to deliberately trigger or structure the future. If we are centered in choice, or *choice-centered*, instead of clinging to constancy, perhaps we can navigate through the chaos of the ever-changing universe. That's my little window on the truth. I hope it's useful to you.

Choices We Can't Consciously Control

Surely we can't choose everything in our lives, can we? No. There are layers of choice that regularly impact my life and yours. At your core are the choices made by your soul. These include the time, place, date, and socio-economic context of your birth, as well as the configuration of genetics that you inherited from your parents. These choices are beyond your conscious control, because, aside from genetic engineering, there's not much that you can change about your birth patterns. You can only learn to accept them.

Equally unchangeable are the choices that you couldn't make for yourself when you were younger. As a child, you were dependent on others for your survival. You were restricted by your age and immaturity, so that the element of choice seemed largely lacking for many years. In some cases, the choices that others made for you were healthy and protective. At other times, their choices dulled your spirit, hurt your body, or limited your self-expression. Unfortunately, just as you can't choose different birth circumstances, you can't really undo the choices that others have made for you in the past. You can only celebrate the positives and heal from the negatives.

At your current stage of life, others may still be making choices that concern you. If your best friend suddenly chooses to ignore you, you feel it! If your mother screams at you over the phone, you react. If my partner accepts a job two thousand miles away without telling me, I raise some questions. If someone is raped, mugged, or killed, we all feel enraged and incredulous about it. Although these present-day scenarios may seem different from our birth or childhood circumstances, they still describe situations in which choices have been made that are out of our control. Predicted or not, these kinds of decisions have an impact on us. We can chalk them up to fate. We can whine, cajole, beg, threaten, manipulate, or negotiate in order to get others to change. But we can't really be sure of directing or affecting someone else's behavior or situation. No matter what we do, there is no absolute guarantee that fate—in the form of another person—will do what we want.

Choices We Can Consciously Control

What's left? What can we control? Ourselves. Essentially, we can consciously act and react as we learn to use our inborn abilities, disabilities, and attributes creatively. The word "consciously" is important because it implies the personal awareness and responsibility of choice-centered living. When we want to create a new direction, we can consciously act, as we deliberately make decisions that set things in motion. When we need to respond to world events or to someone else's behavior, we can consciously react to the situation. All in all, what we can do is to choose our own self-concepts, emotions, thought processes, and behavior. And, the more choices we have in each situation, the more we can influence what happens.

Sam's case is a good example. Like many people, Sam is a single, working parent. He's hired 18-year-old Tina to watch his two children for the summer. For the third time in two weeks, Tina has called at the last minute to say she isn't coming. Tina always apologizes and has a good excuse, but it's still frustrating. Sam scrambles around to find another sitter, but ends up staying home from work. If this happens too often, he knows he'll feel the pinch in his commission check. He's thought of firing Tina, but the children adore her. He feels trapped. It seems that his only choice is to put up with Tina, miss work, and deal with the lack of money. More choices would help.

Maria's district manager, Bob, is just plain inefficient. He takes three meetings to accomplish what could have been done in one; at every meeting, she sees ways to get more done, faster. He also takes forever to implement the things he promises. Last month, he promised Maria a raise, but it still hasn't appeared in her paycheck. While she knows that she'll eventually get her pay raise, the whole situation makes her blood boil. In fact, as Maria simmers, her blood pressure is mounting. Her doctor has warned her not to get so upset, but she doesn't know how else to react. She needs more choices.

Susan has now been dating Tom for about six months. He's been generous and is eager to form a committed relationship with her. Susan likes him a lot, but feels uncomfortable with his persistent criticism of her. He loses his temper frequently and seems to find something wrong with whatever she's doing, thinking, or feeling. Since Susan cringes and feels ashamed every time Tom criticizes her, she's become fearful and defensive around him. She tries hard to live up to his standards, but, no matter what she does, she's afraid that she isn't good enough. She's tried to discuss the issue with him; he thinks it's her problem. Their conversations only underline her feeling of inadequacy. At the moment, Susan feels limited in her choices. She can put up with Tom's behavior and feel bad, or she can break up with him. Neither of these options appeals to her. More choices would be useful.

Joe has decided to become more involved with David, despite the fact that David has AIDS and is beginning to need quite a bit of care. Because Joe is self-employed, he has the freedom to rearrange his schedule in order to be available to David. He can't afford to completely abandon his work, however, and David is needing more and more attention. Joe feels guilty for every hour he spends away from David. He feels equally guilty for every hour he spends away from his office and his clients. Wherever he is, he's thinking about the things he isn't doing in the other situation. Although David is already ill and may eventually die, the current state of affairs could easily continue for a year or two. Joe feels ready to explode with the tension. He's afraid he'll get sick himself if he doesn't come up with some more choices.

More choices—that's what's at the heart of the choice-centered model of living. If we have only one or two possible responses to people and situations, we are fairly restricted in directing our lives. On the other hand, the more choices we have, the more imaginative we can be in creating the results we want. By more choices, I don't mean multiple items of clothing or several people to date. That kind of "moreness" may or may not be appropriate at any given time. The choices to which I refer here are our personal options for acting and reacting in a variety of ways. These choices remind us of the skills, strengths, and positive attributes that we already possess—our personal resources.

More Choices ⟶ *More Resourcefulness*

We have more choices when we can decide how we want to feel, think, or behave in situations that are usually difficult to handle. For example, we make new choices when we elect to respond with humor instead of hurt, or when we talk to ourselves nicely instead of critically. We open up the possibilities for new behavior when we set limits instead of just going along with circumstances. We expand our options when we turn to a spiritual source for comfort or help.

Whether we act at internal, psychological, and spiritual levels, or at external, logical, and behavioral levels, every one of our choices will change the structure of our experience. In response to our new feelings, thoughts, and actions, something shifts in the fabric of the universe and new results occur. If we like the new results, we proceed with the choices we've already made. If we don't like the feedback we get, we can always consider more choices for change.

The Process of Feedback

Feedback is probably the most significant process in life. Feedback is the flow of information from internal and/or external sources that signifies how everything in the universe is responding to our choices.

We utilize this information to evaluate whether our thoughts, feelings, and behavior are helping us achieve our desired results.

Internal feedback consists of our own emotions, intuitions, dreams, sensations, or thoughts. We all experience internal feedback of one form or another. It lets us know whether something is "right" or "not right." External feedback comes from the words, emotions, and actions of the people around us, and from the sequence of events that unfolds as a result of our choices. Both internal and external feedback allow us to evaluate whether we are having the spiritual, emotional, physical, or mental experiences that we want. Moreover, both are constant. As living beings, we are immersed in the flow of feedback twenty-four hours a day, so we may as well make use of it.

Why does it seem so hard to react gracefully to feedback? For many of us, this is a challenge because feedback is *often focused on errors*—what's wrong, what's incorrect, what's "not good enough." In this form, feedback can connote failure and lead to shame or defensiveness. Nevertheless, error-oriented feedback can be valuable when it's not delivered in an abusive manner. And even abusive feedback can give us insight into the person delivering the abuse. In general, error-oriented feedback shows us when we've hurt someone or been hurt, when we've misjudged or been misjudged, and when we've stepped over boundaries or been invaded. In all these cases, feedback based on error lets us adjust and adapt our thoughts, feelings, and behavior.

Feedback *can also be focused on successes*. In this form of feedback, we praise each other, give compliments, and show appreciation. Normally, success-oriented feedback is what most people prefer. It makes us feel "good enough," on-track, and capable. However, it can also be problematic. If we only notice the successes, we may miss critical information that could indicate future needs or predict potential breakdowns.

In the long run, we can utilize all kinds of feedback. It's useful to pay attention to both internal and external feedback, and to both error- and success-oriented feedback.

Feedback is the process that allows us to fine-tune our choices.

Sam, Maria, Susan, and Joe are all getting feedback messages that let them know that something different needs to be done. Sam needs to give Tina some error messages. Maria needs to give her boss some success messages and a subtle error message. Susan needs to give herself some success messages and ask for some success messages from Tom. Joe desperately needs to give himself success messages.

Just by paying attention to various forms of feedback, we can change a situation. Feedback allows us to adapt ourselves in order to create the bodies, spirits, minds, and emotions that we want. More specifically, it is an invaluable resource when choosing how to construct rewarding vocations or careers, healthy lifestyles, interesting opportunities for personal expression, and satisfying relationships.

Satisfying relationships. Most of us want them. Some of us think they will fall in our laps—or not—as fate sees fit. Some of us, however, are beginning to think that we can actually make choices that will help us consciously and deliberately create wonderful interactions with others. If you're on this path, the rest of this book is for you. It will show you how to relate from a choice-centered perspective, and how to use the tarot as a form of feedback.

Exercises

1. Think, write, or talk with a friend about your model of the truth. To which windows and doors and speakers do you pay attention? Does your model have a name? Did you invent it or is it a publicly recognized model of the "nature of things"?

2. Consider a specific situation that feels "fated" to you. What do you think or feel about it? What are some of the advantages, for you, of living by fate? What are some of the disadvantages?

3. Consider a specific situation in which you know you are empowered to make choices. What's your reaction to this experience? What are some of the advantages, for you, of living by choice. What are some of the disadvantages?

4. Think about a situation that seems confusing right now. Consider the kind of feedback you're giving to others. Is it success- or error-oriented. Would it be helpful to change the feedback messages that you're sending?

5. Think about a time when you received error-oriented feedback about a choice that you made. You could have recognized the error

because of your internal response or because of the external signals from people and events. How did you react to it? How was the error message useful to you? What have you done (or will you do) differently next time?

6. Think about a time when you received success-oriented feedback about a choice that you made. You could have noted the success because of internal or external feedback. How did you react to the success message? If there were any disadvantage to it, what were they?

2

Choice-Centered Relating

W hen we shift the focus from the larger context of living to the more specific arena of relating, the process of feedback, as described in the previous chapter, is vitally important if we are to interact in a choice-centered way. In addition, there are four essential attitudes that enhance choice-centered relating. They are *curiosity, balance, appreciation, and flexibility*

Curiosity allows us to wonder what we can do to change, impact, or enhance our interactions with others. If we avoid thinking or acting while we live in hope or fear about someone else's behavior, we're definitely out of control, waiting for fate to unfold. If we move through the world hoping or fearing that we, ourselves, will (or won't) change, we're still not in touch with our own creativity and power. On the other hand, if we become curious about what's possible, we open ourselves to opportunities and options. If we wonder about someone's behavior, we detach a little and move away from feeling emotionally invested in their decisions. If we ask ourselves what else we might do or think or feel, instead of remaining locked in to the current pattern, we've already opened a door into more choices.

By becoming more curious, Susan begins to question what Tom is really wanting when he is critical. As a result, instead of reacting defensively to his criticism of her fried chicken, she asks him what he specifically wants. She goes on to wonder how he can have that particular taste experience even if she isn't the one to provide it. Curiosity also leads her to ask how she can possibly value herself, even if Tom doesn't like her chicken. When she puts it that way, the whole thing seems suddenly humorous, she feels a lot less ashamed, and finds a sense of balance.

Balance, another useful attitude to have when we want to expand our behavioral options, often emerges from curiosity. A sense of emotional or mental balance helps us step back, acquire perspective, and tune in to other parts of a frustrating situation. Although there are a number of attitudes that can be balanced, the one that I find the most useful is the balance between seriousness and lightheartedness.

By seriousness, I don't mean grimness. I mean the ability to be appropriately respectful about current circumstances. If your child has leukemia, your husband is an active alcoholic, or your friend is mentally ill, no amount of denial will make the reality go away. We have to attend to these kinds of situations in a serious manner. A good way to handle serious situations is to make a list of the things you can't control (and let them go) and a list of the things you can control (and do them).

We can also balance our seriousness with lightheartedness. By lightheartedness, I don't mean superficiality or lack of responsibility. I mean the attitude that allows us to laugh a little at ourselves and our situations. A good way to "lighten up" when the current crisis may not need to be so serious is to try stating it as a newspaper headline. "Smithville Woman Has PMS" or "Chicago Man Late to Dinner" don't really make it as headline news!

By putting his situation in headlines, Sam is able to release some of his tension. "Single Dad Stays Home with Kids," and "Babysitter Doesn't Show" really aren't monumental crises in the grand scheme of things. Sam still needs to come up with a solution for the problem but, by finding his balance, he feels less overwhelmed and more creative in problem-solving. Perhaps, he can even appreciate the day spent with his children while he figures out what to do next.

Appreciation is another key that can open the door to choice-centered living and relating. When we find the parts of an existing situation that can bring us joy, satisfaction, or learning, we begin to assess and evaluate even our negative experiences in a more positive light. When we value individuals for their unique characteristics and remember what we like about them, we can sometimes find a way past their faults. When we actively appreciate our own positive qualities, we become less inclined to beat ourselves up.

> *Appreciation is a really useful attitude for Maria. When she stops to remember what she likes about her district manager, she remembers his sense of humor, his warmth, and his willingness to stop and talk about anything that's bothering his staff. She notices that, although the meetings are definitely not result-oriented, they are opportunities for everyone to air their concerns. She realizes that in some ways, this style creates a positive attitude within the district. In appreciating herself, Maria realizes that her ability to streamline projects is really a gift. Instead of being angry with her manager, she begins to feel good about herself and a little more tolerant of his management style. Although nothing has changed at work, Maria's blood pressure is going down and she's beginning to be more flexible about how things "should" be done.*

Flexibility brings us to more choices in a very direct manner. We are flexible when we consider that there is more than one way to approach anything we're doing. To remember this, we can replace the old adage, "If at first you don't succeed, try, try again," with, "If at first you don't succeed, try something else." While curiosity, balance, and appreciation free us from feeling stuck, flexibility actually allows us to consider various plans of action.

> *Joe has always kept his work at the office, leaving it behind when he comes home. This has been a good system for several years. It has allowed him to have a personal life and avoid becoming a workaholic. By becoming curious and willing to be flexible, Joe starts to consider "something different." He realizes that, for this phase of his life, some of his work can be accomplished at home. He can set up his computer in the spare bedroom and get a lot done while David's napping or watching TV. He can still go into the office to meet with his clients, but that only takes twenty hours a week. Joe knows that, as David's condition changes,*

working at home could become difficult. So he's reminding himself that this is a solution "for now." By remaining flexible, he'll be able to come up with other ideas as needed.

Susan, Sam, Maria, and Joe made some seemingly simple shifts in attitude that are surprisingly powerful keys for change. We can all use the tools of curiosity, balance, appreciation, and flexibility to open our minds to the possibilities that could be in front of us. Obviously, these changes of attitude don't necessarily solve the problems. They do, however, make us feel more confident about solving the problems. The more we use these attitudes, the more choices we'll find in our relationships.

The Process of Relating

The word "relationship" is actually somewhat inappropriate to use in this context, because "relationship" is a noun—a thing. By calling something a relationship, we imply that we can find one, put it in the car, and take it home to keep. For example, when I was 19, I thought that getting married was the essential factor in relating. Somehow, I imagined that if I just acquired a husband, the rest of my life would fall into place. Surprise, surprise! Four years and one divorce later, I knew that there was more to relating than just the act of marriage. You, too, may have been tremendously disappointed in "getting" a relationship, only to discover that it's the beginning of a process, not a goal to be achieved. Calling something a "relationship" can set us up to think in terms of acquisition rather than discovery. In reality, relating is an ongoing dynamic that involves the natural rhythms, sudden changes, and gradual growth of each individual involved. Everyday speech being what it is, most people (including myself!) use the word "relationship" in conversation and writing. If, however, we can remember that there's a process implied by the word, our relationships can become more dynamic.

When we experience our interactions with others as processes (not things) we can be more realistic about our expectations and more hopeful about the changes that we, and the others in our lives, might make. We can appreciate each other and acknowledge that, individually and together, we will evolve. We can accept what "is" with a sense of balance, and avoid feeling trapped by it. We can become curious and flexible about the changes that occur within our relationships instead of feeling terrified by them. Moreover, we can utilize the process of feedback as an aid to the process of relating.

When we experience our personal interactions as processes (not things), we also discover that we can have an impact on the quality of our experience. If relationships are things that happen to us, they are essentially out of our control—very much in the "fate" model of thinking. On the other hand, if they are organic processes, we have important choices to make. We can decide how we will:

- Think, feel, and act in order to have the experiences and feedback we want;

- Respond and react to the feelings, thoughts, and behavior of others.

What we can't do is change anyone else. We can inform, reinforce, punish, or otherwise create opportunities for others to change, but in no way can we actually guarantee that others will change. Focusing on what we want others to do is fairly unproductive. In fact, surrendering our expectations of others can be extremely liberating. When we are able to allow others to act and react in accordance with their own needs while we diligently attend to our own actions and reactions, we create honest, healthy models for relating.

Models for Relating

What, exactly, is a model for relating? Is it a role model? An ideal for all of us? Since every person and every relationship is unique, there is really no ideal, perfect model for relating that we can set as a goal. Moreover, we know that, just as models of the truth are in constant flux, models of the truth about relating also change with every person, era, and culture. However, models *do* exist in our minds. Consciously or not, we operate from internal paradigms composed of images, feelings, sensations, and sounds. Your models and mine are created from a combination of all of our experiences:

- *Adults that we knew when we were children:* As children, we assimilated and internally recorded adult styles of relat-

ing with little evaluation or censorship. We simply
absorbed what they did, thought, and felt.

- *People we've known—or still know—as adults*: As we
look around our world, we notice and observe what other
people are, or aren't, doing in their relationships. With our
more mature minds, we evaluate their experiences and
resolve to interact "just like that," or "never like that."

- *Famous people or public figures*: Although we may never
aspire to be on the cover of a news journal or a women's
magazine, we are continuously exposed to how "those
people" live and what they do with each other. At some
level, that information lets us know what is and isn't
acceptable.

- *Fictional people in stories, books, magazines, television,
and movies*: Both cartoons and real-life dramas have provided us, and continue to provide us, with romanticized
concepts of idealized relationships. They also deliver trag-
ic, melodramatic, crisis-oriented, and even healthy notions
to our absorbent minds.

- *Our own imaginations, dreams, and intuitions*: To everything we've seen, felt, heard, and experienced, we add the
richness of our own thoughts, feelings, hopes, fears, and
expectations.

Our brains catalog all this input as it comes in through our senses,
assigning bits and pieces to our conscious and unconscious models
for partnering, parenting, learning, or teaching. Whether we're aware
of it or not, our internal models tend to dictate what we notice about
others, whom we attract and pursue, and how we interact with different kinds of people. They tell us when to be surprised, disappointed, or excited, and whether we're experiencing love, pain, or disgust.

My favorite example of a model for relating begins with the
phrase: "*If you loved me, you would_____.*" The rest of the sen-
tence varies according to the person:

—talk more or listen more;

—buy me traditional flowers and candy, or get me something
unique;

—follow a schedule, or be more spontaneous;

—travel with me, or stay home with me;

—have children with me, or help me avoid having children;

—participate in my work, or leave me alone to work;

—clean the house, or let the house be untidy;

—be more appreciative, or assume you can count on me;

—hold my hand, or give me space;

—be available, or play hard to get;

—flaunt yourself in front of others, or flaunt yourself only for me;

—monitor my drinking, or let me handle my addictions on my own.

It's amazing how often I, and probably you, still pull out those tired, old models without thinking. I'm shocked and hurt when someone doesn't match my inner model, assuming that it's a deliberate "I don't like you" message. You see, I assume that everyone's models match mine.

In fact, most of the time, most of us go along assuming that the whole world operates according to our models. Yet, for most of us, most of the time, our parents, friends, children, and partners have no hint as to what we expect them to do. Quite often, they only meet our "love" criteria by accident. As a result, it's useful to uncover, identify, and share our models with the significant people in our lives, so that we can move toward relating more effectively.

Uncovering Unconscious Models

Maria was confused by the way her romantic relationship with Mark was progressing. During the two years in which they had dated, Mark had periodically taken breaks from her and dated other women. He'd always come back to her. Once they were living together, she thought his behavior would change. There were two pieces in her unconscious model for a partner relationship that created this expectation. She thought that living together meant commitment, and commitment meant monogamy.

When, after three months of living together, Mark spent a weekend with another woman, she was hurt, baffled, and furious. According to *her* model, she had a right to be! Mark was surprised at her reaction. In *his* unconscious model living together meant "I like you best right now," and that did not necessarily mean monogamy.

With half of their furniture sold and a signed, year-long lease, Maria and Mark felt boxed in. If either had identified or discussed their differing models ahead of time, they might have made a different decision about moving in together. In the light of this behavioral feedback, they will have to balance their appreciation for each other and for themselves, and figure out if either of them can be flexible.

Because we all carry unconscious models about our relationships, it's useful to bring them into the light and look clearly at them—as early in the process of relating as possible. In that way, we can make conscious decisions about whether and how to honor the models, share them with others, or change them. Here's one quick way to find your unconscious models:

- Name the type of relationship you want to explore;

- Think of some relationships of this type that you have experienced or observed;

- Finish these sentences in as many ways as you can:
  In these relationships, one person (or I) always _____.
  In these relationships, the other person always _____.

- Change the beginnings of these sentences and keep the parts you added so that they read:
  Unconsciously, I think it's true that I should_____.
  Unconsciously, I think it's true that most people want to_____.

Specific examples of this procedure are:

"I always give in to other people's preferences," would become "Unconsciously, I think it's true that I should give in to other people's preferences."

"My partner always ignores me," would become "Unconsciously, I think it's true that most people want to ignore me."

This process can help you get started exploring your unconscious models for relating. Once you have uncovered these models, it becomes easier to use the tarot (or therapy) to revise and adapt them if you so desire. When adapting your models, remember that what you think is true is only one view of the truth. What are the others?

Creating Conscious Models

Sam's real estate business was growing to the point where he needed a professional assistant. Since he had not had good luck in choosing a babysitter for his kids, he was wary of just choosing someone he "liked." Instead, he decided to be very specific about the kind of assistant he wanted. First, he thought about all the criteria for doing the job well. He wanted his helper to pay good attention to detail, be familiar with computers, be interested in real estate, have a tight sense of time, scheduling, and deadlines, and possess the ability to interact pleasantly with people. That was a good start, but, somehow, it wasn't enough. He could imagine that many people would meet these criteria, yet still not be right for him. So, he began to think about other personality traits that he wanted in an assistant: a sense of humor, an enjoyment of children (at least of *his* children!), and a quality of maturity. If he found all those things *and* he liked the person, he thought he would be doing well.

As he began to place his ad, a colleague stopped by. In talking with her about hiring an assistant, she jokingly commented that his ad sounded like a "personal" ad and asked him what he was offering to this fabulous assistant. Sam began to ask himself how he wanted to behave as a boss. He had never been a boss before, so he thought of various bosses he had encountered and about his own personality. In the end, his ad said:

> *Realtor seeking assistant. I am goal-oriented, driven, very direct and sometimes abrupt in my communication, usually funny, occasionally depressed and grouchy. I love my children and sometimes they come to the office with me. I believe in working hard, playing hard, and taking regular vacations. I need an assistant who has a sense of humor, can stay calm when I go through mood swings, is very familiar with computers, likes children, is curious about real estate, reliable about schedules and deadlines, and enjoys interacting with a variety of people.*

You can use your wealth of personal experience to create models and find relationships that are healthy and satisfying for you. One way to create a conscious model is to follow Sam's example and go through the following steps:

- Name the type of relationship for which you want a model;

- Think of qualities that you want the other person to demonstrate;

- Think of personal qualities that you want to demonstrate in this relationship.

We create conscious models, just as we create unconscious ones, from all of our experiences, real and imagined. Because they are clearly identified, our conscious models can be more easily utilized, evaluated, reorganized, and fine-tuned than those that are unconscious.

When we uncover what we thought we wanted and discover what we really want, it's so much easier to find, attract, create, or redefine the relationships that are important to us. As you uncover and discover your models, remember that your criteria are your own. What's appropriate for you with a lover may not be appropriate for your best friend with her husband. What's inappropriate for your sister with her children may be wonderful for you with your kids. It's your choice.

Exercises

Choose a relationship in which you're having some difficulty right now and go through the following exercises.

1. Try being curious about the relationship. Imagine several positive and negative reasons why the other person is behaving as they are. Ask yourself, "What might cause this situation to improve?" or simply "How could this situation naturally improve, to my surprise?" Notice whether you feel more resourceful in your approach to the situation.

2. Inject a little balance into the situation. Ask yourself how important this will be in 50 years (or 50 days). Try the headline test to determine the seriousness of the crisis. If it's not too serious, practice

becoming more lighthearted. If it *is* pretty serious, evaluate what you can control and what you can't. Take action on what you can control. If the headline actually makes sense, call a crisis hotline or get other help immediately. Notice whether your resourcefulness increases as you find balance.

3. Take a few minutes to appreciate the qualities you value in the other person. Remember to appreciate your own fine attributes as well. Make a list of ten or fifteen strengths represented by each person involved. Pay attention to the ways in which the available qualities and resources can be combined, integrated, and used in the current situation. Do you feel more resourceful, now?

4. If you feel stuck in a repetitive pattern of interaction, consider becoming more flexible and "trying something else." Explore three or four other ways in which you could respond to the situation. When you imagine acting in these ways, is your resourcefulness enhanced?

5. Think of the unconscious models of relating that are being expressed by you or the other person. Use the exercise that appeared earlier in this chapter to discover how your unconscious models contribute to the stress of the situation.

- Finish these sentences in as many ways as you can:
  In these relationships, one person (or I) always
  _____.

  In these relationships, the other person always
  _____.

- Now, change the beginnings of these sentences and keep the parts you added so that they read:
  Unconsciously, I think it's true that I should_____.
  Unconsciously, I think it's true that most people want to
  _____.

6. Create a conscious model for how you'd like to interact with this person (or this type of person). Think of qualities that you want the other person to demonstrate. Think of personal qualities that you want to demonstrate in this relationship.

3

Choice-Centered Tarot

When you use the tarot in a choice-centered way, you give yourself an opportunity to improve your models for interaction. Through the cards, you can also gain ideas and insights into ways to become more curious, balanced, appreciative, and flexible. However, before you can use the tarot creatively, you need to know something about it.

Like Sam (with his psychic) and Maria (with her computer), we have a choice with the tarot cards. We can elect to use them in a future-predicting, fortune-telling manner. In fact, there are many books on the market today that demonstrate this approach. This is not one of them! "Choice-Centered Tarot" is just what the phrase suggests: a utilization of the cards that focuses on personal choice. The choice-centered tarot, as applied to relating, supports us as we create (instead of predict) healthy futures with the important people in our lives. My goal here is to give you an opportunity to approach your life and your relating with more empowerment.

In general, the tarot is a system that can beautifully reinforce the choice-centered paradigm, give us feedback about our lives, and help us utilize the four keys to relating. Just by asking questions we employ the key of curiosity. By asking choice-centered questions (more on this later), we acknowledge that there's more to know than what we perceive at a conscious level. By being open to what the cards say, we admit that we want insight and feedback from another source. That kind of open-mindedness is incredibly useful when we're trying to resolve relationship issues. By reminding us of the hidden (or obvious) issues that we might be missing, the cards often help us find the balance that allows us to utilize feedback. By using the insight from tarot readings, we can get some distance from the dilemmas at hand and become more lighthearted, or more serious, about them.

Since each tarot card can represent a personality attribute, it's easy to use the cards when we want to have more appreciation for ourselves and for others. We can actually ask: What can I appreciate about her? What is my greatest strength as I interact with him? Moreover, many tarot card readings have flexibility at their core. They include questions that emphasize optional or new behavior: How else can I respond to my mother? In what new ways can I effectively approach my boss about a salary increase? How can I handle my frustration with my teenager more effectively?

You and I can ask the cards any number of questions about our lives and relationships. The key is to understand how to ask these questions and to learn how to interpret the answers that the cards reveal.

The Tarot Deck

The tarot is a framework for describing the processes and issues of life: one of many windows or doorways into the truth. The system is symbolized on a set of 78 cards, each with its own set of symbols. Over the centuries, various taroists and philosophers have discovered, chosen, and revised the symbols that appear on the cards according to their personal understandings of the meanings. Some have even changed the number of cards in the deck. In fact, from the 1970s on, there has been a particularly exciting tarot renaissance that has resulted in the creation of multiple new decks full of innovative symbols. While many of these tarot decks show some commonality in terms of symbols, therefore, others differ greatly from tradition. At this point in time, I don't think there is any value to claiming that there is one "correct" deck, with a "correct" set of symbols. Instead, it's more useful to work with tarot decks that appeal to you because of their size, shape, colors, or images. I suggest that you find a deck that you like and get to know it. As you continue to work with the cards, you can always add other decks to your collection and switch decks according to your mood or question. If you don't yet have a deck, this would be a good time to get one!

Once you have a deck, look through it and notice the various categories of cards that appear. If your deck is similar to most, it is composed of two primary sections called the Major and Minor Arcana. Since the word "Arcana" means mysteries or secrets, the tarot is said to be a description of the major (greater or more momentous) and minor (lesser or more daily) secrets of the universe.

The Major Arcana

Each of the 22 cards of the Major Arcana has a unique title: The Empress, The Fool, The Star. These titles are not repeated in any other part of the deck. In many instances, these cards have been renamed by taroists to reflect their preferred interpretations. In some cases, extra cards have been added to the Major Arcana. Most authors and tarot artists, however, still utilize the classic 22 cards and their traditional names.

With regard to interpretation, many taroists group the Major Arcana cards into sequences that represent life lessons, stories about the search for meaning, or universal cycles. For example, the cards can be seen as three groups of seven cards or seven groups of three—plus The Fool. The Fool can come at the beginning of the Major Arcana—showing the divine innocent beginning the journey—or at the end—showing the state of divine innocence that can result from moving through the journey of life.

Although I've found many of the grouping systems useful and interesting, in my work, I've chosen to interpret the cards of the Major Arcana as 22 separate concepts. Brief explanations for these cards and the traditional roman numerals that symbolize them are shown in Table 1 (pages 30–31). In some decks the numbers for Strength and Justice are exchanged; if this is the case in your deck, ignore the number and attend to the interpretations.

Table 1. Concepts of the Major Arcana.

0 (OR XXII) THE FOOL: FAITH
Upright: having faith in others or the world
Reversed: having faith in self or spirit

I THE MAGICIAN: DISCERNMENT
Upright: discerning what's happening externally
Reversed: discerning what's happening internally

II THE HIGH PRIESTESS: SPIRITUALITY
Upright: pursuing named spiritual path
Reversed: practicing private contemplation

III THE EMPRESS: NURTURANCE
Upright: nurturing others
Reversed: nurturing self

IV THE EMPEROR: POWER
Upright: demonstrating worldly power
Reversed: experiencing personal power

V THE HIEROPHANT: MORALITY
Upright: publicly demonstrating a set of morals
Reversed: privately living by personal morals

VI THE LOVERS: COOPERATION
Upright: cooperating with others
Reversed: cooperating with parts of self

VII THE CHARIOT: CONTROL
Upright: controlling the external action
Reversed: directing inner experience

VIII STRENGTH: SURVIVAL
Upright: holding on to physical survival
Reversed: maintaining psychological survival

IX THE HERMIT: KNOWLEDGE
Upright: finding the truth about life
Reversed: finding the truth about self

X THE WHEEL OF FORTUNE: CAUSE/EFFECT
Upright: setting something in motion in the world
Reversed: turning it over to the universe

Table 1. Concepts of the Major Arcana (continued).

XI JUSTICE: EQUILIBRIUM
  Upright: creating balance or harmony in the world
  Reversed: creating internal balance

XII THE HANGED MAN: WAITING
  Upright: waiting for external cues
  Reversed: waiting for internal readiness

XIII DEATH: TRANSFORMATION
  Upright: transforming something in the world
  Reversed: transforming the self

XIV TEMPERANCE: CREATIVITY
  Upright: creating something tangible
  Reversed: creating an inner experience

XV THE DEVIL: STRUCTURE
  Upright: establishing worldly structure or limits
  Reversed: establishing personal limits

XVI THE TOWER: CATALYST
  Upright: shattering the external structure
  Reversed: exploding the internal structure

XVII THE STAR: RESOURCES
  Upright: directing the flow of abundance
  Reversed: receiving the flow of abundance

XVIII THE MOON: GUIDANCE
  Upright: receiving signals from the world
  Reversed: receiving guidance from within

XIX THE SUN: REBIRTH
  Upright: redoing something
  Reversed: rebirthing the self

XX THE JUDGEMENT: GRADUATION
  Upright: graduating to the next level
  Reversed: psychologically moving on

XXI THE WORLD: CHOICE
  Upright: recognizing options in the world
  Reversed: opening inner doors

The Minor Arcana

The 56 cards of the Minor Arcana are divided into four 14-card suits, similar to those in a deck of regular playing cards. The four suits are usually called Wands, Swords, Cups, and Pentacles. I will use these names in this book. In some decks, however, they've been renamed in accordance with the author's philosophy and you can easily translate if your deck uses different titles.

The number, or *pip* cards within the suits go from ace (one) to ten. The face cards, which are called the *court* cards in the tarot, are the Page, Knight, Queen, and King. Names for the court cards have also been changed in a number of decks, so check yours to find the equivalents. The cards of the Minor Arcana are titled with their pip/court value and their suit designation. So cards such as the Three of Pentacles, the Page of Wands, or the Ten of Cups are all Minor Arcana cards.

Table 2. Concepts of the Four Suits of the Minor Arcana.

WANDS: self-discovery and self-expression
> *Upright*: self, identity, name, role
> *Reversed*: self-image, self-concept

CUPS: emotional and intuitive awareness or interaction
> *Upright*: emotions, relationships
> *Reversed*: intuitions, altered-state experiences

SWORDS: thinking and cognitive expression
> *Upright*: ideas, communication; educational experiences
> *Reversed*: beliefs, values, self-talk

PENTACLES: physical experience and manifestation
> *Upright*: physical objects and experiences; health, money, work, sex
> *Reversed*: safety, security, groundedness

Table 3. Concepts of the Cards of the Minor Arcana.

ACES: beginning, conceiving, starting, initiating

TWOS: confirming, affirming, choosing, deciding

THREES: planning, preparing, projecting, detailing

FOURS: doing, manifesting, solidifying, creating

FIVES: adapting, adjusting, challenging, changing

SIXES: cycling, repeating, maintaining, patterning

SEVENS: expanding, varying, experimenting, stimulating

EIGHTS: contracting, organizing, structuring, limiting

NINES: flowing, moving, integrating, processing

TENS: hesitating, waiting, taking time out, pausing

PAGES: risking, daring, hazarding, jumping in

KNIGHTS: focusing, concentrating, fixating, intensifying

QUEENS: maturing, fulfilling, ripening, arriving

KINGS: releasing, completing, sharing, letting go

Interpreting the Minor Arcana is simplified if you know that each card's meaning emerges from its number and suit. Each of the four suits, associated with the four elements, emphasizes an area of life (see Table 2). Each number has a specific function, ranging in meaning from conception (Ace) to completion (King), as shown in Table 3. By combining the meaning of a number with the subject matter of a suit, you can formulate an interpretation for a card. For example, by combining the information in Tables 2 and 3, you can come up with the following:

Three of Swords	planning for communication
Seven of Cups Reversed	experimenting with intuition
Page of Pentacles	risk-taking regarding health
King of Wands Reversed	releasing an old self-image

To get used to combining the meanings, practice a few for yourself. Take the processes that describe the numbers and apply them to the life areas that are designated by the suits. You'll see that it's fairly easy to figure out interpretations for the Minor Arcana cards.

Rules for Reading the Tarot Cards

As you move closer to reading the cards, there are three rules I'd like to share with you. These are my personal rules. You may find taroists who disagree with me and, in the end, you'll have to decide whether they make sense for you. These are the conventions that will remain consistent throughout this book.

Rule 1

The cards reflect their core meanings, regardless of orientation. However, their orientation does influence their interpretation.

When you select cards from the deck, you'll find that some emerge upright (U)—the symbols are rightside-up—and some emerge reversed (R)—the symbols are upside-down. Even in a round deck, you can see that the orientation tends toward being either upright or reversed. Each taroist chooses how to handle the change in meaning that can come about by these changes in orientation. Some interpret the upright cards as positive and the reversals as negative. Some see the uprights and reversals simply as opposites (upright means X, reversed means not-X). Some choose to ignore the orientation and interpret all the cards as if they were upright all the time. My procedure is to recognize that each card has a core, neutral meaning, regardless of orientation, and, as you can tell from the interpretations given on page 33, I think that orientation does affect the emphasis of interpretation.

I find that the upright cards are expressed outwardly. They are more objective, obvious, public, conscious, or measurable:

The Empress U: Nurture others
Five of Pentacles U: Adjustments in health or money

The reversed cards are expressed inwardly. They are more subjective, subtle, private, unconscious, or even vague.

The Empress R: Nurture self
Five of Pentacles R: Adjustments in psychological security

Rule 2
All the cards are neutral; there are no good or bad cards.

Each card's core meaning is essentially neutral in value. There are none that are intrinsically good or bad. Instead, depending on how you frame your questions, you slant the interpretation of the card in a positive or negative direction. Questions that can lead to a negative interpretation of a card are:

What's the obstacle in this situation?
What's the biggest problem here?
What is this person's most negative characteristic?
What blocks me from moving forward?

Questions that can lead to a positive interpretation of a card are:

What's my biggest resource in this situation?
What's my strength?
What is this person's most positive characteristic?
What supports me as I move forward?

When you are interpreting a block, the meaning of the card *is* the block. It's not avoiding the card that is the problem. Doing what the card symbolizes is the problem, if it's your obstacle. For example, the negative interpretations of these cards are:

Six: Repeating the cycle in a predictable way is the obstacle
Queen: Well-established pattern of relating (or relationship) is the problem
Empress R: Nurturing (pampering) self too much is the negative characteristic
Fool: Naively trusting others too much is the block

On the other hand, positive interpretations of the same cards could be:

Six: Repeating the cycle in a predictable way is the resource
Queen: Well-established pattern of relating (or relationship) is the strength
Empress R: Nurturing self is the positive characteristic
Fool: Having trust in others is the support

Let me re-emphasize: when interpreting a card in the position of a block or an obstacle, the meaning of the card is *the problem*. When interpreting a card in the position of a resource or strength, the meaning of the card is *the support*.

Remember, too, that upright cards tend to show observable obstacles and resources. These can be reflected in external circumstances, the behavior of other people, or the actual behavior of the person receiving the reading. Reversed cards show the strengths and stumbling blocks that exist on a psychological level. They may refer to feelings, attitudes, or ways of processing information and experience. Occasionally, a reversed card will show behind-the-scenes manipulation by someone else or some sort of secret behavior, but, most of the time, reversed cards relate to the inner experience of the client.

Rule 3

Each card's core meaning will emerge for you over time.

Most taroists begin by utilizing someone else's interpretations of the cards, just as you may do when you read this book. Don't be surprised if, over a period of time, you begin to develop your own sense of each card. This is your intuition and your own inner knowing at work. Eventually, you'll find core meanings for all the cards that make sense for you.

The Choice-Centered Tarot Process

In my first book, *Choice Centered Tarot*, you'll find a detailed description of the process of consulting the cards. Rather than repeat myself here, I'll give you a summary of the procedure and some examples. If you want more, I refer you to my previous book, but, I think you'll be able to use the following steps whether or not you've read the other book.

You can use the cards either by yourself or with others. Your consultations can take place in a kitchen, on an airplane, over the phone, or in a professional office. No matter how you consult them, there are six steps to a choice-centered tarot reading:

1. Identify your primary concerns; set the topic;

2. Clarify and clearly frame your specific question(s);

3. Write the question(s) in a layout pattern; number the positions;

4. Mix and lay out the cards;

5. Interpret the cards relative to your question(s);

6. Get feedback and/or summarize the reading.

Step 1
Identify your primary concerns; set the topic.

This first step may seem so obvious as to be silly, but it's quite important. This analogy always helps me to take it more seriously. If you go to a healer and say, "Here I am, guess where it hurts," chances are good that this person can check you here and there, run some tests, and make a pretty good, educated guess about your aches and pains. It may take some time (and cost some money), but, eventually, you'll be able to determine whether or not your healer is a skilled diagnostician. After that, you can begin to resolve the problem. If you give your healer some clues or hints at the beginning, however, you may be able to speed up the diagnostic process and move much more quickly and economically into healing.

Working with the cards is similar. If Susan simply says, "I want to know about my relationships," she will probably find out various useful and interesting things about her life and relationships. If she identifies her concern as, "my relationship with my daughter," or, even more specifically, as, "communicating with my daughter about her weekend plans," Susan's chances of quickly getting useful feedback are increased. This is not to say that she, or you, might not want a more general reading. If this is the case for you, "relationships in general" may be your topic. If not, try narrowing your topic to the issue that's truly on your mind. The resulting reading will be much more specific.

Step 2
Clarify and clearly frame your specific question(s).

Once you've decided on your topic, list one or more questions related to that issue. Frame the questions so that they begin with words like "how," "what," and "why." Leave room for open-ended, descriptive answers. For example, Susan may only have one question: "What is the best thing for me to do regarding my daughter's weekend plans?" She may have additional questions that could help her clarify the situation: "What kind of experience will she probably have if she does go?" "What kind of experience will she probably have if she stays home?" "How can I best approach my daughter about this weekend?"

On the other hand, Susan may have some major processing to do regarding her daughter's plans, processing that may involve a whole series of questions.

"Why am I so worried about this weekend?"
"What's important to her about this weekend?"
"What does she really need from me right now?"
"How can I feel better if she does go?"
"How can she protect herself if she does go?"
"How will I feel if I talk to her tonight?"
"How will I feel if I wait to talk to her until Friday night?"
"What will her worst response probably be if I tell her not to go?"
"How can I best deal with (or avoid) that worst response?"
"What will her best response probably be if I tell her not to go?"

All of these questions are choice-centered. Depending on her level of concern, Susan can ask one, a few, or all of the questions in order to get insight into existing and possible future conditions, some choices about how to approach the situation, and some comparisons between alternate courses of action.

You may have noticed that there are no yes/no questions and no hard-core predictions about what will happen. If Susan were doing a more fate-oriented, predictive, or oracular reading, she might have asked:

"Will my daughter straighten up?"
"When will we have peace at home?"
"What will my daughter do this weekend?"
"Should I tell my daughter not to go?"

As you can see, the choice-centered questions invite more depth and understanding. They also leave Susan with a feeling of power. Based on the feedback of the cards, she can make choices about how she wants to behave and what she wants to say. The choice-centered questions allow Susan (and you) to keep the external climate in mind and steer a course within it. The answers to the predictive questions could leave Susan (and you) feeling flat and powerless, waiting passively to discover what will happen.

Notice that both sets of questions include some curiosity about the future, but that curiosity is expressed in two different ways. The oracular questions about the future assume that the future can only unfold in one way and that the universe, through the cards, is revealing that precise outcome. The choice-centered questions compare possible futures without predicting what will happen. They give information and feedback about the possible or probable results of actions, so that someone, in this case Susan, can decide whether or not to take those actions. This is extremely useful and empowering. I encourage you to use the choice-centered form of questioning. Many examples of these kinds of questions are given throughout this book. Some are listed in the exercises at the ends of the chapters.

Step 3

Write the question(s) in a layout pattern. Number the layout positions.

After you've identified your questions, create a layout plan that encompasses all of them. If my layout plan involves more than one or two cards, I always write it out on paper so that I don't have to carry it in my mind. Most of the time, I even write out the short layouts to clarify the true questions I'm asking. Figure 1 shows three possible layouts for the group of questions about Susan's daughter's weekend (see pages 40–41).

You can see that by choosing different groups of questions, sequencing the questions and assigning different numbers of cards to each question, the emphasis of the consultation shifts. Each of these layouts will give Susan useful information. If this were your reading, you could choose or create the plan that most closely matched your questions and priorities.

Notice that I've numbered the layout positions in figure 1. After you draw a plan, it's helpful to number the layout positions in an order that makes sense to you. This gives some direction and sequence to the consultation. It also lets you know where to place each card in step 4.

Step 4

Mix and lay out the cards.

With your layout plan nearby, mix the cards in whatever fashion appeals to you. Shuffling, cutting, and stirring on the table are some

LAYOUT PLAN A

```
┌─────┐
│     │
│  1  │
│     │
└─────┘
```

What is the best thing for me to do
regarding my daughter's weekend plans?

LAYOUT PLAN B

```
┌─────┐
│     │
│  6  │
│     │
└─────┘
```

What is the best thing for me to do regarding
my daughter's weekend plans?

```
┌─────┐              ┌─────┐
│     │              │     │
│  4  │              │  5  │
│     │              │     │
└─────┘              └─────┘
```

How will it be for her if she goes?   How will it be if she stays home?

```
┌─────┐              ┌─────┐
│     │              │     │
│  2  │              │  3  │
│     │              │     │
└─────┘              └─────┘
```

How could I feel better if   How could she protect herself
she does go?   if she goes?

```
┌─────┐
│     │
│  1  │
│     │
└─────┘
```

Why am I so worried about this weekend?

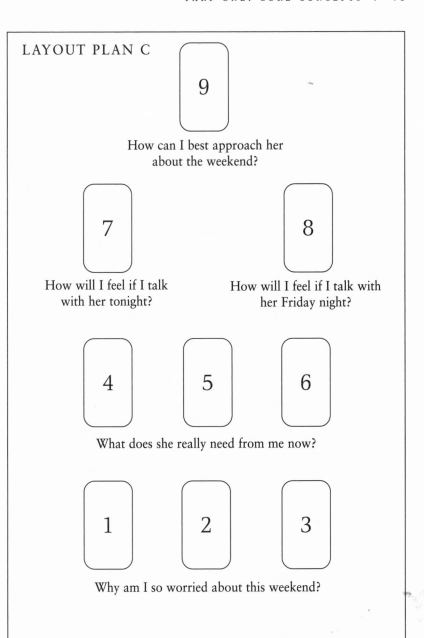

LAYOUT PLAN C

9

How can I best approach her
about the weekend?

7

8

How will I feel if I talk
with her tonight?

How will I feel if I talk with
her Friday night?

4 5 6

What does she really need from me now?

1 2 3

Why am I so worried about this weekend?

Figure 1. Three possible layouts for Susan's questions about her daughter's plans for the weekend.

of my favorite techniques. If you are doing a reading that involves more than one person and all are present, have everyone involved mix the cards. If you are the reader, you can do a final mix to integrate the cards. If you are a participant in the reading, you might want to do a final mix or stir together. If you have a particular ritual or system of mixing the cards that works for you, use it. Many people like to meditate or light a candle before using the cards, shuffle a specified number of times, or cut the deck into two or three sections and then recombine the cards. Others simply stir them on the table. Do whatever feels right for you. It's your way of tuning in. If you want to concentrate on your questions or make your mind blank, go ahead. If you feel kind of casual about the whole thing, that's okay, too. The universe understands your intention. Use rituals if you want, but don't worry if you have no rituals—just mix the cards until you feel ready. Don't get stuck on whether the cards "feel" ready. Just relax and stop mixing when you feel it's right. You'll be fine.

Pick the cards that will respond to your questions. You can choose them in sequence off the top or bottom of your pile, or you can pick them randomly from within the deck. Sometimes I spread the cards across the table, sometimes I heap them in a sloppy pile, and sometimes I put them in a tidy stack and choose them, in order, off the top. It depends on my intuition or my whim. If you're just getting started, try one system for awhile to see how it works for you. This can help you avoid concern about how you're choosing your cards.

As you draw cards from the deck, turn them over in the order and design of your layout pattern. Here's another potential panic spot. Do you turn the cards end-over-end, left-to-right, or right-to-left? Your choice could make a difference in whether the card is upright or reversed! Again, just relax. Flip the cards in whatever way feels most natural to you and don't think about it too much. Let your intuitive self be in charge. After you've chosen all your cards, you will have an interesting spread that represents the answers to your questions.

Step 5
Interpret the cards relative to your question(s).

Now you're moving into the fun part—reading the cards. Consider each card in turn, phrasing the question in your mind or asking it aloud. Then describe the meaning of the card and apply it to the question asked. If the question is "What is her worst response," you'll be giving the card a negative slant. If the question is "What is her best response," you'll interpret that card with a positive slant. As an example, here are sample interpretations of Susan's reading using Layout Plan B from figure 1 (see page 40). In this case, I haven't used complex interpretations of the cards like the ones given in Part Three. Nevertheless, you can see that with this simple keyword analysis, Susan got some useful feedback.

INTERPRETATION FOR LAYOUT PLAN B

Card 1: Why am I so worried about this weekend?

Queen of Swords R: Worried about the maturity of daughter's internal beliefs and values

SUSAN: *Yes, I'm not sure if she can handle a weekend away with older teenagers. What if she's not mature enough to handle the temptations that come up? What if her values are too mature for her age? Are her beliefs strong and healthy enough?*

Card 2: How could I feel better if she goes?

Five of Wands U: Ability to adapt herself or her situation independently.

SUSAN: *I would feel much better if she had her own car and could leave whenever she wanted.*

Card 3: How could she protect herself if she goes?

Two of Pentacles U: Affirm her physical safety in tangible ways.

SUSAN: *I think having her own car and her own money would help.*

Card 4: How will it be for her if she goes?

Page of Pentacles R: Experience risks with regard to her sense of psychological safety or groundedness.

SUSAN: *I guess the weekend will be a real test for her to discover how she emotionally handles situations that challenge her values. It doesn't sound like the risks are actually physical . . . more that she could feel insecure.*

Card 5: How will it be for her if she stays home?

> Ten of Pentacles R: Experience a holding pattern or a feeling of indecision about her sense of psychological safety or groundedness.

SUSAN: *If she doesn't go, she won't really know how she would handle such a situation. She'll just feel uncertain about it.*

Card 6: What is the best thing for me to do regarding my daughter's weekend plans?

> Lovers R: Listen to all the different internal responses to the situation and find a way to honor them all; let "inner voices" collaborate.

SUSAN: *One voice says, "Let her go and test herself," and the other voice says, "It's too dangerous." How can I find collaboration between these two inner voices?*

Two Additional Cards: How can I find collaboration between these two voices?
> Ten of Pentacles R: Put the concern about psychological security on hold.
> Eight of Pentacles U: Organize something practical at the physical level.

SUSAN: *Okay, I'll let her go, but I'll make sure her car is in good shape and that she has enough money.*

> Sometimes a tarot reading leads to an additional question. In this case, Susan wanted to know how to follow the advice of the Lovers R, so she simply added two more cards to her layout. When you are doing readings, you can always add extra cards to help you clarify or extend the meaning of a question you've already answered.

Step 6
Get feedback and/or summarize the reading.

All along the way, it's important to get feedback from yourself (or the other person) about whether your interpretations actually make sense. After all, a tarot reading is based on a relationship between you and someone else, or you and your inner self. Every relationship depends on the feedback process. Moreover, given a person's ability to make choices and the number of possible interpretations for each card, it's often appropriate to give three or more options before you get feedback. If you've paid attention to feedback all along, summarizing the reading takes very little time and is often quite helpful.

In your summary, remember the core issue that you've been exploring and notice how all the parts fit together. In some cases, feedback at the end of the reading may *be* the summary. Throughout this book, you'll find feedback and summaries written in a variety of styles and forms, because each consultation is unique. As you read them, you'll be able to see that there are a number of different approaches to take. The important thing is that some kind of agreement about the message of the reading is reached. A summary of Susan's reading might look like this:

> *Susan, you weren't sure whether your daughter was mature enough to handle a weekend away with older teenagers. You said you'd feel better if she had her own car and enough money to be able to make independent decisions and leave the group if she wanted. The weekend looks like an opportunity for her to test her values in a somewhat challenging situation without any real physical danger. You can honor your conflicting inner voices about the weekend by letting your daughter go while making sure that she takes her own, safe car and plenty of money.*

How the Tarot Works

This section might better be called "How on Earth Does This *Really* Work?" None of us truly knows what happens to make tarot readings function. My theory is that, by deciding to use the tarot cards, we agree with the universe (call it divine inspiration, inner self, higher power, or whatever) on a means of communication and a specific language—the language of tarot. Once you've chosen the tarot as your guide, you then enter into a process that allows you to get feedback and information from the universe through the cards. In some way, the "force" of the universe, or of your deepest, most knowing, self, activates your autonomic nervous system to shuffle, cut, and choose the cards that will clarify or answer your questions. That's the best explanation I can give.

What I do know is that the cards have worked consistently for me, my clients, and my students over the course of several decades. As long as they're useful, I keep employing them. If they ever become irrelevant, I'll discard them. I encourage you to consider the cards with a combination of skepticism and open-mindedness. Test them as you work with yourself and others. Then evaluate how, or if, they apply to you and your life.

Feeling Ready

You may want to do a few practice readings for yourself before you jump into tarot consultations. You can use some of the layout questions from Susan's readings, or those at the end of this section. You can also make up your own. At first, you may want to limit the number of cards in your layout patterns. It's easier to integrate a reading involving five or six cards than it is to pull together an interpretation for fifteen or twenty. If you have a great many questions, you can design a series of two or three layouts that build on each other. Or you can simplify them. On the other hand, in order to enrich your interpretation, you may find that you need to add more cards to a simple reading, just as Susan did. Feel free to do so. Trust yourself. After all, this is just a conversation between you and the friendly universe.

Sample Layout Questions

Here, and at the end of each succeeding chapter, you'll find a list of sample questions that are relevant to the material presented in the chapter.

> What can I do to enhance this relationship?
> How can I react differently to this person?
> Why am I worried about _____?
> What will be my experience (or someone else's experience) if
>   I make this choice?
> How can I approach this person about this issue?
> What's important to me about this choice?
> What do I need from this person right now?

What does this person need from me right now?
What is my best action regarding _____?
How will it be for me if I_____?
How will it be for me if I _____ instead?

SAMPLE LAYOUT

Overall, how can I enhance this relationship?

What will by my experience if I choose to ask for what I want?

What do I need from   What does "X" need from
    "X" right now?   me right now?

Exercises

1. If you are new to the tarot, spend some time with your tarot deck. Organize the cards by the Major and Minor Arcana.

- Note whether traditional titles or adaptations are used in your deck.

- Put the cards of the Major Arcana in numerical order and identify each one. Think about how the symbols on your cards reflect (or don't reflect) my keyword interpretations.

- Become familiar with the symbols for the four suits of the Minor Arcana. Do your Minor Arcana cards have story-telling pictures or just the symbols for the suits? If your cards tell stories, can you figure out how the images could reflect the keywords in this chapter?

2. Think about Rule 1: The cards reflect their core meanings regardless of orientation. However, their orientation does influence their interpretation. Ask a one-card question—perhaps one from the sample list above. Pull one card from the pack. Think about its upright interpretation and how it applies to you. Then think about the reversed interpretation. Do they both make sense? Does one make more sense? Do this two or three times, or until you feel comfortable with switching between upright and reversed interpretations.

3. Think about Rule 2: All the cards are neutral; there are no good or bad cards. Look through your cards and find some that seem to look "negative" to you. Interpret them as obstacles or problems. Now, switch your interpretation to a neutral, or even positive, frame of reference. Then find some cards that look more "positive" to you and interpret them as resources and supports. Think about them from a neutral or negative perspective. Pull ten or fifteen tarot cards in a row and interpret them as blocks. Remember that the meaning of the card is the problem. Now interpret the same cards as resources.

4. Think about Rule 3: Each card's core meaning will emerge for you over time. Choose two or three cards, at random, from your deck. Without referring to my book, or any other book, consider what the cards say to you. How do you intuitively respond to them? How are these particular cards relevant to your life at this time?

5. Think of a relationship about which you have some questions. Follow the 6-step reading process for a particular issue within that relationship:

    1. Identify your concerns; set the topic;
    2. Clarify and clearly frame your question(s);
    3. Write the question(s) in a layout pattern; number the positions;
    4. Mix and lay out the cards;
    5. Interpret the cards relative to your question(s);
    6. Give yourself feedback and/or summarize the reading.

Issues and Examples

In Part Two, you'll find four groups of concerns that generally arise within the experience of relating: finding and creating new relationships, enhancing or healing existing relationships, long-term relating, and reaching closure when we end relationships. For each issue, I discuss the theory or theme and give examples of tarot readings that can give insight about it. Throughout, the tarot will illuminate the way!

4

Finding and Creating New Relationships

The tarot can be used to develop the four key attitudes for relating, uncovering unconscious models, and designing conscious ones. Through the tarot, we can create opportunities for new people or new patterns of relating to enter our lives.

As you learned in Part One, the four key attitudes for relating are:

Curiosity • Balance • Appreciation • Flexibility.

Whether you're already involved in significant relationships or seeking them, you can actively develop these attitudes—and the tarot can help!

Jon used the reading in Layout 1 (see pages 51–52) to explore ways to develop his skills as he waited for his future partner to come along.

LAYOUT 1. *Jon's practice of the four key attitudes in preparation for a partner.*

How can I develop or practice?

1	2	3	4
Curiosity	Balance	Appreciation	Flexibility

INTERPRETATION

Card 1. Curiosity

Knight of Swords R: Focus on important values of self and/or other person.

Ask self "What are the deep important values behind this behavior?"

Card 2. Balance

Eight of Wands U: Maintain some independent and personal boundaries.

Card 3. Appreciation

World R: Remember to value all of own many and wonderful qualities.

Card 4. Flexibility

Strength R: Do whatever it takes to maintain psychological survival.

Extra Card: To determine how psychological survival can help you be flexible.

Five of Swords R: You'll have to adapt and adjust your inner thinking and the ways you talk to yourself. See things differently in order to cope (and survive) in a partner relationship.

Using the Tarot to Uncover Unconscious Models

In Part One, we explored the ways in which our unconscious models impact our behavior and expectations in relationships. Here is an example of how Abigail used the tarot to uncover some unconscious models. She realized that she was disappointed in her experience with her 2-year-old. Although, at a conscious level, she thought it was ridiculous, she kept feeling that little Ben wasn't "doing it right." Somehow, he wasn't matching her model. Since she was curious about her unconscious model of parenting, she did the reading in Layout 2 (see pages 53–54).

LAYOUT 2. *Abigail's and Ben's unconscious models of parenting.*

| 1 | 2 | 3 |

What are the factors of my unconscious model
about parenting Ben at age 2?

| 4 | 5 | 6 |

What are the factors of Ben's unconscious model
for being a 2-year-old?

INTERPRETATION

Cards 1-2-3: What are the factors of my unconscious model about
parenting Ben at age 2?
The Empress U: Give lots of nurturing attention
King of Swords R: Share personal values and philosophy
Queen of Swords R: Mature, private verbal communication;
demonstrate inner values

ABIGAIL: *I thought that, even at age 2, Ben would pay close attention to the values I'm living out. I thought that, even if it was in
babytalk, I could share with him many of my ideas about life. I
thought there would be many peaceful moments of holding him,
feeding him, and taking care of him.*

Cards 4-5-6: What are the factors of Ben's unconscious model for
being a 2-year-old?
Two of Pentacles U: Affirm physical being
Eight of Swords R: Restrict or limit private communication
Knight of Cups R: Focus on feelings or psychic interactions

BEN: *Ben moves all the time, rarely stopping to be held. He grabs food on the run, hardly acknowledging the provider's presence. He doesn't talk much, but demonstrates his feelings strongly and sends Abigail lots of messages in the dreamstate.*

Abigail and Ben have very different unconscious models about interacting as a mom and a 2-year-old. Abigail expects tender, serene moments of holding, feeding, and discussing the meaning of life in babytalk. She also expects Ben to watch her behavior and notice her interactions with others. Ben is more interested in how fast he can move, or how far he can throw his ball. When he hurts, he cries; when he's happy, he laughs out loud. When he's asleep, through dreams, he lets his mom know how much he loves her and likes being her son.

Using the Tarot to Create Conscious Models

In Part One, I described three steps that can be used to create conscious models for relating. Here, I'll give you some sample tarot readings that illustrate these steps.

Step 1
Name the type(s) of relationship for which you want a model.

You can do a tarot reading, such as the one in Layout 3, to help you identify some of the relationships that might interest you (see page 55). Tom, who has just retired at age 60, isn't even sure of the kinds of relationships he wants now. In this reading, he is exploring those that he might want in his life. Although the question for this kind of reading is quite general, it can give you some good ideas. In addition to doing this reading, you can glance through the descriptions of "people" at the beginning of each suit given in Part Three, or browse through the Major Arcana interpretations given in Table 1 (pages 30–31). This will give you more food for thought about all the different types of people who may enter your life.

LAYOUT 3. *The new kinds of people Tom might want in his life.*

| 1 | 2 | 3 | 4 |

What are the new kinds of people that I might want
in my life, now that I'm retired?

INTERPRETATION

Cards 1-2-3-4: What are the new kinds of people that I might want
in my life, now that I'm retired?

Page of Swords U: Adventuresome travel companion; someone who takes risks with learning new things

The Hermit U: An expert; a wise man or woman

Six of Pentacles U: Someone who can help me keep my
finances in balance; a regular sexual partner

Ten of Swords U: Other retired people; people on sabbatical;
people who can take time out from the usual routine

TOM: *I definitely want a travel companion. Ideally, this person
would also be a regular sexual partner who is either retired or can
easily take time to travel. I definitely need an expert accountant. And,
I would really like a wise teacher/mentor who can help me learn new
philosophical things. This helps me identify three people: travel/sex
companion; financial expert; teacher.*

Step 2
Think of qualities that you want the other person to demonstrate.

One way to organize your lists of attributes is to use issues related to the Major and Minor Arcana to help you brainstorm. You can
look at the brief descriptions in Tables 1, 2, and 3 (see pages 30, 32,
and 33), or the detailed descriptions given in Part Three. Figure 2

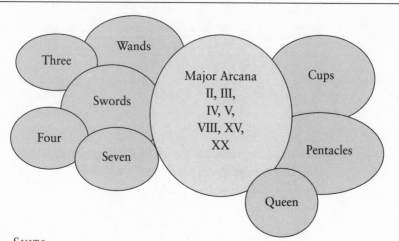

SUITS
Wands: Taller than me, not too thin, outgoing personality, upbeat energy
Cups: Emotionally balanced, done some homework in past relationships
Swords: Smart, good communicator
Pentacles: Financially secure, physically active, enjoys sex, healthy

PIPS
Three: Good planner
Four: Follows through on manifesting plans
Seven: Enjoys variety and experimentation
Queen: Mature

MAJOR ARCANA
II—The Magician: Clear-thinking
III—The Empress: Nurturing and self-nurturing
IV—The Emperor: Has a solid career
V—The Hierophant: Similar religious background: Unitarian
    Universalist concepts
VIII—Strength: Can take care of herself*
XV—The Devil: Has good boundaries and honors others' boundaries
XX—Judgement: Already graduated from college

---

*With Paula's use of feminine pronouns, the gender of her preferred partner becomes obvious. If you are doing readings for others, it's important to check on gender with regard to intimate relationships, so that you can use the correct pronouns. If you are not sure of gender, you can use phrases such as "this person" or "your partner."

Figure 2. Paula's tarot-based groups of qualities.

shows two examples of tarot-based groups of attributes that Paula made when imagining her ideal partner (see page 56). Both the list and the diagram include the same information; they're just organized differently. She simply went through the topics related to the Minor Arcana suits and numbers, and the key ideas for each Major Arcana card, noting the factors that seemed important to her. Layout 4 on pages 57–58 shows a tarot reading she did to help uncover important attributes that she might have missed or needed to really emphasize.

LAYOUT 4. *Attributes for Paula's future partner to demonstrate/not demonstrate.*

| 1 | 2 | 3 | 4 |

Crucial attributes for future partner to demonstrate

| 5 | 6 |

Attributes that the future partner should *not* demonstrate

INTERPRETATION

Cards 1-2-3-4: Attributes future partner should demonstrate:
> Sun R: An ability to learn from past emotional experience and do things slightly differently the next time; a play therapist?
> Nine of Wands U: Capacity to maintain personal, independent direction over time; firefighter? camper? pioneer spirit?
> Ten of Cups R: Ability to put personal feelings on hold when needed; someone with a sense of emotional perspective
> Queen of Cups R: Inner emotional maturity; psychic skills; well-developed intuition

Cards 5-6: Attributes future partner should not demonstrate:
The World: Should not always be looking for other options.

Additional Question: Other options with regard to what?
Nine of Cups U: Other on-going relationships
High Priestess R: Should not be vague or out of touch; should
not be so involved in spiritual world that the needs of this
reality are ignored; should not be withdrawn

PAULA: *My last partner had a mental illness that resulted in wild bursts of emotion and dramatic mood swings. She refused to stay on her medication so I also had to take care of her a lot. She was incredibly needy. Sex got to be boring because all the energy of the relationship went into dealing with her emotions. When she finally left me, it was actually a big relief. I don't want to repeat that pattern!*

It's clear that Paula wants a live-in lover/partner who is emotionally mature, with an independent spirit. So, she's looking for a person who is not too emotionally dependent, yet monogamous. She also wants her partner to be able to put strong emotions "on hold," when necessary, in order to gain perspective.

Step 3
Think of personal qualities that you want to demonstrate in this relationship.

In addition to understanding what she wants from her partner, it's critical for Paula to identify the personal qualities and attributes that she wants to express in her partnership. Paula could do a tarot-inspired list similar to the one she did for the partner (see figure 2, page 56). She could also do a reading similar to the one shown in Layout 4 (page 57). Layout 5 shows her reading about herself (see page 59).

LAYOUT 5. *Attributes for Paula to demonstrate/not demonstrate.*

| 1 | 2 | 3 | 4 |

Crucial attributes for Paula to demonstrate.

| 5 | 6 |

Attributes that Paula should *not* demonstrate.

INTERPRETATION

Cards 1-2-3-4: Attributes Paula should demonstrate
    Empress R: Ability to nurture and take care of self
    Nine of Cups R: Capacity to let intuition flow; to tune in on
       an on-going basis
    Judgement R: Ability to let self grow into new stages of
       awareness and development
    Four of Cups U: Outwardly express feelings as needed

Cards 5-6: Attributes Paula should not demonstrate:
    Six of Pentacles U: Should not be too boring/predictable re:
       sexuality; should not maintain current financial patterns
    King of Swords R: Should not let go of core values and ethics

PAULA: *I want the freedom to take care of myself, not just take care of her; I'm doing a lot of psychic work right now and I want to be able to pursue my growth there. And, I want to be able to express my feelings, not just pay attention to hers.*

Personally Preparing for Relating

Once you've identified the specific kind of relationship you desire, uncovered your unconscious models, and created your conscious ones, you can ask a very basic question: "What can I do to create the relationship I want?" Even a one-card layout can show you the next step. As you read the card(s) bear in mind how these general factors of interpretation relate to *preparing* for something:

- If most of the cards are upright, your preparation involves external behavior and obvious action of the sort described by the cards.

- If most of the cards are reversed, an inner, or more personal process of change or reflection may be needed.

- If Major Arcana cards appear in significant number or significant positions, a big life change may be necessary.

- If one suit of the Minor Arcana seems emphasized, it's important to consider the issues related to that suit.

In his search for a new partner, Jon had already determined that he wanted to live monogamously. He also knew that he wanted someone with whom he could share his interests in gardening, art, and nesting. Since Jon is a recovering alcoholic, he wanted his partner to be clean and sober. He wanted a woman who was close to him in age and who didn't have (or want) any children. Jon wanted to be able to express his affection and to communicate about everything under the Sun. He especially wanted to share his spirituality with his partner. And he wanted to feel free to attend his AA meetings and to avoid his own tendency to argue. He had other wants and needs, but these were the basics. Layout 6 shows a very simple layout that describes the steps that Jon can take to find his partner (see page 61).

LAYOUT 6. *Jon's search for the right partner.*

| 1 | 2 | 3 |

What should I do to find a new partner?

INTERPRETATION

Cards 1-2-3: What should I do to find a new partner?
  The High Priestess R: Make sure my own spiritual life is in
  order.

JON: *I could, in fact, "turn it over" to my higher power, trusting that
the universe will bring my partner to me.*

  Queen of Pentacles U: Do the things you already do well.
  Continue to demonstrate mature skills and abilities in physical world: exercise, sports, physical hobbies or activities,
  health care, financial planning, or work-related talents.

JON: *I have a passion for gardening, a pursuit that uses my body as
well as having a physical result. In fact, I'm president of our local
Rose Club. And, I don't know if it counts for health care, but I have
very good habits about safe sex. I think I'm extremely responsible in
that regard.*

  Justice R: Maintain my own inner equilibrium

JON: *Well, that's a good point. Usually, I jump right in and get too
involved, too fast. This time, I want to be more careful.*

The Major Arcana cards in this reading are also the reversed
cards, showing that the most important, or life-changing, steps for
Jon to take are internal. He needs to make sure that his personal
spirituality and sense of balance are firmly in place. After that, if
he continues to do what he's already doing, chances are good that
a healthy partnership will come his way.

The reading showed that Jon needed to prepare for his partner primarily on an internal level. Because this was a choice-centered reading, I didn't predict whether Jon would find a partner or when. However, Jon was left with a sense of purpose, direction, and action. You can do similar readings for yourself. Notice that they generally help you to feel actively engaged in seeking a relationship, rather than passively waiting for one to appear.

Identifying and Addressing Obstacles and Resources

How many times have you gotten yourself prepared for something—such as finding the right partner—only to bump into the "yes buts," and the "what ifs," and the "that's not possible" arguments and experiences. These are the obstacles that we face when creating our lives by choice. The impediments can be internal (reversed cards), arising from attitudes and beliefs, or they can be external blocks (upright cards) that seem to confound and confront us. In either case, naming them is the first step to transforming these obstacles into opportunities for new and creative choices.

Naming our resources is just as important. We frequently forget the internal strengths, skills, and perceptions that empower us in a variety of situations. We may also neglect external resources in the form of people, money, time, energy, or things that can make our paths easier. When we remember to "count our blessings," we often feel—and become—more resourceful and capable.

The tarot can assist us in identifying and avoiding obstacles. It can also help us understand how to name and utilize resources. In Jon's case, he felt that the issue of maintaining his equilibrium was difficult and crucial. Layout 7 shows a reading for him about this issue.

Layout 7. Maintaining Jon's equilibrium in his quest for a partner.

| 1 | 2 | 3 | 4 |

Blocks to maintaining
internal equilibrium

Supports for maintaining
internal equilibrium

INTERPRETATION

Cards 1-2: Blocks to maintaining internal equilibrium

> The World R: A capacity to imagine all the possibilities of what could happen to him as a result of having a partner; a tendency to think that his personal and emotional world will open up in incredible and multiple ways if he finds a partner.

> Queen of Cups U: An already established, mature relationship that gets in the way of him keeping his balance; or a well-ingrained emotional pattern that threatens his stability.

Cards 3-4: Supports for maintaining internal equilibrium

> Page of Swords R: An ability to take risks with his beliefs and attitudes; an ability to reinforce himself by daring to talk to himself in different ways.

> Six of Pentacles U: Continuing with regular physical habits; keeping up his regular routine of working, exercising, eating healthfully, and taking care of his home and garden.

With an equal number of upright and reversed cards, Jon's key to maintaining his equilibrium was a balance of inner and outer processes. Jon said that he tended to fantasize about how his full inner potential could be unlocked with the right partner. He realized that these impossible expectations got in the way of his maintaining his balance in new relationships. This could be the emotional habit (Queen of Cups) that was already established for him. However, he also mentioned a dear friend who overreacted and felt abandoned whenever he got a new lover. This usually threw him off-balance. He found that it was a daring and exciting adventure to believe that he could unlock his own potential. When he reminded himself that he could grow and develop on his own and that he was not dependent on a partner, he felt more stable. The idea of maintaining his self-care routines also made him feel balanced and secure.

Interviewing and Evaluating Candidates

When it comes time to actually evaluate whether someone is a possible candidate for a particular kind of relationship, you can use layouts that simply ask which of your needs will (or won't) be met if you interact with a specific person in a particular way. You can also ask the tarot a variety of other questions that will let you know whether a person is really appropriate for you.

When Jon began dating Kim, a woman who he thought might be a match for his partner criteria, he wanted more feedback from the tarot. He met Kim at a horticulture conference and, although Kim had a different specialty, she was equally passionate about green growing things. Kim liked to talk and travel. In fact, she had been a travel agent for three years. Jon was a little nervous about the instability of a commission-based job, but felt reassured that Kim really liked her work and intended to keep at it. Kim is two years younger than Jon and has no children or dependents. While she has never been an alcoholic, she has been working on issues related to incest recovery for the last several years and has no problem with choosing to be clean and sober. So far, so good! In terms of his resources and obstacles, Jon told his close friend that he didn't intend to abandon her. He maintained his day-to-day work and health routines. And he made every effort to believe that Kim could be a companion in his growth, but not the cause of it. So Jon felt that he'd done his homework and was ready for this relationship to be "it." He wondered if there was anything he hadn't considered. The layout and interpretations in Layout 8 depict his next set of questions (see pages 65–67).

LAYOUT 8. *Jon's new relationship with Kim.*

> **7**

Probable result in 6 months if Jon and Kim continue to move along in the way they have been.

> **5**

> **6**

What Jon needs to ask Kim in order to clarify their relationship.

What Jon needs to ask himself about this relationship.

> **3**

> **4**

Changes Jon may need to make in order to make this relationship work.

> **1**

> **2**

Core need of Jon's that can be met in this relationship.

Core need of Jon's that might not be met in this relationship.

INTERPRETATION

Card 1: Core need of Jon's that can be met
>The Fool R: It's likely that his relationship with Kim will support Jon's faith in himself.

Card 2: Core need of Jon's that might not be met
>Three of Pentacles R: Jon's need to plan for future security with someone might not be satisfied.

Cards 3-4: Changes Jon may need to make
>Page of Cups R: Take more emotional risks within the privacy of the relationship than he's used to taking; really dare to trust his intuition and inner guidance; recommit to maintaining his sobriety.

>Justice R: Truly learn how to establish and maintain his own inner equilibrium.

Card 5: Question to ask Kim
>The Devil U: What boundaries are important to her; what are the musts and must-nots in this kind of relationship for her?

Card 6: Question to ask himself
>Ten of Wands U: Is he really comfortable putting his own independence on hold; is he himself ready to make commitments; is he ready to hold off on his tendency to rush head-long into things?

Card 7: Probable result in 6 months
>The World U: The probability is good that in six months he'll have a world of new possibilities opened to him. He may even get to travel. There will probably be a host of directions in which this relationship could go.

This whole reading was pretty significant, since four of the seven cards were Majors. In addition, all the cards that related to Jon's behavior were reversed, showing that changing or paying attention to his inner experience was important in this relationship. Jon liked the idea that the relationship could support his need to have faith in himself. He could see that Kim might not be able to make long-term plans for security. Although Kim was willing to be completely monogamous, she was not sure about long-term commitment at this early stage. This lack of commitment on Kim's part certainly led Jon to acting on his own intuition. In addition, it reminded him to base his security on recommitting to his own sobriety, not on Kim.

The questions Jon needed to ask Kim were critical to the reading and to the future of the relationship. He needed to find out about Kim's boundaries. Was Kim actually opposed to long-term relationships? Or was she just cautious? What were her limits in terms of the time and energy she was willing to put into the relationship? These were interview questions that Jon still needed to ask. Jon also needed to do a little soul-searching about his own willingness to put his independence on hold and make commitments, but that question wasn't as important as the ones he needed to ask of Kim. Jon found it amazing that the reversed Justice card appeared again, indicating that Kim wouldn't buy into taking care of him. Jon would have to maintain his own balance. Jon decided to proceed with the relationship. However, because of the long-term commitment question and the Ten of Wands soul-searching, he decided to hold back on his own tendency to commit to people too quickly.

Discovering, Setting, and
Honoring Boundaries

A boundary is a limit, fence, or margin that you place around your own, or someone else's behavior. The four main types of boundaries are as follows:

- You must not/must treat me in a certain way if you are to spend time with me.

Examples:

You must not talk to me in that tone of voice.
You must pay me if you expect me to help you any more.

- You must not/must engage in certain activities if you are to spend time with me.

Examples:

You must not drink or drug around me.
You must attend my child's basketball games if . . . "

- I must not/must interact with others in certain ways if I am to stay emotionally healthy.

Examples:
I must not rescue this person again.
I must have some time by myself every day.

- I must not/must do certain things when I interact with others if I am to maintain my own health.

Examples:

I must not have sex with people who have not been tested.
I must go to bed by eleven, no matter what my partner does.

It is important in establishing relationships to remember to set only the boundaries you can honor and honor the boundaries you set.

The only challenging thing about boundaries is that we're often tempted to renegotiate them. We set limits on eating or spending behavior, and then go over them. We tell people that we won't talk to them when they're drunk, and then make exceptions. We warn people that we will end the relationship if they abuse us, and then give them more chances. We commit to exercise or meditation regimes, and then slack off. It's human nature. However, if you set too many boundaries without honoring them, you (and others) will stop believing that the boundaries are real. Therefore, it's useful to only set boundaries that you can honor and to honor the boundaries that you set. If you're not sure about your ability to follow through on a certain boundary, try some of these techniques:

- "Try it on" for a short, defined period of time; then reevaluate.

- Talk to someone you respect, get feedback.

- Get regular support from a sponsor, parent, or counselor to help you remember to honor boundaries.

- Give yourself a (healthy) reward if you honor the boundary for a certain amount of time.

- Do it with a buddy so you can share experiences and reinforce each other.

If you clearly know and understand your own boundaries and those of someone else, the likelihood of clear expectations is increased. Instead of wondering whether something is okay and possibly triggering moments of discomfort, you can know what's allowable in a given relationship. It's worth it to ask people about their boundaries and to explore your own. Bear in mind, however, that people often have unconscious boundaries. These only emerge, often with great emotion, when they are crossed. At that point, we can only do our best to clarify the limits—for ourselves and others—and to honor them as gracefully as possible.

In Jon's reading in Layout 8, he discovered that he needed to have a conversation with Kim about her boundaries (see pages 65–67). He needed to discover whether Kim had limits regarding commitment, time spent together, activities shared, and so forth. Layout 9 (page 70) shows a reading in which Jon explored the boundaries he needed to honor in Kim.

LAYOUT 9. *Jon's boundaries in relating to Kim.*

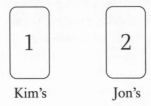

Kim's   Jon's

What are the most important boundaries for
Jon to honor while relating with Kim?

INTERPRETATION

Card 1: Kim's boundary to be honored by Jon:
   Judgement U: Time for Kim's maturation and growth into
   new levels; opportunities for Kim to graduate.

Card 2: Jon's boundary to be honored by Jon:
   Queen of Pentacles R: Mature capability of keeping himself
   grounded and secure.

> It turned out that Kim wanted to pursue educational opportunities
> in the field of travel so that she could advance her career. It was impor-
> tant to her to be able to attend conferences and classes whenever pos-
> sible, without any disagreement or complaints from Jon. Jon's need to
> take care of his own security was clearly established in earlier readings.
> In order to do that, Jon might need to set a firm internal boundary that
> ensured that he not ask Kim to be his security blanket.

Imagining Future Probabilities

In the reading shown in Layout 8, I got into the tricky area of the
future (see pages 65–67). This is because part of Jon's decision about
Kim rested on the probable outcome of dating her. When choosing
whether or not to engage in a new relationship, you may also want
to know something about the probable results of getting involved.

Notice that I usually include the word "probable" when talking about the future or defining a future layout position. By labeling it in that way, I agree with the universe that I am looking for a probability, not a prediction. If Jon continued to use his skills to stay grounded, chances were good that The World would result in six months. If he decided to force Kim into early commitment, forget his own self-care routine, or even start drinking again, he could have changed the probability. Jon could have responded to this information by being afraid of messing it up. Instead, he focused on the positive value to be gained by keeping himself emotionally healthy. Jon knew that he could probably have The World future if he kept his own boundaries and took care of himself. This gave him confidence and a sense of personal empowerment. It also kept him in the mode of experiencing relating as a process. He was not just waiting around to see if the future happened. He began to actively create it.

In general, the purpose of approaching the future as a probability is to encourage people to continue to take responsibility for creating the future they want. Notice, as well, that I put a time frame on the future in this reading. I didn't try to give Jon a final or ultimate outcome. We didn't ask or answer the question: "Will this relationship work forever?" By giving a six-month frame on the question, it put the future into a manageable perspective. It gave Jon a sense of what he needed to do for now, without locking him into a "forever" mentality inappropriate in this relationship. In the early stages of most relationships, it often seems most useful to look at short-term future possibilities.

Sample Layout Questions

How can I develop my curiosity/balance/appreciation/flexibility?

What are the factors in my unconscious model for this kind of relationship?

What are the factors in my conscious model for this kind of relationship?

Who are the kinds of people that I want in my life right now?

What are the qualities I seek in the other person at this time in my life?

What are the attributes the other person must have?

What are the attributes that it would be nice for the other person to have?

What are the attributes of the other person that are negotiable?

What are the attributes that the other person must not have?

What are the qualities I want to express in this kind of relationship at this time?

What are the attributes that I must express with this person?

What are the attributes that I'd like to express with this person?

What are the attributes of mine that are negotiable in terms of expression?

What are the characteristics of mine that I don't want to express?

What can I do next in order to find this kind of person?

What am I doing that supports me in finding this kind of person?

What am I doing that blocks me from finding this kind of person?

What strengths can I count on as I approach this type of relationship?

What blocks get in my way as I approach this type of relationship?

What do I need to change about myself to be ready for this kind of relationship?

What will help me make the changes I need to make?

What stops me from making the changes I need to make?

What are my resources with regard to these changes?

What are my obstacles with regard to these changes?

What needs of mine will probably be met in this new relationship?

What needs of the other person am I meeting?

What do I need to ask this person?

What do I need to ask myself?

How will I probably experience this relationship in six months if I proceed?

How will I probably experience this relationship in three
weeks if I proceed?

What do I need to remember if I want this future to
happen?

What do I need to avoid if I want this future to happen?

Sample Layout Combining Some Questions

What are the three most important qualities
that I seek in a new lover?

What are the three most important qualities that
I want to express with a new lover?

What blocks me from making   What supports me in making
the changes below?   the changes below?

How can I change myself to be ready for a new lover?

Exercises

1. Do a reading to discover how you can develop your curiosity, balance, appreciation, and flexibility—in general and in specific types of relationships.

2. Identify the unconscious model that you carry for an important relationship in your life. Do a reading to uncover the factors that create this model.

3. Identify the conscious model that you would like to experience for this relationship. Specify the attributes that you want to experience in the other person. Specify the attributes that you want to express yourself.

4. Choose a relationship that you want to create. Do a reading to discover the internal and external actions you can take in order to manifest that relationship.

5. Think about the resources and obstacles that could affect your quest to create a specific relationship. Do a reading to discover what blocks you from taking the steps or making the changes you want to make. Find out what supports you in taking those steps or making those changes.

6. Think of a relationship that you're considering as a possibility. Do a reading to discover the needs that would (and would not) be met in that relationship.

7. Consider the boundaries that you might need for a specific relationship or type of relationship. Do a reading to explore which boundaries you want to set regarding behavior or attitudes they must demonstrate (must not demonstrate), and behavior or attitudes you must demonstrate (must not demonstrate).

8. Look at the probable future for a specific relationship. Give yourself a short-term time frame (6 months or less) and interpret the future that could unfold in that time if you do what you know to do. You can include layout positions that outline what you need to do and what you need to avoid in order to make that future happen.

5

Enhancing or Healing Existing Relationships

Relationships are terrific testing grounds for the skills we've already learned and are still determined to learn. Yet it's within the excitement or stress of our important relationships that we often forget to apply what we know. The tarot can help us recognize the interactive "games" we play with each other and remind us to take care of ourselves with our significant people. The cards give signals that indicate that we should move forward or slow down within our relationships, taking responsibility for our own "stuff," communicating more clearly, making changes, and asking for changes in the other person.

If a relationship needs some change or enhancement, it could be that some kind of "game" is being played among the two or more people who are involved. By "game" I don't mean scrabble or volleyball, but rather a kind of dysfunctional interaction that is seductive and compelling, yet ultimately harmful to everyone. Unhealthy interpersonal games take on a variety of shapes and sizes, but my psychotherapist friends inform me there is really only one game that is played in endless permutations. I call it the "Only Game in Town."

The Only Game in Town

The Only Game in Town is a triangular pattern of interaction, commonly explored in therapeutic settings, called the victim-rescuer-persecutor dynamic (see figure 3, page 77). The Only Game in Town can be played with two or more people. Each person can choose one role and stay in it or switch roles at any time. Periodically, people engaged in a game also call in outsiders to play some of the roles. Some classic scenarios of the game follow:

Game 1
Two people go around and around on the triangle, changing roles frequently and engaging others as needed.

> Man (persecutor) physically and verbally abuses woman;
> Woman (victim) calls police;
> Police (rescuer) arrest man;
> Man (now the victim) feels shamed;
> Woman (now rescuer) drops charges;
> Man (now victim) is grateful and apologetic;
> Woman (still rescuer) feels that only she can help him change; waits for him to change; observes that he's not changing or grateful; (now persecutor) criticizes or nags him;
> Man (now victim) feels blamed, challenged and resentful; (now persecutor) verbally and physically abuses woman;
> Woman (now victim) calls police . . . .

Game 2
Three people take different roles and, more or less, stick to them with occasional excursions into other roles.

> Mom (victim) is bedridden for chronic pain, feels hopeless, whines and complains about her situation; suffers silently and loudly, is martyr-like and apologetic about her needs; (persecutor) blames her parents and her ex-husband for abusing her; blames local chemical plant for toxins in her system.
> Daughter (persecutor) blames Mom for suffering so long without getting well, tells her what she ought to do to get better; criticizes Mom's approach to healing, nags and bullies her to take medication; (rescuer) files lawsuit against chemical plant.

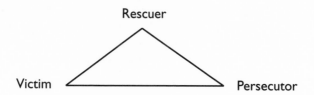

VICTIM: Feels or is blamed; controls others by having crises and needing attention; asks for help or advice, then often says "yes, but . . ."

Attitudes/Behavior: Crying, sick, tired, overwhelmed, hurt, helpless, abused, hopeless, addicted, childlike, unrecognized, undervalued, grateful, apologetic, martyr-like, "poor-me," self-sacrificing, demanding, whining, loudly suffering, wailing, complaining, resentful.

RESCUER: Reroutes blame from victim to persecutor; controls by handling crises; suggests actions, solutions, and answers.

Attitudes/Behavior: Comforting, sympathizing, sustaining, helping, nurturing, reassuring, supporting, enabling, care-taking, fixing, accommodating, suggesting, hand-holding, righteously indignant, advocating for, championing, defending, patronizing, healing, saving, fighting for, filing lawsuits for, getting revenge.

PERSECUTOR: Blames others; controls by enforcing own will; demands actions, new behavior, different attitudes.

Attitudes/Behavior: Nagging, withholding, "gently" remonstrating, gossiping, spreading rumors, "accidentally" burning dinner, "unconsciously" bumping or hurting someone, "forgetting" to do things, suggesting, questioning, abusing, perpetrating, exploiting, criticizing, attacking, using, battering, defiling, blaming, judging, finding fault, detracting, censoring, interrogating, bullying, hitting, shoving, taking charge of space with words or body, name-calling.

Figure 3. The Only Game in Town.

Son (rescuer) blames Dad for abuse, sister for criticizing, and chemical plant for toxins, takes care of Mom, is sympathetic; jumps to satisfy every need, worries, accommodates, comforts, nurtures, suggests healers; reassures her, cooks and cleans for her; (victim) sacrifices own plans for sake of Mom.

Game 3
Two people switch roles as needed to get what they want.

Mom (persecutor) angrily tells teenage daughter that she can't go to the mall with her friends unless she cleans up her room.

Teenage daughter (victim) claims that it's so unfair, she has to work too hard, none of her friends have to do so much, she's being abused; (persecutor) yells that Mom is so unreasonable and doesn't understand, that Mom is mean, a bad mom.

Mom (victim) feels hurt and maligned, says that she's just trying to set some mature boundaries and it's not too much to expect; after all, it's hard to be the mom of a teenager.

Teenage daughter (victim) crying, says she just wants some time with her friends, who are only in town for the weekend.

Mom (victim) feels apologetic and (rescuer) says she'll help with the cleaning so it can get done quickly and daughter can go to the mall.

Obviously, these are just examples of the game. Everyday, most of us act it out in some way with some people. In fact, it may be impossible to have a game-free relationship. It is useful to understand the game, however, so that, when our relationships falter or need help, we can analyze what's going on and step off the triangle.

How do you step off the game's triangle? When you recognize that you're enmeshed in a game with someone and use your curiosity to figure out who's playing what role in what sequence, sometimes the ah-hah! of it is enough to change the pattern. When you need to be more proactive, however, the four keys come in handy (see Table 4, pages 79–82). They are useful, as you may remember, because they return us to choice. Along with the process of feedback, they will return you to choice from each of the roles in the Only Game in Town. As victim, choice reminds you that you don't have to stay there; you're not inextricably stuck. As rescuer, it reminds you that

Table 4. The Four Keys of Relating Applied to the Game.

KEY: *Curiosity*
Wonder how you're engaged in the game; notice the situations, behavior, and comments that tend to engage you in it.

ROLE:	ACTION:
Victim:	*Think*: I wonder what I can do to help myself?
	Say: "I'm curious about how I'll get out of this situation."
Rescuer:	*Think*: I wonder how he/she will decide to handle this? It's not my decision.
	Say: "I have a lot of faith in your skills and abilities. I'm curious about what you'll do."
Persecutor:	*Think*: It's not up to me to control or manage this situation.
	Say: "I'm sorry if I've been giving you a hard time with my expectations. Actually, I'm curious about what you might come up with—on your own."

Table 4. The Four Keys of Relating Applied to the Game (cont.).

KEY: *Balance*

Get some perspective on the relative seriousness (or silliness) of the situation; laugh at yourself a little; remember that you are the only one who can keep you centered.

ROLE:	ACTION:
Victim:	*Think*: Is this a true headline-making crisis? What can I actually do about it? Honestly, what's out of my control? What kind of help do I really need? How can I repay it?
	Say: "This is the situation. This is the part I can handle. I'm mature and skilled enough to do it. I will need some help with this part. Are you willing and able? How can I pay for it, repay you, trade something I can do?"
Rescuer:	*Think*: The world won't end if I can't help. What's reasonable for me to do in terms of time, energy, and money? How can I help without hurting myself or invading his/her territory?
	Say: "This is the situation as you've described it. I'd like to help and I need to take care of myself as well. This is what I can do."
Persecutor:	*Think*: I don't need to control this situation. This is not about me and my security. I can let go.
	Say: "I tend to get involved with criticizing your actions. I'd like to back off, take care of me, and let you handle it on your own."

Table 4. The Four Keys of Relating Applied to the Game (cont.).

KEY: *Appreciation*

Value yourself and the other person; let go of blaming; pull out your strengths to help you deal with the situation.

ROLE: ACTION:

Victim: *Think*: What am I learning from this? How can I grow, now? Which of my gifts and strengths can I value and appreciate? Who's been helping me? How can I appreciate them?

Say: "I really appreciate your help. It makes a big difference to me. I'm also learning to . . . on my own. My own strength is increasing."

Rescuer: *Think*: This person has a bunch of strengths and resources that I haven't been acknowledging. She/he's stronger than I think. I'm a good helper, but I might help most by letting go of my tendency to give advice or take over.

Say: "I really admire, value, and appreciate these specific skills and resources of yours. I bet you can use them in this situation. Meanwhile, I'm going to back off and let you handle it. I have confidence in you."

Persecutor: *Think*: I have a lot of good ideas and I may really disagree with what he/she is doing, but it's not my life. My job is to handle my own behavior, my own anger and my own critical nature—and I can do that.

Say: "I may not agree with you or your decisions but it's not my life. You need to do what seems right for you."

Table 4. The Four Keys of Relating Applied to the Game (cont.).

KEY: *Flexibility*

Try something else; if that doesn't work, try something other than that; keep experimenting until you are satisfied.

ROLE: ACTION:

Victim: *Think*: I have lots of options and resources. If my first action doesn't work, I'll think of something else. If the first person I call can't help, I'll think of someone else. I'll be surprised at how many different solutions I can generate.

Say: "I would love and appreciate your support and help in this situation because I value your ability. If it's not appropriate for you to help at this time, I do have other resources."

Rescuer: *Think*: What are the many different kinds of things I can do? If I can't do what she/he initially asked, what other resources and people can I suggest?

Say: "I can't help you in the way you suggested. This is what I can do. Would it be helpful? Here are some ideas of other people/resources. I'll leave you the list so you can make your own decisions whether to use them."

Persecutor: *Think*: What else can I do besides being critical or blaming? How can I contribute some confidence or love to the situation? What else can I be doing besides invading his/her territory?

Say: "I'm used to critiquing your behavior and choices—and I'm trying to get out of the habit. I'd like to support you. Meanwhile, I also need to attend to my own life."

---

the victim does have options and that you can help—or not; you're not obligated. As persecutor, choice reminds you that you have other ways to respond to situations in which you usually become angry or resentful.

Once you have returned to choice, the way out of the game is to set a boundary for yourself or for someone else. (For a review about boundaries, go back to page 68). The way to get off the Game Triangle is, therefore, fairly simple to describe—sometimes more challenging to do!

- Use the four keys to relating and the process of feedback to return yourself to an experience of choice.

- Set a boundary for yourself or someone else and honor it.

When dealing with the game, remember to give and receive feedback in a way that honors and respects both people. Remember that both error and success messages contain "information" that can be useful in helping us to evaluate our choices.

When Jan broke up with Mike, she vowed never to repeat the same dysfunctional patterns. She was determined to take some time for herself, to avoid intimate relationships for a while, and to figure out how she had played the game, so she could change her behavior in the future. Her reading about the game is shown in Layout 10.

LAYOUT 10. *How Jan participated in the Game with Mike.*

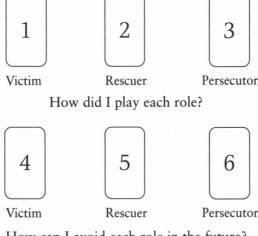

1	2	3
Victim	Rescuer	Persecutor

How did I play each role?

4	5	6
Victim	Rescuer	Persecutor

How can I avoid each role in the future?

INTERPRETATION

Cards 1–2–3: How did I play each role?

Victim:

> Five of Wands U: Uncertain of identity in world; erratic representation of self to others
>
> JAN: *I would say, "I'm just not sure of how to be myself around Mike and his cool friends," while feeling sorry for myself. I wanted Mike to rescue me and make me feel at ease.*

Rescuer:

> Hermit U: Knowing or understanding what's going on; having some distance or perspective on the situation
>
> JAN: *I would feel and say, "I understand what's really going on. You're just hurt, scared, and untrusting because of how your ex-wife treated you. I know all about these things from my own therapy. I'll give you the benefit of my knowledge."*

Persecutor:

> Queen of Swords R: Well-developed set of beliefs and values; long-standing form of private communication
>
> JAN: *"I think I always talked down to him, assuming I knew more about his pain, struggles, and circumstances than he did. It probably made him feel that I didn't respect him much. And, really, I didn't respect him very much."*

Cards 4–5–6: How can I avoid each role in the future?

Victim:

> Sun U: Do something done in the past, but differently; become more playful or lighthearted
>
> JAN: *"In the past, I've been able to handle uncomfortable social situations by suggesting a game or something fun to do. It's easier for me to relax when doing something, than when just sitting around."*

Rescuer:

> Eight of Swords U: Limited or less communication
>
> Jan: *"I could really just be quiet, listen, and become curious about what the other person is doing or feeling . . . I don't need to start right in with a lecture, even a caring and understanding one!"*

Persecutor:

Star R: Channeling resources and energy into the self; receiving

JAN: *"I can make sure that I am getting my own needs taken care of . . . then, I don't have to get so angry if I think the other person isn't taking care of me correctly."*

Essentially, Jan felt socially uncomfortable around Mike and his friends but superior to Mike in terms of personal growth, therapy, and awareness. She wished he would rescue her from her social discomfort and she played both the rescuer and persecutor when it came to his lack of therapeutic experience.

In future relationships, she plans to focus more on fun activities, a little less on conversation, limit some of what she says and listen more, and pay good attention to taking care of herself.

Taking Care of Yourself

When a new lover, child, collaborator, or mentor comes into your life, the easiest thing to lose is self-care. You may become so involved with exploring the ramifications of the new interaction that you forget your personal maintenance needs. For a little while, this is fine. You are meeting other needs for growth or expansion and it seems okay to let maintenance slide. As relationships proceed, however, you may find that you can't continue to function healthfully unless you remember to support your individual stability. If you become curious and flexible about ways to meet your needs and keep your boundaries, the tarot can help you remember to consider yourself.

When Jan got involved with Robert, she was conscious that she wanted to avoid playing the game and remember what she'd learned from her relationship with Mike. She was especially conscious of wanting to take better care of herself. Specifically, she was concerned about having enough time for herself, alone. The reading in Layout 11 is about her self-care (see page 86).

LAYOUT 11. *Jan's self-care in her relationship with Robert.*

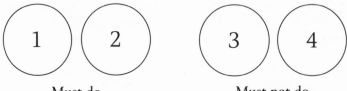

| 1 | 2 | 3 | 4 |

Must do   Must not do

How can I best take care of myself in my relationship
with Robert, especially regarding time alone?

INTERPRETATION

Cards 1-2: What Jan must do to take care of herself:
> Seven of Cups U: Interact with a variety of people and
> express a variety of feelings and emotions.
> Justice R: Keep inner sense of balance and equilibrium.

Extra Card: How can I keep the internal balance?
> Star Sideways (round cards!): Make sure energy, resources,
> and time come from you to others and from the universe
> to you.

Cards 3-4: What Jan must not do in order to take care of herself:
> Sun R: Do not repeat old patterns (even in slightly new
> forms), especially personal patterns of thinking and feeling.
> Eight of Swords U: Do not become too rigid or limited with
> regard to communication or Schedule.

JAN: *This makes sense to me. I have a tendency to focus on one rela-*
tionship and leave all my other friendships behind. I guess it isn't just
time alone I need. I also need time without Robert, with my other
friends. Still, the Justice card does emphasize keeping my internal
equilibrium with a balance of output from me and input to me. I
know the input's from painting, meditating, exercising, and my clos-
er friends. I'll try to be a little flexible and not so rigid about my
schedule of away-from-Robert time. At the same time, I do want to
let go of my old pattern of thinking that this is the only relationship
for me and that it will disappear if I take even a moment for myself!

When Julia's second baby arrived, she knew she had to do something. With her first child, she had been busy, but she'd managed to find a little bit of time for herself in the evenings. With two, she was afraid that, when she went back to work, she'd stop taking care of herself at all. It was such a high priority for her to take care of them that she experienced a real struggle within herself when she took time out. She also knew that she needed to know how to maintain some self-care. Her reading is shown in Layout 12.

LAYOUT 12. *Julia's self-care with her two children.*

What are the important things I can do
to take care of myself?

INTERPRETATION

Cards 1–2–3: Important things to do in order to take care of self:
Lovers U: Collaborate with others.
King of Swords U: Let go of the routine and schedule.
Eight of Pentacles R: Organize self around comfort and
security.

JULIA: *You know, I don't tend to ask for help. My husband is gone a lot on business and I guess I think I shouldn't ask for outside help when he's not available. But I do have two good friends with children. Maybe we could trade off on child-care sometimes. Letting go of the routine will be hard, but I have been considering working thirty hours instead of forty at my job. It would be tight financially, but it could be worth it. And, I want to make my home more comfortable for me. I have already planned a weekend to reorganize things so that my books and recliner have a little corner of their own—a spot for me!*

Although Jan had already established many criteria for the relationship she was entering, Julia was almost taken by surprise. It was only
after her second child was born that she realized that her self-care
was slipping. Both of them were able to increase their self-care after
getting insight from the tarot. You, too, can use the tarot to explore
this important part of relating.

Red Flags and Green Flags

As the process of relating proceeds, you'll find that signals arise to
let you know when to proceed and when to slow down. I call the
uneasy feelings or discordant words and sounds red flags, because
they remind us to stop, ask questions (be curious), change our reactions (be flexible), or choose new actions. The comfortable sensations and harmonious verbal interactions are the green flags that
give us the go-ahead to proceed to stronger commitments. Red and
green flags can come from another person's words or actions. They
can also come from our own internal feelings, thoughts, and mental
images.

Jan had been involved with Robert for about eight months when
she began to wonder whether she was ignoring important clues about
their interaction. Before she moved into a more serious level of commitment, she wanted to pay attention to the signals that were coming
her way. Layout 13 (pages 89–90) shows her reading.

LAYOUT 13. *Red flags and green flags for Jan and Robert.*

5	6
What signal coming from Robert is an important green flag for Jan?	What signal coming from within Jan is an important green flag for Jan?

3	4
How can Jan react appropriately to the red flag from Robert?	How can Jan act appropriately in response to her own red flag?

1	2
What signal coming from Robert is an important red flag for Jan?	What signal coming from within Jan is an important red flag for her?

INTERPRETATION

Card 1: Red Flag from Robert:
> Queen of Swords U: Talking as if he "knows it all" and dominating conversations.

Card 2: Red Flag from inside Jan:
> Ten of Swords R: Putting her own opinions and beliefs "on hold" and avoiding knowing (or sharing) what she really thinks.

Card 3: Appropriate reaction to Robert's "know it all" conversation style:
> Five of Wands R: Challenge herself to respond more assertively.

Card 4: Appropriate reaction to her own tendency to hold back:
> The Chariot R: Take charge of her own runaway thoughts and feelings and remember that she's in control of her inner world. After she has discovered her own opinions, she can then decide whether or not to share them.

Card 5: Green Flag from Robert:
> Four of Swords R: Robert's capacity to act on his deeply held beliefs.

Card 6: Green Flag from within Jan:
> Two of Swords R: Jan's increasing ability to internally affirm what she knows.

It seemed that the biggest issue in their relationship surrounded Robert's rather strong philosophy and his tendency to dominate with his communication style. Jan, in trying not to repeat her pattern with Mike, was holding back and deferring to his opinion. In fact, she often avoided even knowing what she felt or thought about something in order to avoid conflict. Jan needed to take time to discover what she thought, realize that she could steer her own course based on her own beliefs, and truly choose to have her own opinions. After that, she could decide whether or not to share her ideas with Robert.

In Jan's case, the key issue had to do with philosophy and communication style. The details of the interpretation arose from analyzing the cards in the red-flag positions from a negative perspective and interpreting those in the green-flag positions in a positive light. Since the cards themselves are neutral (Rule 2), this is a situation where the form of the question slants the meaning of the card. In other readings, the following red flags could be interpreted in these ways:

- Queen of Cups R: Long-term substance abuse

- Six of Pentacles U: Dysfunctional work, money, or health habits

- Knight of Pentacles U: Physical aggressiveness

The same cards, as green flags could be interpreted like this:

- Queen of Cups R: Spiritual or intuitive maturity

- Six of Pentacles U: Steady employment; good health habits

- Knight of Pentacles U: Athletic ability; focus on health

As you look for the red and green flags in your relationships, remember to apply the appropriate negative (red) or positive (green) interpretations to the cards in those layout positions.

Taking Responsibility for Your Own "Stuff"

As we mature in our relating skills, it becomes increasingly important for us to take responsibility for our own "stuff." At one level, this can mean taking charge of personal money, laundry, cars, or other physical possessions—the practical things represented in the tarot by upright Pentacles cards. As adults, most of us try to manage our own Pentacles things, or to make agreements with others about them. For example, whether you actually clean your house, do your laundry, wash your car, trade with someone for these services, or pay someone else to do them, you are still managing the care of your own life. Agreeing with someone that he will cook dinner and you will vacuum is managing your life. When you are sick, overwhelmed, or going through a rough patch, you can ask for help and still assume responsibility for your world, knowing that, at some time in the future, you will be willing to return the favor. Assuming that someone else will always pick up after you, bail you out of financial trouble, or buy gifts for your family—without prior negotiation and agreement—might not be managing your own life. These Pentacles responsibilities are fairly obvious, although we all occasionally become unconscious or less-than-graceful about managing them.

The trickier things to manage are represented by the rest of the cards. In addition to the upright meanings I've already mentioned, the reversed Pentacles tell us that we are responsible for our own levels of security and groundedness. The Wands remind us to take responsibility for our own identities, roles, self-esteem, and self-expression, while Cups help us remember to honor and take care of our own feelings, as well as our emotional and intuitive responses to life. The suit of Swords reflects the degree to which we manage our schedules, as well as our opinions, communication patterns, and personal values and beliefs. Each of the Major Arcana cards describes a specific life lesson that we can learn or experience as we mature. Like it or not, we find that we are responsible for managing all the tangible and intangible "stuff" of our lives. We certainly have choices to make about how we handle it, whether and when we enlist the help of others, and whether we manage our lives gracefully or resentfully. One way or another, however, the responsibility comes back to us.

Many of the struggles in our relationships come down to the issue of deciding who's managing what. The attitudes of appreciation (How can I value myself and my ability to handle my stuff?), of curiosity (How can I manage my stuff better?), and of flexibility (How can I manage my stuff differently?) are especially useful when negotiating "stuff management." There are also several ways of looking at this issue with the tarot. You can choose a specific category and ask what you need to do (or not do) in order to assume your appropriate share of responsibility in that regard. The short reading in Layout 14 is an example of this kind of reading. In it, Julia sorts out how much to participate in cleaning her older daughter's room.

LAYOUT 14. *Should Julia clean her 8-year-old daughter's room?*

```
┌───────┐          ┌───────┐
│       │          │       │
│   1   │          │   2   │
│       │          │       │
└───────┘          └───────┘
```

Key task for Julia to do. ——— Key task for Julia not to do.

INTERPRETATION

Card 1: Key task for Julia to do:

Six of Pentacles U: It's appropriate for Julia to establish an overall, reliably workable system of organization and repeatable set of tasks to be done and to do some (or all?) parts of the cleaning on a regular basis.

Extra Card: Which parts of the cleaning should Julia do?

Judgement U: Adult responsibilities

Card 2: Key task for Julia *not* to do:

Three of Pentacles U: It's not appropriate for Julia to plan the details of how the tasks should be accomplished.

JULIA: *I think the adult responsibilities are things like cleaning her shades and lights, and spring cleaning.*

Julia needed to make sure that, at a practical, physical level there were defined and predictable expectations. This could include a list of tasks to be accomplished and a daily or weekly time in which they need to be accomplished. It is also appropriate for Julia to take care of "adult" responsibilities in the cleaning.

At this stage, it's not appropriate for Julia to worry about the details of how Sally plans to clean up her room. Julia can make sure Sally has organizers and enough places to put her toys, set the goals and expect that they will be met at a certain time. It's up to Sally to figure out how to approach the job.

Communicating Clearly

I have noticed that we often put more effort into understanding those who come from other cultures, or who speak other languages, than we put into our important relationships. In the case of the true foreigner, we assume that they may not use words in the same ways we do, that culturally based assumptions about commitment or fair play or work ethics may not be the same. In cross-cultural situations, we may even find the differences between the equivalencies below to be amusing or intriguing:

Arriving exactly at the scheduled time = polite
Arriving one to two hours after the scheduled time = polite

Soon = 15 minutes
Soon = 3 days
Soon = 1 month

Can you meet me at 3:00 to discuss this issue? = I want to talk with you.
How are you doing? What are you doing this afternoon? = I want to talk with you.

No, I don't need any more = I really don't need any more.
No, I don't need any more = keep asking me, I'll say yes later.

I'll call you later = I will definitely call you within 24 hours.
I'll call you later = don't call me, I might call you someday.

Having sex with someone else = betrayal and lack of commitment
Having sex with someone else = bringing new energy back to the relationship.

Christmas = big family holiday with fifty relatives present
Christmas = small intimate gathering with closest family
Christmas = highly religious experience
Christmas = gifts and celebration
Christmas = someone else's holiday, irrelevant to me

Grandmother's rocking chair = prized possession to be saved at all costs
Grandmother's rocking chair = old item, ready to be sold

Tidy house = respect for self and guests
Tidy house = rigid, uncomfortable formality

Hug = casual friendliness
Hug = intimacy

Loving me = always being home for dinner
Loving me = picking up my dry-cleaning
Loving me = always interrupting yourself to listen to me

When a cross-cultural component is not involved, or when we think we've mastered the nuances of someone else's culture, we frequently forget to check on the meaning of words, experiences, and behavior. Because we think we are speaking the same language, we forget to be curious about whether we are interpreting another's verbal or non-verbal signals correctly. Then, we have the opportunity to take offense or lay blame when the other person doesn't act or react in the ways we expect.

I've found that it can be very helpful to imagine that most other people are foreigners and that we have to create mental models of their culture. Over time, we may develop consistent translations, so that we're more certain, more often, of interpreting the messages correctly. However, even in long-term relationships, a little double-checking can be useful. The best way to make sure you're on the same wavelength is to be curious. Ask questions that make general words and behavior more specific:

> "When you say soon, what does that mean in hours or days?"
> "If I say I'll call you later, I mean by Friday."
> "For me, Christmas means these recipes, these people, this level of gift giving . . ."
> "When you say that you don't care if I go without you, is it your expectation that I *will* go or that I will then, graciously, *not go?*"
> "When you hug me, what does that signify?"
> "How, specifically, will you know that I love you?"
> "How will you know that I value your participation?"

Whether interpreting the signals that are unique to cultures of many people or a culture of one person, it is crucial to remain curious and to stay appreciative of all the people and cultures involved. These attitudes, combined with flexibility, allow us to sustain a mood of respectful attention as we interact. When someone else's language or behavior is bothering or puzzling you, use these attitudes, and a sense of balance or proportion, to discover what their words and actions mean to them. Jan did the reading in Layout 15 in order to translate and understand some of Robert's behavior.

LAYOUT 15. *What does Robert's behavior mean?*

1	2	3
Know-it-all style of communication.	Staring off into space when listening to Jan.	Consistently being 15-30 minutes late for dates.

INTERPRETATION

Card 1: Know-it-all style of communication:
   Ten of Swords R: Personal, philosophical holding pattern; could mean he's developed what he thinks is true so far and is not re-evaluating it, or moving on to further development; could indicate "being stuck" in a point of view.

Card 2: Staring into space when listening to Jan:
   Eight of Swords R: Doing internal processing and organizing of what Jan's saying; could be literally making mental diagrams and pictures to represent her thoughts; could also be internally organizing what he wants to say next.

Card 3: Consistently being 15-30 minutes late for dates:
   Six of Cups U: Emotional habit; tends to do it with everyone.

Extra Card: Why is being late useful for him?
   King of Pentacles R: Gives him time to let go of insecurity (maybe it makes him too insecure to wait for someone else?).

Jan was curious about three of Robert's behaviors. As it turned out, they had a common theme—something about giving himself time to sort out ideas or feelings. When he does his know-it-all communication pattern, he's simply repeating the thoughts he's had before, not thinking new thoughts in the moment. When he stares into space, he's either organizing Jan's thoughts or his own. And, by being late for dates, he gives himself time to release any nervousness or insecurity.

Changing Yourself

There comes a time in many relationships when we want things to be different from what they seem to be. We wish that he would do this differently, that she would do more of that, that they would take more responsibility, that others wouldn't respond or react in that way. We've discovered that wishing doesn't make it so. In fact, if we want things to be different, we are the ones who have to make the choice to feel, think, or behave differently.

When we elect to do something differently, we have the choice of transferring behavior or of adding new behavior. Transferring behavior means applying something that you tend to do in one situation to a different situation. Perhaps you already know how to listen carefully to your spouse. You might transfer that behavior by listening more carefully to your employee or boss. Adding new behavior, on the other hand, implies learning to do something that you haven't done before, in any context. Examples of this can be learning to balance a checkbook or discovering how to assert yourself with someone who's being rude to you. Whether you are transferring or adding behavior, the choice is still in your hands. You are the one who is changing.

Don had been business partners with Brad for about a year when he began to feel that he was shouldering too much responsibility. Upon reflection, he realized that his own control needs set the tone for the partnership. He wanted to add a new behavior: sharing control. Layout 16 (pages 98–99) relates to Don's decisions about making some changes in his working relationship with his business partner, Brad.

Layout 16. Don's adding a new behavior—sharing control.

Positive   Negative

How will I feel if Brad handles the bookkeeping and billing
without my feedback or intervention?

Positive   Negative

How is Brad likely to handle it?

Positive   Negative

What's the probable impact on business in the next 6 months,
if Brad handles the bookkeeping?

INTERPRETATION

Cards 1–2: How will Don feel about Brad handling bookkeeping?
  Positive: Devil R: Good feeling about setting some inner
  boundaries and sticking to his own resolve.
  Negative: Ten of Swords U: Uncertain sensation of leaving
  communication "on hold," not fully letting go, but not
  involved.

Cards 3–4: How will Brad handle it?

Positive: Five of Cups U: Able to adapt appropriately to interacting with people (including Don) differently—on an emotional level.

Negative: Moon R: May rely too much on own instincts and inner sense of things—perhaps not get enough feedback from others.

Extra Card: How can I give Brad feedback without taking over?

Knight of Cups U: focus on feelings and doing it together.

Cards 5–6: Impact on business in next 6 months:

Positive: Two of Swords U: Good affirmation of communication between the business and those outside; probably firm agreements with customers or vendors.

Negative: Lovers U: Some inappropriate collaborations or agreements.

Extra Card: What kinds of inappropriate agreements?

Nine of Cups U: Maintaining ongoing relationships that aren't good for business (perhaps people who aren't paying bills?).

DON: *I could see Brad letting people off the hook because he's a friendly guy and he hates confrontation. I really do want to let go of some of the responsibility in our partnership. I think it's good practice for me, because I want to learn to share the load. Given this reading, I don't think that bookkeeping and billing is the place to start. Since he's really good at collaborating with people, I'd feel a lot better letting go of the burden of sales. I think I'll propose that at our next meeting.*

Don was quite committed to changing himself by adding the new behavior of "sharing control." In this reading, he found that his first thought about what to share might have lead to disappointment. With these results, he may have felt uncertain about whether he really *should* share the responsibility. By keeping his commitment to change, but revising the subject of change, he ended up with a solution that felt right to him.

When you do readings about changing yourself, you can begin, like Don, with an idea of what you want to change and then explore the impact. You can also start by asking a general question such as:

> "What thoughts, feelings, and behavior could I transfer from other relationships and situations to this one?"
>
> "What thoughts, feelings, and behavior could I add that would help me and help this relationship?"

In each case, you'll be exploring if and how it's appropriate for you to make changes in yourself, not for the sake of the other person, but for the sake of improving your relating skills and your interactions with that person.

Inviting Someone Else to Change

If you've made all the personal changes you want to make and still wish another person would also make some adaptations, it's sometimes worth it to gracefully invite the other person to transfer or add new behavior. While there's no guarantee that the other person will honor your request, if it's reasonable and the other person is emotionally healthy and committed to the relationship, you may get what you want.

"Gracefully invite" is the key phrase in the above paragraph. Asking people to end existing behavior is more challenging than asking them to transfer existing skills or add new ones. Of course, if you need someone to end abusive or harmfully inappropriate behavior, you may want to invite him or her to change *and* set your own boundaries at the same time.

Jan experimented with various ways of responding to Robert's "know-it-all" communication style and finally decided that she wanted to invite him to make a change. Layout 17 helped her figure out what to ask and how to ask it (see pages 101–102).

LAYOUT 17. *Inviting Robert to change how he communicates.*

2	3
What communication style could Robert transfer?	What communication style could Robert learn?

1

How can I best approach Robert about changing his communication style with me?

INTERPRETATION

Card 1: Best approach to Robert?
Ten of Swords U: On a vacation or day off work, say something like: "Let's take some time out to talk about how we communicate with each other," or "I really need you to listen carefully to me without responding for a while."

Card 2: Communication style to transfer?
Three of Wands R: Style he uses when he's planning what to say in his mind, before speaking out loud to someone else.

Extra Card: What style is that?
Ace of Cups U: Approach the other person as if it's a brand new relationship and he knows nothing about what this person thinks or feels.

Card 3: Communication style to learn?
Queen of Pentacles U: That of somebody who's mature (maybe someone at his workplace?) whom he respects.

When Jan thought about these cards, she realized that, when Robert meets someone new, he's always very curious about who they are and what they know. He listens carefully to what they say and holds back on giving his own opinion until he knows them better. Jan thought she could invite him to treat each conversation with her as though he were interacting with someone new. Although she couldn't think of anyone at work that could be a model for new behavior, Robert did have a favorite professor in college who was very good at debating and also good at conceding points to others. He might act as a model. Despite the reading, Jan said that she knew that Robert might not respond to her ideas—that she was running the danger of repeating her "I'm the therapy expert" pattern. Just understanding more about the possibilities, however, helped her feel more balanced and flexible.

Evaluating the Costs and Benefits of Change

Sometimes, when we choose to change or invite someone else to change, the whole situation shifts. People begin to respond in new ways and the benefits are obvious. Sometimes, when changes occur, we find that others move on or that we've outgrown them, and the costs or losses are more obvious. There's always a risk involved with change, so when we are deciding if and how to change, we need to consider the possible results. We need to weigh the costs and benefits of change in order to decide if the outcome will be worth the effort. In Layout 18, Julia thinks about changes she could make, now that she has two children.

LAYOUT 18. *Should Julia switch to 30 hours a week?*

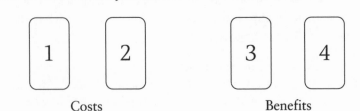

Costs   Benefits

INTERPRETATION

Cards 1–2: Costs of switching to 30 hours a week:
  Page of Cups U: Temptation to become re-involved with other people.
  Queen of Pentacles U: Need to be very mature and responsible about money.

Cards 3–4: Benefits of switching to 30 hours a week:
  Page of Pentacles R: Recommitting to a kind of psychological security and groundedness that she used to have.
  Five of Wands R: Adapting her self-concept in a positive way.

JULIA: *The benefit of groundedness is obvious to me, but I hadn't realized that so much of my self-concept was attached to work. It probably would be good for me to adapt that idea of myself a little. As for the costs, I used to spend a lot of time having coffee with my friends and, if I had more time off, I might be tempted to do some of that. That's a kind of renewal, too, so I don't think it's that bad of a cost. The need to be mature about money is a big one for me. I hate having to budget, but I think the change might be worth it.*

In addition to "costs/benefits" you can use several other words and phrases that might more accurately give you the feedback you want. For example, Layout 16 includes some "positive/negative" questions that give feedback about the results of change. Advantages/disadvantages are also good words to use. Additionally, you can focus on the costs and benefits of change by asking more specific questions:

• What will be the cost to me of making these changes? Time? Money? Energy? Emotion? Sense of self? Health?

• What will be the benefit to me of making these changes? Time? Money? Energy? Emotion? Sense of self? Health?

The value of doing a cost/benefit reading is that it gives you information and insight from which you can make a decision. It's useful to remember that, if you ask for negatives, you'll get the worst ones that exist. It's up to you to evaluate how much the identified costs or disadvantages will affect you. In Julia's case, the financial negative was definitely an issue, but the social one wasn't as great. Similarly, if you ask for positives, you'll get the best that are possible. If those benefits or advantages aren't strong enough for you, change might not be worth it. It's still up to you to make the choice after evaluating the relative impact of the positives and negatives.

Getting Outside Help

Even after we've done a great deal of personal and interpersonal work, there are occasionally times when we need outside help in order to support or enhance our important relationships. This can be in the form of family therapy, couples counseling, spiritual guidance, mediation, or even business coaching. If you decide to seek outside help, remember to keep the four essential attitudes in mind:

- Curiosity: Wonder what *might* happen instead of having a preconceived agenda about what *should* or *will* happen;

- Balance: Be serious about the important issues; handle the others lightheartedly;

- Appreciation: Value yourself, the other person, and the counselor;

- Flexibility: Be open to new ways of looking at things and to transferring or adding new behavior.

Jan finally got to the point of wondering whether some kind of counseling might help her and Robert to sort out a few things. Robert was pressing her to make a commitment, but she wanted to resolve some of their communication issues first. He was willing to get some help. Layout 19 shows their process for deciding about counseling (see pages 105–106).

LAYOUT 19. *Should Jan and Robert get counseling?*

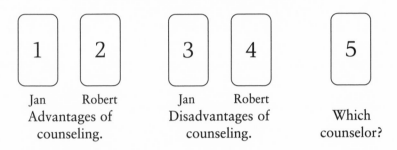

Jan	Robert	Jan	Robert	
Advantages of		Disadvantages of		Which
counseling.		counseling.		counselor?

INTERPRETATION

Cards 1–2: Advantages of counseling:

> JAN: Knight of Swords U: Concentrate and focus on what she needs to say.
>
> ROBERT: Ace of Swords U: Plant seeds for communicating in a new way.

Cards 3–4: Disadvantages of counseling:

> JAN: Knight of Cups R: Focus on deeply held feelings and emotions that could be upsetting; she could become obsessed with processing her feelings.
>
> ROBERT: Three of Wands R: Think about himself and his self-image in different ways and plan how to be the new self out in the world; he might only plan for the new identity without being able to manifest it.

Card 5: Which counselor?

> Queen of Pentacles U: Someone mature and experienced, with good professional credentials; probably someone who could be paid through the insurance provided at work, someone whose approach is practical, not only theoretical.

JAN: *Yes, I would want to dig deep into my feelings—so maybe I could do that in some individual counseling and just work on the communication issues together.*

ROBERT: *Yes, I could see that it might be more challenging to apply what I've learned than to think of it in the first place. I always like to reflect on things long before I act. However, I feel pretty committed to Jan and I think this work would be good for me, in any case. So, I'm willing to work hard at it. We'll have to pay for the therapist through my insurance at work and that has to be a psychiatrist or Ph.D. psychologist. Maybe we can compare several of them by using the tarot cards.*

In this case, Jan and Robert decided to go ahead with couples counseling, while Jan proceeded with some individual counseling on her own. They also decided to do a further tarot reading that would allow them to compare several therapists (see Layout 20).

LAYOUT 20. *Choosing a counselor.*

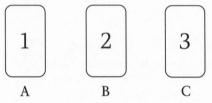

A   B   C

Working style of each therapist.

INTERPRETATION

Card 1: Working style of therapist A:
   Seven of Cups R: Very intuitive; explores lots of deep feelings, creative.

Card 2: Working style of therapist B:
   Nine of Wands R: Deals with individual needs; wants to establish an on-going sense of self-esteem for each person.

Card 3: Working style of Therapist C:
   Four of Cups U: Pays attention to actions and interactions between people; encourages people to express emotions.

All three therapists had good reputations but, upon seeing the cards, Jan and Robert felt that therapist C would be most helpful to them. They thought she might be able to help them really work on the active dynamics between them. Jan decided to consult therapist A on her own to do the deep emotional work that she wanted to do.

Remember, when choosing any kind of professional, it's critical that you feel right about your connection with that person. Although Jan and Robert were leaning toward therapist C, they intended to interview all three of them. The tarot can be combined usefully with your own knowledge and insights when making choices about helpers (or anything else!) in your life.

Sample Layout Questions

What must I do in order to take care of myself in this relationship?

What must I not do in order to take care of myself in this relationship?

What can I emphasize in order to nurture myself?

What can I emphasize in order to nurture this person?

What can I de-emphasize in order to nurture myself?

What can I de-emphasize in order to nurture this person?

What kinds of resources will help me take care of myself in this relationship?

What kinds of obstacles might prevent me from taking care of myself in this relationship?

What are the red flags coming from this person?

What are the green flags coming from this person?

What are the red flags, coming from within me?

What are the green flags, coming from within me?

What changes could I make in myself in order to improve this relationship?

What useful behavior can I transfer from other relationships to this one?

What new behavior could I add that would help me and help the relationship?

How can I gracefully invite this person to _____ ?

How will I feel if this person changes and does _____?

How is this person likely to handle it?

What's the impact on the _____ area of my life if I elect to change?

What are the (benefits, advantages, strengths, positives) of _____ ?

What are the (costs, disadvantages, weaknesses, negatives) of _____ ?

What is the working style of this person?

Sample Layout Combining Some Questions

What helps me to take care of myself within this relationship?

| 1 |

What prevents me from taking care of myself within this relationship?

| 2 |

What are the benefits of being more aggressive in pursuing this relationship?

| 3 |

What are the costs of being more aggressive in pursuing this relationship?

| 4 |

Exercises

These exercises are really just topics for readings. For each one, create a layout of one to six cards that explores the issues (or more if you feel ready for bigger readings). You can use the questions in the list above or invent your own. Feel free to explore the same relationship in all of the readings or to explore several different ones, putting the name of the person involved in the exercises below.

1. Identify how you're engaged in the Only Game in Town.

2. Get out of the game (off the victim-rescuer-persecutor triangle).

3. Take better care of yourself while interacting with [name the person].

4. Explore the red flags/green flags in your relationship with [name the person].

5. Take responsibility for your own "stuff" while relating with [name the person]. ("Stuff" can be objects, tasks, emotions, thoughts, behavior.)

6. Translate the meaning of [name the person]'s words and/or behavior.

7. Change yourself in the context of relating to [name the person] (transferring behavior; adding behavior).

8. Invite [name the person]to change (transfer behavior, add behavior).

9. Calculate the costs and benefits of making changes (disadvantages/advantages, negatives/positives).

10. Get help for yourself (or for others in the relationship).

11. Compare helpers.

6

Long-Term Relating

By now, you know that I view relationships as mobile, growing processes, not as static things. Because we, and our important relationships, evolve and change over time, it's not surprising that some relationships do end or change form. It's also not surprising that the choice-centered approach tends to raise the question of permanency and commitment. An acknowledgment of change doesn't have to mean the end of long-term relating. In fact, most of us want to construct relationships that last over time. This means that we're challenged to create stable structures that allow for creative changes and transitions. We need to consider some important factors when building lasting relationships, and find ways to identify and name our relationships, and explore processes for defining commitment. This requires that we find a balance between intimacy and autonomy, that we stay on-purpose, and that we periodically assess our progress.

The conscious and unconscious models of relating presented in Part One tell us what we expect and desire from different kinds of interactions. They provide us with general templates for our professional, friendship, romantic, and family dynamics. They don't, however, specify the details for any particular relationship agreement made with a specific person. To do this, we need to analyze the verbal and nonverbal agreements that we've made—or would like to make—with these individuals. Essentially, we have to name the relationship and then agree on what that name means.

Amanda and José had been dating for about four months when they realized that they wanted and needed to define what they were doing together. They began with the one-card reading in Layout 21 and moved on to the three-card reading shown in Layout 22 in order to define and describe their relationship (see pages 112 and 113). You'll notice that, in the second reading, they begin by naming different configurations that might be possible for their relationship, and then use the tarot to evaluate which feels right.

LAYOUT 21. *Naming the relationship.*

$$\boxed{1}$$

What is the nature of our relationship?

INTERPRETATION

Card 1: What is the nature of our relationship?
The Moon R: We were intuitively guided to come together.

AMANDA: *Yes, I've sensed all along that we were meant to be together.*

JOSÉ: *I somehow think we have a purpose, something to do together.*

LAYOUT 22. *Defining the relationship.*

1	2	3
Short-term sexual.	Long-term sexual with commitment.	Long-term sexual and business with lots of commitments.

INTERPRETATION

Card 1: Short-term sexual:
   Nine of Cups R: Flows easily, tends to be on-going, intuitive, private.

Card 2: Long-term sexual with commitment:
   Three of Wands R: Involves private planning and figuring out a joint sense of who we are together; sense that there would be a further "action" (Four of Wands).

Card 3: Long-term sexual and business with lots of commitment:
   Queen of Wands R: Mature sense of who we are together; still private.

Extra card: What would move the relationship to a more public form?
   Three of Pentacles U: Plan details for new approach to money, home, sex, health.

AMANDA: *I think our sexual interaction is fine as it is and I'm all for long-term commitment. I guess we should talk about living together or finding some space for the health-care partnership we talked about.*

JOSÉ: *I'm thinking we should rent a big house and run your massage practice and my acupuncture practice from home. Then, when it all gets working, we can buy a place.*

At first, it looks as if it would be easy for this to be a short-term sexual relationship. On the other hand, it might never end. It might just continue. Although the first card has a nice feeling to it, it tends to point to the longer-term commitment. The long-term sexual relationship seems to have a "what next" sense about it. They are still figuring out or planning what to do together. By adding business to their relationship, it seems to come into its maturity. In order to make it more publicly defined, they may want to make some plans for a new direction in money, home, health, or sexual interaction.

Defining Commitment

When we arrive at a point of commitment in our interactions with others, we usually respond pretty emotionally to the whole concept. Whether it's a romantic, family, or business commitment, we imagine what it means in terms of curtailing our freedom or assuring our security. We may react with relief, excitement, or even fear. One reason for this strong feeling is that the word "commitment" is huge and abstract; it can be defined in so many ways. In most relationships, it's useful to uncover the operative definition for commitment—and to make sure that all parties agree on it!

José and Amanda knew that their emotional commitment involved sexual monogamy, living together, and sharing money and other resources. They weren't sure how to define the commitment of their business collaboration. Layout 23 shows the reading in which they explored that partnership (see page 115).

LAYOUT 23. *Defining the commitment. How would it be to create various types of business relationships?*

1	2	3

Two separate businesses	Legal partnership	Corporation
Share office/equipment	Share office/equipment	Share office/equipment
Refer clients to	Refer clients	Refer clients
each other	Joint bank account	Corporate account
Separate finances	Take equal draws	Salaries

INTERPRETATION

Card 1: Separate Businesses:
   Queen of Cups R: Mature emotional interactions; relationship would be private.

Card 2: Legal Partnership:
   Magician R: Continual process of clarifying the difference between reality and illusion; partners might have differing perceptions about what's going on.

Card 3: Corporation:
   Five of Swords U: Certain amount of challenge, upheaval, argument, or active discussion.

AMANDA: *Wow. I think we should keep separate businesses for now. Just get our personal relationship solid and share office space.*

JOSÉ: I agree!

The Dance of Intimacy and Autonomy

Once a commitment has been made and is well-defined, the dance of intimacy (or closeness) and autonomy (or separateness) begins. This dance can take several forms. Some people balance these two poles of relating by having periodic fights. They use struggle as the emotional transition from a time of closeness to a time of separateness, or as a signal to return to closeness after feeling separated. Other people move through serial partnerships, ending relationships when they need more autonomy and finding new partners when they're ready for intimacy. Some people base an entire relationship on either intimacy or autonomy, ignoring the other need. Some are able to transition gracefully from intimacy to autonomy, and then back to intimacy within one relationship. To a large extent, the form of the dance varies according to a person's awareness of it. People who feel guilty about their needs for autonomy or resentful of their needs for intimacy struggle with the dance. Most people, when they realize that every relationship involves a balance between closeness and separateness, find ways to honor both needs.

After Rachel moved away from her parents' home, she became aware that the dance between herself and her mother needed to be rechoreographed. She was committed to maintaining a close connection with her mom. She'd agreed to talk with her on the phone at least once a week and to spend a day with her once a month. She realized, however, that the dance of intimacy and autonomy involved more than a commitment and a schedule. At this stage of her life, she needed to figure out how much to share with her mom and how much to keep private. Layout 24 shows her consultation.

LAYOUT 24. *Balancing intimacy and autonomy. How much sharing/ privacy are appropriate for Rachel in her relationship with her mom?*

1	2	3
Issues to share	Issues to keep private	Signal that lets me know when to transition between intimacy and autonomy

INTERPRETATION

Card 1: Issues to share:
 Wheel of Fortune R: Plans that I've already put in motion by myself.

Card 2: Issues to keep private:
 Seven of Wands U: Experiments with my identity and playful activities out in the world.

Card 3: Signal that lets me know to transition:
 Justice U: Transition when I've shared about the same amount as my mom—keep our relationship in balance.

Extra Card: How can I know when the sharing is balanced?
 Nine of Cups R: Intuitive sense of feeling like moving on; follow natural flow.

RACHEL: *You know, when I'm talking with my mom, I always reach a point where I feel that it's time to quit telling her things. But she pushes me to share more and I end up telling her more about my social activities than I want her to know. Then, she gives me advice that I don't want to hear. I know that I should pay attention to my feeling and just stop. On the other hand, I don't mind telling her about career, social, or vacation plans I've already put in motion. In that case, I don't need her feedback and it's too late for her to influence me anyway!*

Staying on Purpose

Our reasons for relating seem to group themselves into three categories, based on the time frame of experience that is important to us at a given time. Specifically, our relationships seem to focus on the past, present, or future in the following ways:

Past: In these relationships, the purpose is to repeat, idealize, or heal the past. Consciously, or unconsciously, we focus on the emotional, spiritual, mental, physical, or material experiences of the past.

Present: In these relationships, the purpose is to fully experience our aliveness in the present. In them, we focus on the joyful or painful intensity of the moment. We explore ourselves and others as we exist today.

Future: In these relationships, the purpose is to creatively manifest the future. Here, we focus on what we are imagining and planning for the future. We interact with those who can support us as we move forward, or with those with whom we might actually co-create the future.

At different stages in our lives, we want relationships for different reasons. For example, you may want a partner because you want to heal from incest (past), travel to China (present), or make music together forever (future). You may interact with a mentor to remediate lack of knowledge (past), gain status (present), or create career opportunities (future). You may have a child to make up for past losses, have fun in the moment, or leave a legacy. And these are just a few reasons! I'm sure you can think of others.

If a relationship with a specific person is to last over time, it's essential that you maintain your key purpose(s) for that type of interaction with that person. If the job of your mentor is to help you envision the future, someone who focuses on "the way things have always been done" isn't the mentor for you. If your best friend must be a companion who enjoys board games and movies and doesn't worry too much about the past or the future, someone who's in deep therapy to heal childhood wounds may not be an appropriate buddy. And, if you yourself need to recreate your family struggles in order to heal them, a partner who is focused on creating future financial security may not be right for you at this time.

Obviously, within each time frame category, there are healthy and functional purposes and destructive, dysfunctional purposes. It is easy to assume that healthy purposes make for longer relationships. The healthiness of the purposes, however, does not signal the length of the relationship. Rather, the degree of matching or compatible purposes signals its length.

Two people who are both focused on current and future personal growth may stay together. Two people who both want to forget their past troubles in alcoholic oblivion, however, could also stay together, drunk, indefinitely. A parent who applauds a child's current successes may remain as a primary cheerleader over time. A student who is committed to admiring her egotistical mentor's past successes may be the favored student as long as she wants.

If, on the other hand, one or both of these same people pursue physical, instead of personal, growth, decide to get sober, focus on the parent instead of the child, pay attention to the student's future instead of the mentor's past, or otherwise redefine their purposes, it usually signals a time for reevaluation within the relationship. If the new purpose(s) are matching or compatible, the relating goes forward in a new and, hopefully, improved way. If the new purpose(s) are not compatible, it may be time for the relationship to end or change form. (More on that in the next section.)

Some possibilities for purposes are listed below. In each case, imagine that the central bond of the relationship forms itself around the issue that is described, for one or more of the people involved in the relationship.

Past:
Past identity or name;
Past status, errors, or accomplishments;
Previous role models, parents, or teachers;
Emotional expectations, based on past experiences;
Value systems, religions, or philosophy from the past;
Communication habits or skills developed in the past;
Historical physical skills and abilities (or lack of them);
Historical wealth, possessions, or financial losses.

Present:
Current identity, name, or status;
Experience of exploring/enjoying the spirit of aliveness today;
Current substance abuse, co-dependence, or recovery dynamics;
Current emotional losses or gains;
Experience of immediate mental diversion and stimulation;
Current philosophy, religion, or ideals;
Immediately satisfying health and fitness activities;
Current wealth, possessions, or losses.

Future:
> Future identity or status;
> Opportunities for someone's future self-expression;
> Potential future emotions;
> Depression when goals have been met, but no new goals have been set;
> Learning that can change lives;
> Communications that can occur;
> Abilities or disabilities imagined in the future;
> Potential for future financial gains or losses.

Ian was offered a job in a different department in his corporation. Before he took the job, he did Layout 25 to determine whether the new boss would help him to stay on-purpose with his career.

Layout 25. Staying on purpose. How will Ian's new boss tend to support Ian's future career goals?

1	2	3
Boss's focus on maintaining the past	Boss's focus on getting the job done in the present	Boss's focus on creating future opportunities

INTERPRETATION

Card 1: Boss's focus on the past:
> Seven of Swords R: Interested in exploring and remembering the many aspects of the past; especially values and priorities.

Card 2: Boss's focus on the present:
> Temperance R: Really focused on current creative pursuits; perhaps team-building and collaboration within the department.

Card 3: Boss's focus on the future:

Ten of Cups R: Tendency to hesitate with regard to intuition or creative options for the future; doesn't think about where relationships will go in the long-term future.

IAN: *I really want a job that will be a stepping-stone to my future. So, although I like this boss and the money sounds good, I don't think I'll take the job.*

In general, it looks as if this boss takes his inspiration from the past and focuses on the productivity and team spirit of the present. He seems less interested in his own future or the futures of his subordinates.

Allowing for Change and Re-evaluation

Because people *do* grow and change, we need to account for that option within our important relationships. Even in a relationship that focuses on the past, people may grow to explore different aspects of the past at varying levels of psychological understanding. In present-oriented interactions, we may develop new or different hobbies and interests, even though our focus is still on doing them now. In future-oriented associations, we need to accommodate changes of plans and direction. If we ignore the issue of change, we eventually become frustrated by stagnation or are surprised when someone makes a shift.

One of the best ways to allow for growth is to periodically reevaluate the relationship dynamics together. For new relationships, weekly or monthly discussions may be useful. For relationships in trouble, when people want to allow for the possibility of change, re-evaluation may occur in three, six, or even twelve-month cycles. For on-going, stable relationships, it's useful to have reevaluation sessions at least once a year—and/or every time a new phase or change is reached. Examples of change that might trigger a reevaluation are: having a child, the youngest child leaving home, starting a job, quitting a job, moving, starting a new health or exercise regime, engaging in a new hobby or creative pursuit, taking on volunteer work, or developing a new lifestyle. At the time of re-evaluation, we can ask ourselves:

- What agreements about our interaction have we made unconsciously?

- What agreements have we made consciously?

- Are these agreements still operative? still meeting our needs?

- What circumstances have changed?

- What new agreements do we need to make?

- What can each person do to make it easier for the self and the other?

Ellen and Mariko had been best friends for a long time. When Mariko became pregnant and Ellen decided never to have children, they did a reading to figure out how to maintain their friendship as Mariko's life began to change dramatically. Their primary purpose together had always been to play and have fun in the present. They decided that they needed to add a future element—to check in with each other every six months to make sure the changing relationship was still on-purpose. Layout 26 (pages 123–124) shows their reading.

LAYOUT 26. *Allowing for change and re-evaluation.*

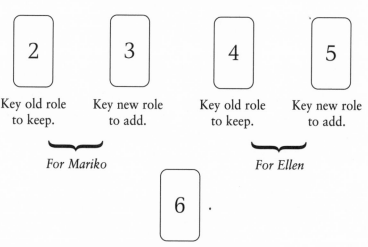

New purpose for this friendship.

Key old role to keep.　Key new role to add.　Key old role to keep.　Key new role to add.

For Mariko　　*For Ellen*

Key question at re-evaluation time.

INTERPRETATION:

Card 1: New purpose:
Queen of Pentacles U: Mature, practical or financial connection; career?

ELLEN: *That actually makes sense, since I have a house-cleaning business and Mariko is planning to hire me to help her.*

Card 2: Key old role to keep for Mariko:
Knight of Wands U: Focus on independent identity.

MARIKO: *Well, I never did everything with either Ellen or my husband. I've always needed a lot of time alone.*

Card 3: Key new role for Mariko to add:
Two of Wands R: Confirm new self-image.

Extra card: Which self-image?
Justice R: That you are a person who can have balance and equilibrium.

Card 4: Key old role for Ellen to keep:
Three of Wands U: Independent self who's making plans for the future.

ELLEN: *I've been saving for a major trip abroad.*

Card 5: Key new role for Ellen to add:
Knight of Pentacles U: Focus on work, money, health, fitness.

ELLEN: *The house-cleaning is a good idea. I see that I might do more exercise and health stuff with Mariko, instead of just going out for fun or shopping. I want to get more exercise anyway and that's always playful and fun for me.*

MARIKO: *That would really support me, because I need to be physically active, although I tend to resist it. If we spent our time together doing physical activities, it would feel so good. And, we could still talk while we exercise! I think it would still be fun.*

Card 6: Key question at reevaluation time:
Queen of Cups R: How is our intuitive relationship maturing? How can we stay emotionally mature as we interact?

> The main thing that Mariko and Ellen needed to remember was to stay focused on the independence that had brought them together as friends in the first place. They both liked the feeling that the other person was not dependent on them. By switching what they did together to something that they both wanted to do and found to be fun (their original purpose), they could still spend as much time together and meet new needs.

Remember that, when you build a long-term relationship that allows for change, there is no substitute for honesty. We need to be honest with ourselves so we know what we need and want at each stage of growth. We need to be honest with each other about the value of the relationship and the new dynamics that may emerge.

Sample Layout Questions

What is the nature of our relationship?

How would it be for [name person, pair, or group] to have a [specify type] relationship?

What was this relationship before?

What is this relationship now?

What can this relationship be in the future?

What are the element(s) (1 or more cards) of commitment for [name person, pair, or group]?

How will [name person, pair, or group] feel if the commitment involved these [name specifics: limits, expectations, demands, boundaries, time frames]?

What will happen to this relationship if these commitment specifics [name them] were changed to [name new specifics]?

What kinds of things must [name person, pair, or group] experience autonomously?

What creates intimacy for [name person, pair, or group]?

How can [name of person, pair, or group] balance intimacy and autonomy?

What was the original purpose of this relationship?

What is the purpose of this relationship now?

What is the purpose of this relationship for [name person, pair, or group]?

What will support [name person, pair, or group] to stay on purpose?

What will tend to block [name person, pair, or group] from staying on-purpose?

How does [name person, pair, or group] focus on the [past, present, or future] in this relationship?

What does [name person, pair, or group] need to do in order to accommodate change [specify] in this individual or situation?

How can [name of person] make sure to allow for their own changes in this relationship?

How can [name of person] make sure to allow for the other person's changes?

What does [name person, pair, or group] need to ask when reevaluating the relationship?

Sample Layout Combining Some Questions

```
┌─────────┐                    ┌─────────┐
│         │                    │         │
│    1    │                    │    3    │
│         │                    │         │
└─────────┘                    └─────────┘
```

How can I best experience   How can I best experience
healthy autonomy in   healthy intimacy in
this relationship?   this relationship?

```
          ┌─────────┐
          │         │
          │    2    │
          │         │
          └─────────┘
```

What is the purpose of this relationship in terms of my future?

Exercises

As in the previous section, these exercises are topics for readings. Do as many as are relevant in your life at this time. You can use any of the layout positions that appear in any part of this book.

1. Identify or name the relationship.

2. Define commitment for [name of person].

3. Define commitment for [pair or group].

4. Balance intimacy and autonomy for [name of person].

5. Balance intimacy and autonomy for [pair or group].

6. Stay on-purpose for [name of person].

7. Stay on-purpose for [pair or group].

8. Allow for change/reevaluation in [name of person].

9. Allow for change/reevaluation in [pair or group].

7

Reaching Closure

For a variety of reasons, some relationships end. We know that no significant relationships are ever completely erased, because anyone who has ever been important to us is always a part of our lives. However, the structure of the relationship—the kinds of contact and the frequency of contact—may alter radically. We experience this change of form as an ending. The tarot can help you understand the processes of grieving, of exploring the indicators that influence us to end or keep a particular relationship, of ending relationships gracefully, and of moving on.

Grieving

Grieving is the emotional process of experiencing an ending. This process has been researched, documented, described, and defined in the past few decades and found to have predictable stages. These stages seem consistent across cultures, genders, ages, and contexts. While I've presented the stages in a sequence in Table 5 (see pages 130–131)—and, indeed, they often occur in about this sequence—I've also found that people tend to cycle around in the phases. Denial always seems to come first. Then we seem to move in and out of bargaining, anger, and isolation, revisiting the various feelings in no rigid order. During that time, we may even momentarily hop

Table 5. The Stages of Grieving.

STAGE	REACTION	THOUGHT
Denial:	Pretending nothing has changed; Avoiding awareness that the situation is serious; Acting as if there is no need for any action or change.	"He's not really an alcoholic." "He isn't seeing someone else." "I can't imagine that she would steal from the company." "She's not really going to die."
Bargaining:	Making deals with yourself, other people, or Spirit/God; Coming up with partial solutions; Making some concessions for the sake of some security.	"If he'll only drink on weekends, we can continue." "Maybe if I were sexier, he wouldn't see her." "If she pays it back out of her next paycheck and *promises . . .*" "If we do this and this, maybe we can keep her alive for a few more months."
Anger:	Feeling furious about being betrayed or abandoned; Experiencing rage that cir-cumstances have changed; Lashing out in many directions (not just at the person).	"He's such a jerk; I can't see why I ever liked him." "You will not ever do this again because I'm leaving!" "How could you do this to us?" "Don't you understand that my mother is dying! Are you totally uncaring?!"

Table 5. *The Stages of Grieving (continued).*

STAGE	REACTION	THOUGHT
Isolation:*	Feeling depressed or ashamed; Feeling sad, withdrawn, or lonely; Experiencing and seeking comfort privately.	"I don't want to talk to anyone about your drinking; I'm so embarrassed." "I'm so depressed about his affair, I just can't face anyone." "It makes me feel so sad that she could do this." "Just leave me alone, I'll handle her death by myself."
Acceptance:	Coming to terms with the truth; Letting go of what "was" and embracing what "is," or what "will be"; Arriving at some peace or relief about the situation.	"Well, it's true, he is an alcoholic." "He really has been seeing someone else. Now, what shall I do about it?" "She must repay us, with interest—and lose her job." "My mom is really going to die. How can I make her more comfortable?"

*I.e., sadness, withdrawal, depression, shame.

back to denial or hop forward to acceptance. It's only when we feel complete with the middle three experiences that we finally move to a more permanent acceptance. Even then, on the anniversary of the ending, we may cycle through parts of the grieving again. I've found that, for serious relationships, the intense part of the grieving experience takes about two years. For less important relationships, it takes less time. In either case, it's a natural process and can't really be short-circuited or avoided.

An interesting thing that I've discovered is that grieving can happen before or after the official "ending" of a relationship. Some people, in some circumstances, go through an intense process of grieving before they file for divorce, quit the job, or send the child out on her own. By the time the separation actually occurs, they have come to acceptance and are ready to let go. Other people, in the same circumstances, don't even begin grieving until after the ending: after the divorce is final, after they've left the company, or after the child has gone. Of course, many endings occur when people are in the middle of the grieving process. When two people are ending their relationship, if they are at different stages of grieving, they can feel hurt and confused by the other's response. For example, one who has grieved "before" the ending may think that the "grieve-after-the-ending" person is holding on too much and becoming maudlin. At the same time, the "grieve-after" person may feel that the "grieve-before-the-ending" person is now heartless and uncaring. What's true is that, if an ending occurs, both people grieve in some way, at some time.

Judith was grieving the loss of Marian, her excellent assistant of ten years. Marian hadn't left yet, but she was pregnant and planning to become an at-home mom. At first, Judith ignored the fact that, in a few months, Marian would be gone. As Marian's belly grew, however, Judith couldn't stay in denial any longer. She began to bargain: Maybe Marian could work part time and bring the baby to work? Maybe Marian could work if Judith paid for childcare? Marian's response was "no." She had waited a long time for this baby and was really committed to staying home. As Judith felt the anger welling up and found herself lashing out at her husband and children as well as Marian, she chose to get some help. In talking with a therapist, she began to understand the process of grieving. To support herself, Judith did Layout 27 (see pages 133–134).

LAYOUT 27. *Grieving the loss of Marian.*

| 1 | | 2 |

What's the best thing I can
do with my anger?

What's the worst thing I can
do with my anger?

| 3 |

How can I handle the isolation
phase productively?

| 4 |

What will help me come to
acceptance?

INTERPRETATION

Card 1: Best thing to do with anger?
King of Swords R: Release it in private communication: i.e.,
talk to yourself, write in a journal, or talk to therapist.

Card 2: Worst thing to do with anger?
Star R: Don't pour a lot of energy into your own feelings;
avoid reinforcing the anger.

Card 3: Handle isolation productively?
Temperance R: Create something privately, just for yourself.
Writing? Art? Music?

Card 4: Come to acceptance?
Ten of Pentacles U: Take some time off from work.

JUDITH: *Actually, I'm pretty comfortable financially and I was thinking that I needed a break. I had been hoping that Marian would handle things while I took time off. On the other hand, I think I can just take a sabbatical. I'll simply tell people that I'm not available for a month at the time that Marian leaves. That way, I can actually spend some time with Marian and her baby, rest up myself, do some writing, and think about my future direction. I like this plan!*

The Ending/Keeping Indicators

In my years of working with people, I've found that a process of evaluating pros and cons happens concurrently with grieving. It's the logical or thinking experience that accompanies the emotional experience of grieving. Throughout grieving, people weigh and balance the "ending the relationship" indicators against the "keeping the relationship" indicators.

Ending: Evidence that shows me that I should (or can)
           let go;
         Something that tells me it's time for an ending;
         Feeling "it's right" or "I'm ready" to move on.

Keeping: Evidence that shows me that I shouldn't (or can't)
           let go;
         Something that tells me to maintain the relation-
         ship as it is;
         Feeling that "it's right" or "I'm ready" to stay.

The ending/keeping indicators are composed of all the parts of relating that I've described so far. They are listed below. You will know whether to let go if it seems to you that, too often, too many of these experiences are not happening in the ways you want. You can look down the list and notice which of these factors are not satisfying for you. Then ask yourself how many, and which, factors must be disappointing before you end a relationship. For some people, one red flag or boundary violation is too many, because that particular one carries so much weight. For other people, several disappointments have to occur, half of the time, in order to reach an acceptance of ending. For still others, all of issues in the list would have to become ending indicators—all of the time—before they let go. Ultimately, it's a subjective decision.

Keys to Relating: Use of curiosity, balance, appreciation, flexibility;

Process of Feedback: Ability to give/receive information about reactions, thoughts, and feelings;

Attributes: Opportunities to experience and express crucial personal characteristics;

Obstacles and Resources: Ability to identify situations/attitudes that help/hinder the relationship and take appropriate action;

Boundaries: Ability to identify and honor each other's limits and boundaries;

Future Probabilities: Imagine various futures with/without each other;

The Only Game in Town: Identify the Game as it arises; use keys, feedback, boundaries in order to neutralize it;

Self-Care: Identify and honor individual needs;

Red and Green Flags: Handle the red; acknowledge the green;

Own Responsibility: Understand and value your emotions, ideas, spirit, body, things;

Other's Responsibility: Other takes responsibility for their emotions, ideas, spirit, body, things;

Change: Transfer behavior or add new behavior;

Invite the Other to Change: Ability to gracefully invite without playing the Only Game in Town;

Costs/Benefits of Change: Believe that the benefits of change exceed the costs;

Outside Help: Get the kind of help that will heal the relationship;

Identify the Relationship: Name *this* relationship for what it is at this time;

Commitment: Define and agree;

Intimacy/Autonomy: Find appropriate balance at this time;

Stay on Purpose: Support/match the purpose(s) of both (all) people;

Change and Re-evaluation: Allow and plan for it.

Carmen was uncertain about her relationship with a volunteer community action group that supports people with AIDS. She had been involved with this group for about a year and they wanted to her to sit on the board of directors. Carmen wasn't even sure she wanted to continue her current role, much less take on more responsibility. She used the tarot to discover the pros and cons that existed in her relationship with this group (see Layout 28). She knew where she stood on some of the ending and keeping indicators, so the reading covered her areas of uncertainty.

LAYOUT 28. *Ending/Keeping indicators. Should Carmen terminate her relationship with the volunteer group?*

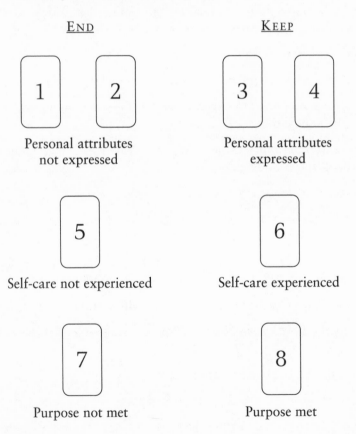

 END   KEEP

1	2

Personal attributes
not expressed

3	4

Personal attributes
expressed

5

Self-care not experienced

6

Self-care experienced

7

Purpose not met

8

Purpose met

INTERPRETATION

Attributes not expressed:
Card 1:
> Hanged Man R: Take action when she feels internally ready.

Card 2:
> Five of Pentacles R: Make adjustments and adaptations in own sense of security.

Attributes expressed:
Card 3:
> Seven of Swords R: Lots of dialogue about interesting philosophy within group.

Card 4:
> Nine of Wands R: Sense of being part of on-going direction that expresses self-image.

Self-care not experienced:
Card 5:
> Chariot U: Sense of holding the reins or directing the fast-moving action.

Self-care experienced:
Card 6:
> Tower R: Changes in beliefs about self.

Extra Card: Which beliefs?
> Nine of Pentacles R: I will always be grounded and stable; my life will always be secure.

Purpose not met:
Card 7:
> World U: Opportunities for many new directions and contacts; experience of diversity.

Purpose met:
Card 8:
> Page of Wands R: Dare to commit to higher level of own self-image.

CARMEN: *I've really grown up this year. I used to think that only gay men and drug addicts got AIDS. Now I know that, in addition, lots of other people get AIDS, too. I've had to defend myself to my family and friends who thought I was crazy for doing this work, and stand up for myself. I really see myself as an activist. On the other hand, most of the people in this group are white, middle-class volunteers. And, we serve white, middle-class people. As a Hispanic, I want to work with a more diverse group and serve the needs of more people. I want to have more of a voice. Being on the Board would give me more of a voice but the diversity is still not there. I think I'll find a different AIDS group.*

In this reading, three of the four Major Arcana cards fall in the "end" side of the chart. This, alone, would tend to indicate that there are many important reasons for Carmen ending her relationship with this group.

	END	KEEP
My attributes not expressed:	Hanged Man R Five of Pentacles R	
My attributes expressed:		Seven of Swords R Nine of Wands R
Self-care not experienced:	Chariot U	
Self-care experienced:		Tower R
My purpose not met:	World U	
My purpose met:		Page of Wands R

To be specific, Carmen needs to act on her own timing and adjust circumstances to enable her to feel secure and these needs aren't met in this group. She's also not accomplishing her purpose of meeting and interacting with a diversity people, and she doesn't sense that she has any influence over the pace or direction of the group. On the other hand, she gets to talk about her ideas and values with other members of the group, she has dared to express herself as someone who believes in this group's mission—and has continued in an on-going way for a year! And, she has realized that her life isn't as secure as she thought: in meeting the people they've helped, she's come to realize that disaster can strike anyone.

Carmen used the tarot to uncover and clarify her ending/keeping indicators. Anna, on the other hand, thought she knew her indicators pretty well. She just needed some additional insight and information from the tarot about the probable outcome of two courses of action: divorce and staying married. She had been married to Dan for twenty-five years when she began to wonder if two attributes that were part of her definition of marriage would ever be manifested with Dan. She was missing the fun of going out with friends as a couple and the pleasures of intimate communication.

After years of changing herself and inviting Dan to change, these two attributes were still weak in her marriage. In addition, although she had gotten help from books and from a counselor, he resisted getting help and seemed to sabotage her attempts to meet her own needs autonomously. Her original purpose for the relationship—raising a family—had already been accomplished. At this point in time, as she identified her new purpose of "personal growth and expression," the missing attributes and behavior seemed more critical than ever before. She no longer felt very curious or optimistic about their relationship, just empty. It was hard to lighten up and find the balance in the situation. She found herself being pretty unappreciative of Dan, although she did remember some of his good qualities. She was tired of being flexible and adapting to his needs. Anna was trying to decide whether it was time to end the marriage relationship. She analyzed the ending/keeping indicators as shown in Table 6 (page 140), then did the reading shown in Layout 29 (pages 141–142) to determine the specifics of "future possibilities."

Table 6. *Anna's Ending/Keeping Indicators Before Her Reading.*

INDICATOR	END	KEEP
Keys to relating	No balance, curiosity, flexibility	Some appreciation
Feedback	Could be better	Occasional
Obstacles/Resources:	I feel bored and frustrated.	My positive feelings for Dan
Future probabilities.	I'd be single for a while.	I'd be frustrated forever
Boundaries	Invades my privacy sometimes.	Honors most personal boundaries
The Only Game in Town.	Tend to rescue/persecute Dan as victim	Recognize it more often
Self-care.	I need to take care of myself better	No indicators
Red/Green flags	Red: he won't talk about feelings	Green: he says he loves me
Own responsibility	Not taking care of my spirit well.	Yes—emotions, ideas, things
Other's responsibility	Doesn't take care of emotions	Yes—spirit, ideas, things
Change.	I've changed a lot; he resists	No indicators
Costs/Benefits.	He thinks costs are too high	No indicators
	I think benefits would be high	No indicators
Outside help.	He resists getting help	No indicators
Identify relationship	No indicators.	Monogamous, parenting, marriage
Commitment	Don't understand any more	No indicators
Intimacy/Autonomy	Not enough of either	Used to be more of both
Purposes.	Little going out with friends	No indicators
	Raising-children purpose is waning	Accomplished raising children well
	Little intimate communication.	Lots of intellectual stimulation
Periodic re-evaluation	Never happens	No indicators

LAYOUT 29. *Anna explores future possibilities.*

What will be my probable experience if I get a divorce?

1	2

Six months after
divorce is final

Five years after
divorce is final

What will be my probable experience if I stay in the marriage?

3	4

Six months from now

Five years from now

INTERPRETATION

How will I probably feel if I get a divorce?
Card 1: Six months after divorce is final:
    King of Pentacles U: I'm releasing (or losing?) things such as money or house.
Card 2: Five years after divorce is final:
    Five of Wands U: As if I'm adjusting and adapting myself, my identity.
Additional Cards: Adapting in what way?
    Fool R: Having more faith in myself.
    Ten of Cups R: Setting my intuition and feelings aside, waiting for intimacy.

How will I probably feel if I stay in this marriage?
Card 3: Six months from now:
    Knight of Cups R: Focusing on intimacy, intensely utilizing intuition.

Card 4: Five years from now:
  Lovers R: Collaborating, despite differences, within marriage.

ANNA: *I think I'll tell Dan that I'm this close to filing for a divorce and see what happens. Maybe it will open up communication in some way. Given this reading, I'm willing to give it six months to see if the intimacy improves. I also want to do another reading about inviting Dan to change and about how I can change. He really has a lot of qualities that I want in my partner. I guess I'm not quite ready to let go yet.*

> The Major Arcana card showed up five years in the future, if she stayed in the marriage. It was a card of collaboration and finding common ground. This indicated that there might still be some value in the marriage. Also, it looked as if her need for intimacy might still be unmet if she got a divorce. Conversely, it seemed that there was some hope that the intimacy in the marriage would increase—even in six months.

In the end, given the feedback of the cards, Anna re-engaged her curiosity about what could activate change and an appreciation for her own and Dan's good qualities. She discovered a balance of light-heartedness and seriousness regarding the situation and some flexibility about the ending date. She renewed her determination to give and receive feedback This was enough—for her—to weight the ending/keeping indicator scale in the direction of "keeping" the relationship—at least for six months. Her ending/keeping indicators after the reading are shown in Table 7 (page 143).

With different cards, or for someone else, the decision could have been different. For example, Isaac had a different response to his reading about a similar issue. He had been Josef's business partner for fifteen years. They had enjoyed a good working relationship. When Josef got divorced, however, things changed. Josef wanted bigger draws from their small company. He took many days off and was unfocused while at work. Some days, he even came to work hung over, with alcohol on his breath. Isaac didn't want to end the partnership if this was

Table 7. Anna's Ending/Keeping Indicators After Her Reading.

Indicator	End	Keep
Keys to relating	Not many indicators	More honor, curiosity, appreciation, balance, feedback, and flexibility
Obstacles/Resources	I feel frustrated	I feel creative; have good feelings for Dan
Boundaries	Invades my privacy sometimes	I can be clearer; he usually honors my limits
Future probabilities	Still searching for intimacy	Potential for more intimacy
The Only Game in Town	Tend to rescue/persecute Dan as victim	Recognize it more often
Self-care	I need to take care of myself better	I can improve
Red/Green flags	Red: he won't talk about feelings	Green: he says he loves me
Own responsibility	Not taking care of my spirit well	I can add spirit
Other's responsibility	Doesn't take care of emotions	Yes—spirit, ideas, things
Change:	I've changed a lot; he resists	I'll invite again
Costs/Benefits:	He thinks costs are too high	I think benefits would be high
Outside help	He resists getting help	I'll invite again
Identify relationship	None that apply	Monogamous, parenting, marriage
Commitment	Don't understand any more	Maybe we can define together
Intimacy/Autonomy	Not enough of either	I can be clearer about needs
Purposes	Little going out with friends	Great fun, alone together
	Past purpose (children) waning	Accomplished raising children well
	No agreement on new purpose	Curiosity: want to talk about it
	Little intimate communication	Lots of intellectual stimulation
Periodic re-evaluation	Never has happened	I will reevaluate in six months

Table 8. Isaac's Ending/Keeping Indicators (same before and after).

INDICATOR	END	KEEP
Keys to more choices	No curiosity, balance, feedback	Some appreciation and flexibility
Obstacles/Resources	I feel disappointed and frustrated	I can still make good choices
Boundaries	Dishonored	No indicators
Future probabilities	Find new partner	Lose money and customers
The Only Game in Town	I'm the persecutor, rescuer and victim!	No indicators
Self-care	I need to take care of myself better	No indicators
Red/Green flags	Red: alcohol, absences	No indicators
Own responsibility	Want to take care of all my stuff	No indicators
Other's responsibility	Doesn't seem to take care of any stuff	No indicators
Change	He's changed for the worse	No indicators
Costs/Benefits	I think costs are too high	He wants new customers/market
Outside help	He resists getting help	
Identify the relationship	No longer equal partnership	Used to be equal partnership
Commitment	Don't understand any more	No indicators
Intimacy/Autonomy	Total autonomy, no connection	No indicators
Purposes	Future money-making is threatened	Made money well in past
	Loss of easy rapport	
	Loss of communication	
	Loss of efficiency	
Periodic re-evaluation	No longer happens	No indicators

just a short phase, but he felt that, if the behavior continued, business and his own quality of life would suffer. Like Anna, he wanted some feedback about the future. For Isaac, however, it was enough to get insight into the experiences he'd have if he stayed in business with Josef. He could already imagine how it would be to end the partnership. Layout 30 shows his reading and Table 8 (page 144) shows his ending/keeping indicators both before and after the reading (they didn't change).

LAYOUT 30. *Analyzing future possibilities. Should Isaac stay in business with Josef?*

If I keep the partnership with Josef, what will probably happen to the business?

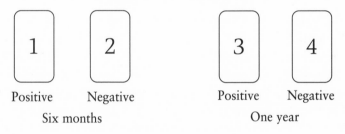

Positive   Negative   Positive   Negative

Six months   One year

INTERPRETATION

Cards 1–2: What will probably happen in six months?
  Positive: Seven of Cups U: We'll expand our partnership, add new people, find new customers, experiment with our relationship.
  Negative: Justice U: We'll be in a state of equilibrium, but maybe no growth.

Cards 3–4: What will probably happen in one year?
  Positive: The Tower U: Radical change in our beliefs and attitudes toward business, customers, and the world.
  Negative: Queen of Cups R: Alcoholic pattern will probably continue, behind the scenes manipulations are possible, a complex, well-developed pattern of subtle or unclear emotional interaction.

ISAAC: *It looks as if, if I stay in business with Josef, our business will change completely. We'll have new customers, which is good, and, eventually, a new outlook, which is also good. However, it doesn't look as if these changes will really lead to more, or improved business. The reality is, I can't stand the idea of working with Josef if he keeps drinking this much. Alcoholism is a huge red flag for me. I'm sorry about his divorce and I've tried to talk to him, but he won't pay attention. He says he wants to have fun. My purpose in having a business partnership is mature feedback and communication. Without it, I'd just as soon work by myself. I feel alone these days anyway. I think I'll take steps to buy Josef out.*

Ending

As I mentioned earlier, a relationship ends when the kinds of contact and the frequency of contact change significantly. In most cases, we think this means we are separating from the other person, that the contact is becoming less intimate and less frequent. Endings can also occur, however, when relationships move on to a *more* intimate stage. People often grieve the dating phase when they make a commitment, or they grieve the old work group when they add new team members. They might even grieve their dysfunctional habits after they've changed them! Although it's easiest to think of ending as "letting go of a person," it may also be "letting go of a phase" or "letting go of a pattern" within the relationship.

Whether you're ending a relationship or ending a pattern of relating, bear in mind that the "official ending" can occur any time before, during, or after the grieving process. Depending on when it occurs, the ending can happen in a variety of ways, ranging from graceful to horrendous. Naturally, if the ending occurs when one or both people are experiencing the anger phase of grieving, it's more likely to be loud or bitter. If one or both are feeling isolated and sad, it will be weepy. And, if one or both are still bargaining, it may not happen at all! If the ending occurs when at least one person is at acceptance, it tends to be more civilized. If both people are feeling acceptance, it's easier yet. Since we can't always control the timing of the ending, it remains to make the transition as graceful as possible—given whatever stage we're experiencing.

Interestingly enough, the keys to relating, those that give us more choices and resources when we are creating relationships, are also the keys that help us end relationships gracefully. We can become curious about how to end the relationship in a graceful manner, appreciate the good experiences or the lessons learned from the relationship, maintain a healthy balance between lightheartedness and seriousness, practice some flexibility in making the ending easy for all concerned, and give or receive mature feedback about the details of the ending process.

Howard was retiring after thirty years with his company. He was ready to move on, but it was also difficult to let go of his friends and co-workers. In addition to making the ending easy, he wanted to honor himself and his co-workers in the process. Howard did Layout 31 (pages 148–149) in order to get some insight into how he could make the transition as gracefully as possible.

LAYOUT 31. *Keys for ending. How can Howard retire gracefully?*

How can I best:

1	2
honor myself?	honor my co-workers?

3	4
be curious about my future?	keep a balance of lightheartedness and seriousness?

5	6
appreciate myself?	appreciate others?

7	8
maintain flexibility?	give and receive feedback?

INTERPRETATION

Card 1: Honor self?
 Tower U: Change beliefs about the world.

Extra card: Which beliefs?
 King of Swords U: Ending of a lifestyle (retirement = ending?).

Card 2: Honor others?
> Chariot R: Remind them that you will hold the reins and guide your own rapidly approaching, somewhat intense, transition out of the company.

Card 3: Be curious about future?
> Page of Swords U: Dare to recommit to a lifestyle you enjoy; take risks with communication, learning, and travel.

Card 4: Balance lightheartedness and seriousness?
> Page of Cups R: Take risks with inner feelings; dare to express intuition; have an adventure with closest people.

Card 5: Appreciate self?
> Queen of Swords U: You have mature knowledge and communication skills.

Card 6: Appreciate others?
> Page of Wands U: They are younger, risk-taking, independent, adventurous.

Card 7: Maintain flexibility?
> Two of Cups R: Affirm intuition or instincts; hold someone's hand as long as needed.

Card 8: Give and receive feedback?
> Justice U: Keep a balance of activities: listening and speaking, doing and observing, moving forward and waiting.

HOWARD: *Most of this really makes sense to me. I've been working on seeing retirement as a new beginning instead of an ending. Actually, I'm excited about taking some educational tours of different countries. Over all, I can see that I need to make the transition more gradually than I realized—trusting the spirit of the young guys I'm leaving behind, but giving them the benefit of my experience for as long as they need it. I'm not sure what the "adventure with closest people" is. I am beginning to share more of my feelings with them, but I'll have to think about an adventure that would be fun for everyone.*

Moving On

When all is said and done and the ending has been accomplished as gracefully as possible, it's time to move on. The three questions that are most relevant to moving on are shown in Layout 32. Harry has already let go of a significant romantic relationship. Now he's ready to move on.

LAYOUT 32. *Moving On. How can Harry move on effectively?*

What is a resource that helps me move on? [3]

What is an obstacle that blocks me from moving on? [2]

How can I most effectively move on? [1]

INTERPRETATION

Card 1: How can I effectively move on?
  Five of Wands U: Adapt the way I present myself to others; adjust my roles in the world (change appearance?).

Card 2: Obstacle?
  Page of Wands U: Sense of risk-taking or fear regarding independence.

Extra Card: How can I overcome the fear?
  Queen of Wands U: Remember your maturity, strength, strong personality and all the ways you've been independent already.

Card 3: Resource?
    Ace of Swords R: Willingness to plant seeds for new values;
    beginning new way of talking to self.

Extra card: Which new values?
    Seven of Wands R: Self-image as an experimenter and playful
    person.

HARRY: *That's it! I'm afraid of being independent, but in my work,
I'm very independent. Maybe I can pretend that being single is a "job
to do." I have been thinking about cutting my hair differently and
getting contact lenses. I guess I'll do it. I've been thinking that I need
to talk more nicely to myself. I tend to beat myself up. I used to be
more playful and willing to experiment when I was younger. Maybe
it's time to reconnect with that part of me.*

When you're ready to move on, you can do a reading such as Harry's.
Then, return to Part One of this book and begin again. Take some
time to reevaluate your conscious and unconscious models for relating. Figure out how to find and create new relationships, improve or
enhance your existing relationships, maintain joyful long-term relationships, and let go when it's appropriate. Remember that the practice of relating provides the practice for relating more effectively.
Have courage and keep relating!

Sample Layout Questions

What have I really learned from this relationship?
How have I grown in this relationship?
What do I still appreciate about [name other person]?
What do I value (cherish, treasure) about myself or [name
    other person]?

What am I denying about this relationship?
How can I move out of denial?
How is denial helping me?

How is denial hurting me?
How can I be more curious about what's really going on?

What is my anger really about?
How can I handle my anger appropriately?
What's the best thing I can do with my anger?
What's the worst thing I could do with my anger?
How can I give (receive) feedback appropriately?

How am I bargaining (probably two cards, if this—then that)?
How can I consider the bigger picture?
Which details are really important in this situation?
How can I be flexible while still taking care of myself?

How am I isolating?
What's at the root of my shame?
What can I do to relieve the sadness?
How can I handle depression more effectively?
How can I achieve solitude instead of isolation?
How can I achieve a balance between lightheartedness and
    seriousness?

What will help me come to acceptance?
What do I still need to do (feel, experience) in order to arrive
    at acceptance?
What are the indicators for ending this relationship?
What are the indicators for keeping this relationship?

Which of my attributes are being expressed (not expressed)?
Which key purposes have already been satisfied in this rela-
    tionship?
Which important purposes have yet to be satisfied in this
    relationship?
Which purposes will probably never be satisfied in this rela-
    tionship?
What are the obstacles that prevent me from letting go?
What are the resources that could help me let go?
Which boundaries are being honored by me or [name the
    person]?

Which boundaries are not being honored by me or [name the person]?

How can I step out of playing the Only Game in Town?
How am I playing the victim in this situation?
How am I playing the persecutor in this situation?
How am I playing the rescuer in this situation?
What will be my probable experience if [name the action]?
What will probably happen in one month (six months, one year, five years, etc.) if I (we) [name the action]?
How can I take better care of myself during this transition?
What are the biggest red flags that move me toward ending this relationship?
What are the biggest green flags that tend to keep me in this relationship?

How am I taking responsibility for my emotions, spirit, thoughts, communication, body, possessions, money?
How do I need to take better responsibility for my stuff—spirit, thoughts emotions, communication, body, possessions, money?
How is [name the person] taking (not taking) responsibility for his/her stuff?
How can I change to heal the relationship?
How can I change to let go more gracefully?
What changes should I invite from [name the person]?
How can I invite [name the person] to change?

What are the costs of letting go?
What are the benefits of letting go?
What are the costs of staying in the relationship?
What are the benefits of staying in the relationship?
What kind of help would be useful right now?

How can I invite [name the person] to get help?
How can I accept that I need help?
What is really the truth about this relationship at this time?
What could this relationship be in the future?
What commitment is appropriate to make?

How can I better balance intimacy and autonomy during the
transition?

Which of my intimacy needs are met (unmet)?

Which of my autonomy needs are met (unmet)?

How does [name the person] support (block) my purpose(s)?

How do I support (block) [name the person]'s purpose(s)?

What are key questions to ask when reevaluating this relationship?

What are the ending/keeping indicators?

Sample Layout Combining Some Questions

1	2	3
victim role	persecutor role	rescuer role

What do I have to do to get out of the Only Game In Town
with regard to "X"?

Exercises

Here are some more topics for readings. You can combine layout
positions to create the readings that will be most useful to you as you
make decisions about ending a relationship.

1. How to enhance grieving.

2. Listing or uncovering the ending/keeping indicators.

3. Exploring future probabilities for this relationship (be sure to indicate time frames).

4. Ending gracefully.

5. Moving on

PART THREE

Tarot Interpretations

In this long section, you'll find meanings for all the tarot cards, with special emphasis on interpretations associated with relating. General interpretations for the tarot are included in my first tarot book, Choice Centered Tarot, *and in many others. The interpretations included here are those that apply more specifically to readings about relationships. These interpretations also include applications and possibilities that I've developed since I wrote the first book. For that reason, they may be useful to you in other kinds of readings as well.*

8

Reviewing the Basics
of Tarot Interpretation

Y ou may already have a sense of the basic principles of interpretation. If so, feel free to move right on to the detailed interpretations in sections 9 and 10. For those who are new to the art, let's review the basics. You may remember that there are three basic rules for interpreting the tarot (see page 34). These are my personal rules, and you may amend them to fit your practice.

Rule 1

The cards reflect their core meanings regardless of orientation (upright or reversed). However, orientation does influence their interpretation. The upright cards are expressed outwardly. They tend to be more objective, obvious, direct, public, conscious, or measurable. The reversed cards are expressed inwardly. They tend to be more subjective, subtle, indirect, private, unconscious, or vague.

Rule 2

All the cards are neutral in value. There are no good or bad cards. Positive and negative interpretations result from the form of the question. If you ask "What's the obstacle or problem in the situation?" it's appropriate to use the negative meaning. If the question is "What's the best step to take with regard to this person?" it leans toward the positive interpretation. In most cases, a more neutral interpretation (the first ones given in the samples) generally apply.

Rule 3
Each card has a core meaning that will emerge for you over time. Trust your intuition.

The Major and Minor Arcana

The Major Arcana cards deal with big life lessons and universal themes that can be applied and experienced in a variety of ways. Therefore, each Major card has its own interpretation, separate from all the others. Many people find that, by sequencing or grouping them in various ways, the Major Arcana cards can tell a story about the quest for the meaning of life.

Proportionally speaking, if a great many Major cards appear in a reading, the issue at hand is probably of some importance or significance in the person's life. A critical turning point could be indicated. If only a few show up, they can indicate the core issue around which the questions revolve.

The Minor Arcana cards reflect the more mundane activities of life: the rhythms of day-to-day reality. Each of the four suits represents an area of life and each of the numbers indicates a specific psychological process and/or a behavioral experience. The interpretations for the Minor Arcana emerge from combining the meaning of the pip, or court, card level with the subject matter of the suit involved. For example:

Sevens = variety, diversity, expansion, stimulation
Cups = emotions, relationships
Seven of Cups = variety of emotions, diversity of
relationships

If a reading contains mostly Minor Arcana cards, it's likely that the focus of the reading is on daily activities and the process of living. These cards help us understand what we're doing and why we're doing it. Further, the Minor Arcana cards may show how, or in what department of life, a person is experiencing the concern represented by a Major Arcana card. Sometimes the Major cards appear in a nest of Minor cards. In that case, it's useful to consider how the meaning of the Major card might shift because of its proximity to a Minor card (or group of cards). Some of the following examples may help you understand how the Minor and Major cards might influence each other in a reading.

Upright Empress with a Wands emphasis: Expression of identity as a nurturer;

Reversed Empress with a Cups emphasis: Emotions regarding self-nurturing;

Upright Empress with a Swords emphasis: Communicating about nurturing;

Reversed Empress with a Pentacles emphasis: Sense of security from self-nurturing.

Upright Lovers with a Cups emphasis: Collaborating with other people;

Reversed Lovers with a Wands emphasis: Getting parts of the self to work together;

Upright Lovers with a Pentacles emphasis: Practical actions of collaborating;

Reversed Lovers with a Swords emphasis: Finding commonality of divergent inner beliefs.

Upright Hanged Man with a Wands emphasis: Waiting for outer circumstances to indicate that it's the right time for independent action;

Reversed Hanged Man with a Cups emphasis: Waiting for inner readiness regarding an action about a relating;

Upright Hanged Man with a Swords emphasis: Waiting for outer circumstances to indicate that it's the right time to communicate;

Reversed Hanged Man with a Pentacles emphasis: Waiting for inner readiness regarding practical financial action.

Upright Devil with a Cups emphasis: Setting external boundaries with other people;

Reversed Devil with a Wands emphasis: Setting internal boundaries about own actions;

Upright Devil with a Swords emphasis: Setting public boundaries about travel;

Reversed Devil with a Pentacles emphasis: Setting internal, personal boundaries about sex.

Remember, these are just examples! By combining various interpretations of the Minor and Major cards, you can find interpretations and insights that will suit your questions.

The remainder of Part Three gives you a detailed summary of the various aspects of each of the cards in the deck. Interpretations are given for both upright and reversed orientations. Using these interpretations, you can experiment with layouts like those given in Part Two that will guide you in choice-centered relating.

9

The Minor Arcana

Each Minor Arcana card is a cross between a number (pip or court card) level and a suit. By understanding the essence of each number and applying your understanding to the suits, you can interpret the whole Minor Arcana for yourself. You can use the key words in Part One for basic definitions. If you prefer more detailed descriptions, the keywords provided on pages 162–164 give you even more choices with regard to interpretation.

In terms of the pip (1-10) and court (Jack, Knight, Queen, King) cards, the levels develop in groups of three, with two choice points at the Ten and King. The Aces are generally about beginnings, Twos about choosing, and Threes about planning. Fours are associated with manifestation, Fives with adjustments, and Sixes with maintenance. Sevens indicate expansion, Eights involve limits, and Nines reflect integration. At the level of Ten, we hesitate while deciding what to do. Pages symbolize risk-taking, Knights represent focus, and the Queens demonstrate maturity. The Kings reflect closure and letting go.

Key Words for the Pip and Court Card Numbers.

ACES
wishing • desiring • considering • conceiving • conceptualizing • imagining • envisioning • initiating • originating • starting • sensing the possibility • seeing the potential • inspiring • instigating • motivating • provoking • stimulating

TWOS
deciding • choosing • confirming • affirming • saying yes • selecting • electing • picking • singling out • preferring • determining • endorsing • accepting • validating • acknowledging • claiming • acquiescing

THREES
planning • promising • preparing • getting ready • readying • intending • composing • listing factors that lead to • adding up to • identifying key elements • studying • symbolizing • designing • outlining • rehearsing • practicing

FOURS
building • constructing • manifesting • creating • taking action • acting • forming • devising • establishing • erecting • revealing • showing • displaying • flaunting • parading • demonstrating • doing something about • taking steps • doing

FIVES
adapting • adjusting • modifying • reconditioning • overhauling • changing • confronting • challenging • fine-tuning • remodeling • creating upheaval • altering • shaking up • behaving erratically or unpredictably • erupting • interrupting • disrupting • disturbing

Key Words for the Pip and Court Card Numbers (continued).

SIXES
keeping • maintaining • repeating • moving cyclically • recycling • behaving habitually, predictably, reliably, consistently • stabilizing • sustaining • perpetuating • supporting • upholding • reiterating • drilling • training • mollifying • calming • appeasing • staying • sticking with it • reincarnating

SEVENS
expanding • stretching • inflating • compounding • fanning • extending • amplifying • elaborating • enlarging • swelling • increasing • dispersing • playing with • exaggerating • experimenting • varying • exploring • diversifying • being curious, open-minded, open-ended • adding to • jumping from one to another

EIGHTS
contracting • narrowing • restricting • organizing • reorganizing • structuring • restructuring • coordinating • controlling • condensing • compacting • limiting • setting boundaries • abbreviating • cutting back • diminishing • systemizing • putting in order • consolidating • centralizing

NINES
integrating • merging • blending • synthesizing • permeating • continuing in an on-going way • resonating with • unifying • flowing • mixing • mingling • intermingling • streamlining • coalescing • behaving with fluency, smoothly, effortlessly, gracefully • streamlining • coming along • taking it easy • relaxing • becoming immersed in

TENS
hesitating • hedging • waiting • avoiding • taking time out • putting things "on hold" • pausing • looking before leaping • wavering • delaying • faltering • stalling • ignoring • buffering • setting aside for awhile • deferring • holding things up • suspending • temporarily separating • procrastinating

Key Words for the Pip and Court Card Numbers (continued).

PAGES

leaping • risking • daring • jumping in • going for it • adventuring • hazarding • gambling • betting • speculating • wagering • behaving boldly, bravely, dauntlessly, fearlessly, courageously • behaving heroically, audaciously, recklessly, gallantly, valliantly

KNIGHTS

focusing • concentrating • obsessing • fixating • staying on-task • targeting • dedicating • motivating • pursuing the goals • riveting • paying close attention to • committing resources to • behaving single-mindedly, passionately, intensely, devotedly • behaving zealously, purposefully, intently, compulsively

QUEENS

maturing • ripening • typifying the quintessential • behaving in a manner that is competent, full-grown, expert • being seasoned, experienced, grizzled, well-versed • being practiced, veteran, qualified, adult, fully familiar • acting hardened, fully trained, weathered • embodying proficiency, capability, accomplishment • embodying mastery, professionalism, skill, talent • embodying flawlessness, effectiveness, expertise

KINGS

letting go • releasing • finishing • ending • quitting • stopping the use of • completing • moving away from • extricating • disentangling • untangling • freeing • surrendering • discharging • disengaging • wrapping up • exhausting • concluding • terminating • grieving • sharing • gifting • giving • passing on • surrendering to • giving in to

The areas of life associated with the four Minor Arcana suits are described on pages 166–171. In general, the fiery suit of Wands is associated with identity, self-awareness, and self-expression. The Wands cards tell us that it's important to know who we are on the inside (reversed) and to demonstrate who we are on the outside (upright). Upright Wands are associated with the ways in which we present ourselves to the world, including personal style as well as clothing or appearance. They reflect our roles in the world and the titles we bear. Reversed Wands connect us to our spirits—the sparks of life inside us. They represent self-esteem and self-image and all the ways we privately experience ourselves.

The watery suit of Cups is associated with emotions, relationships, and intuitive sensitivity. The Cups cards let us know how valuable it is to understand our feelings. They remind us to express our emotions, act on our relationships (upright), and become aware of deeper feelings and intuitions (reversed). Reversed Cups cards are also related to addictions, depression, mental illness, and the process of recovery. In this context, it's useful to remember that addictions can include compulsive behavior regarding such things as sex, money, food, or love, in addition to drug or alcohol abuse.

The airy suit of Swords is associated with thoughts, ideas, concepts, and communication. The Swords cards describe how we take in information, process it, and pass it on to others. They remind us of the value of logic and clear, linear thinking (upright) and the beliefs behind that thinking (reversed). Upright Swords represent the obvious forms of information exchange: spoken and written communication. They are also associated with other forms of networking and connecting, including travel, transportation, computers, and telephones. Time management, schedules, and lifestyle engineering also emerge from this suit. When reversed, the Swords cards reflect the deeper values, philosophies, and beliefs from which our ideas emerge. Reversed Swords can involve private or internal communication and the ways we talk to ourselves.

The earthy the suit of Pentacles is associated with practical matters and the material world. The Pentacles cards let us know how we interact with physical reality (upright) and how we create a sense of safety for ourselves (reversed). They remind us to value our bodies and our survival. Upright Pentacles represent the most tangible side of physicality: money, work, and physical environments, including houses and land. The upright Pentacles cards are also associated with all phases and forms of ill-health and good health, including preventive health measures, physical breakdowns, healings, and recovery. At an interpersonal level, this suit reflects physical contact and covers everything from physical abuse, to hugs, to sexual encounters. When reversed, the Pentacles cards remind us of deeper levels of security. They bring up the issues of psychological protection and raise questions about whether we feel safe or suicidal in our bodies or on the planet. Reversed Pentacles can also refer to long-term stability, as represented by such things as retirement plans and savings accounts. They can point out concerns related to hidden or behind-the-scenes financial or physical activities as well.

The Minor Arcana Suits

WANDS

Upright Self, role, identity, personality, persona, independence, appearance, presentation of self, freedom, individuality, autonomy, liberty, self-expression.

Reversed Self-esteem, self-image, self-confidence, private identity, soul, hidden self, inner self, inner child, personal spirit, core self, psyche, identities from earlier phases of this life or from other lifetimes.

PEOPLE: Self; independent individuals; self-employed people; aggressive, passive-aggressive, or assertive people; isolated or lonely people; self-absorbed people; self-sufficient people; people who appreciate or enjoy solitude; people who show-off; firefighters; hermits; warriors.

PLACES: Warm, sunny, or dry locations; places where people go to be alone; places where fires happen (i.e. fireplaces, camps, forests); pioneering, outdoorsy environments.

THINGS: Fast-moving; long, rolled up, or cylindrical; personalized items; things that reflect or symbolize a particular identity, name or role (i.e. judge's gavel or football player's jersey); furnaces, fuel pipes, fires, fireplaces, stoves, or other heat-related items.

ACTIVITIES: Hiking, climbing, biking, out-in-nature activities; activities to do alone; pioneering experiences; cutting edge or risk-taking activities; activities in which someone is the star, performer, or hero; activities in which personal identity is identified, refined, or expressed; martial arts; unilateral decisions.

INFORMATION: Data about personal identity, including name, titles, roles, identification symbols or numbers; memberships in groups; information about what a person likes to do alone.

FEELINGS: Anger; assertiveness; aggressiveness; drive toward independence; gut instincts; "I can handle it myself, thank you."

CUPS

Upright Emotions, relationships, feelings, sensitivities, affections, kinship, friendships, partnerships, intimacy, liaisons, affiliations, alliances, collaborative or cooperative efforts.

Reversed Intuition, psychic awareness, hunches, instincts, hidden emotions, inner feelings, private relationships, spiritual awareness, addictions, co-dependency, mental illness, depression.

PEOPLE: Others; emotionally expressive people; people who work or interact best in partnerships or groups; lovers; friends; partners; intimates; family members; sensitive or intuitive people; artists and musicians; addicts of any sort; recovering people.

PLACES: Wet or rainy locations; bodies of water such as ponds, rivers, lakes, oceans; places that are near or across these bodies of water; bathrooms, places where plumbing, sewage, or drainage exists; places where people go to meet others; therapy or healing environments; places where people go to have intuitive or meditative experiences; places where people go to act out their addictions or experience their recovery; art and music studios.

THINGS: Things that are wet or are associated with water or other liquids (i.e. pipes, sinks, bathtubs); things that hold liquids; things that have emotional or intuitive significance; things that represent other important people; spiritual items; medications; mind-altering or addictive substances; allergens or toxins; items that support recovery from addictions, depression, mental illness, toxicity, or allergies; tools of creativity.

ACTIVITIES: Sharing feelings; intimate emotional exchanges; water activities including swimming, bathing, soaking, water sports, boating; using mind-altering substances (i.e., alcohol, chemicals, drugs, medications; even sugar, caffeine, nicotine); activities with others; activities in which emotions, relationships, or intuition are the focus; addictive or recovery oriented activities; making music, painting or drawing.

INFORMATION: Data about significant people including names, genders, locations, occupations; rumors about people; information about personal emotions; psychic or intuitive information; information about addiction, recovery, depression, or mental illness.

FEELINGS: Tenderness; empathy; sympathy; neediness; clinginess; drive toward relatedness or couples; "Let's do it together"; desire to binge or behave addictively; urge toward serenity, recovery, or creativity; tendency toward depression or mental illness.

SWORDS

Upright Written, signed, or verbal communication in any form, thoughts, ideas, concepts, talking, conversations, community, lifestyle, schedule, travel, networking, knowledge, data, information, news, facts, meetings, dialogues, exchanges, discussions, written rules and official codes of conduct; rumors, verbal abuse.

Reversed Beliefs, values, philosophy, ethics, doctrines, secret codes, private thoughts, inner dialogue, private conversations, learning style, self-talk, principles, laws, unwritten rules, inner truth, personal codes of conduct.

PEOPLE: Siblings, cousins, co-workers, neighbors; communicators; people who are involved with the processing of data or information; intellectual people; students and teachers; people who like to utilize logical, linear thinking; writers; travelers; foreigners; mail carriers.

PLACES: Airy or windswept locations; places with large expanses of sky; open-air stadiums or theaters; windows, doors, and openings; places of learning and education; bookstores and libraries; places associated with travel and transportation; places related to communication.

THINGS: Things that are full of air or other vapors; things associated with air or air quality (i.e. air conditioning, forced-air heat, pollution control); things used for teaching, learning, or communication, including writing utensils, books, computers, telephones; things associated with travel and transportation, including cars, planes, bicycles; anything electrical or electronic.

ACTIVITIES: Exchanging or presenting thoughts, ideas, concepts; teaching or learning; any educational opportunities; philosophical discussions; arguments and debates; air activities including flying, hang-gliding, hot-air ballooning; writing or communicating in any way; travel of any sort; networking.

INFORMATION: Data about ideas, beliefs, concepts, truths; information about communication systems, including addresses, phone numbers, e-mail, fax; details about daily schedule or routine; travel information.

FEELINGS: Clarity; objectivity; insight; sense of distance; urge to reflect on emotions; urge toward logic; "Let me think about it."

PENTACLES

Upright Physical matter, practical things, health, body, sex, material possessions, money, job, career, profession, property, home, use of resources, realism, reality checks, business, government, tangible experiences, sports, physical or sexual abuse, violence.

Reversed Security, stability, safety, commitments, long-term security, groundedness, commitment to the body, willingness to stay alive, luckiness, traps, suicide, abuse of self.

PEOPLE: Employers, employees, coworkers; people who are involved with money in any way; physical laborers; people who are associated with homes, buildings, or other real estate; people connected to the earth; anyone involved with health, sickness, healing, or sexuality; athletes; craftspeople and three-dimensional artists; rescue workers; those involved with abuse or violence.

PLACES: Earthy or stony locations; places constructed of stone, wood, or concrete; buildings; homes; mountains, hills, plowed fields, or forests; caves, holes, quarries, pits, mines; all places of business; places where money is exchanged or managed; places related to health, exercise, sports, or healing; places associated with sex; places associated with crafts or tactile art.

THINGS: Things that are solid and made of dirt, stone, wood, concrete, fabric, or other human-made products; things associated with gardening, farming, landscaping, recycling or taking care of the Earth; things used for monetary exchange, including checkbooks, credit cards, and cash; gambling; things connected with health care in any way; things associated with arts and crafts.

ACTIVITIES: Touching, hugging, holding; physical or sexual abuse; violence; sexual interactions; exercise or sporting activities; gardening, farming, landscaping; constructing, building, crafting, creating three-dimensional art; healing or health related activities; financial exchanges and any other endeavors associated with money; safety conscious practices; undertakings related to home or real estate; suicide.

INFORMATION: Data about money, property, or real estate; information about sex, sexually transmitted diseases or physical contact; facts about abuse; information about physical or psychological safety; details about health, healing, remedies, medications, exercise, nutrition or doctors; details about gardening, farming, homes, construction, or building.

FEELINGS: Solidity; safety; reliability; groundedness; security; urge to create long- or short-term protection; urge to interact at a physical level; willingness to live; inclination toward suicide; "Let me try it on."

Sample Interpretations for the Four Suits of the Minor Arcana

Remember that you can create your own interpretations by combining the meanings for the pip or court cards with the areas of life associated with each of the four suits. The following are just examples of some possible combinations. If they don't apply to your questions or the issues at hand, make your own delineation that is more specific to your reading (and write them in this book if you want).

ACE OF WANDS

GENERAL:

U Conceiving of a new identity or role in the world; imagining independence; tuning in to the possibility of autonomy

R Considering a new self-image; inspiring self-esteem; sensing the urge toward personal spirit

AS SOMEONE'S POSITIVE ATTRIBUTE:

U Ability to conceive of a new self; envision individuality; tune in to the potential for independence; hike or climb

R Ability to desire a new self-image; wish for personal spirit; consider core self; be outdoors alone

AS SOMEONE'S NEGATIVE ATTRIBUTE:

U Tendency to abort new identity; begin doubtful autonomous behavior; wish for lonely isolation; instigate dysfunctional aggressive behavior

R Tendency to imagine negative core self ; desire a destructive hidden identity; inspire dubious self-esteem; start problematic hidden fires

IF LAYOUT QUESTION HAS A POSITIVE SLANT, THEN:

U Consider new self; conceptualize liberty; sense the urge for self-expression; start the fire

R Conceive of a new self-image; tune in to the potential for self-esteem; imagine a core self; see the potential for enjoying solitude

IF LAYOUT QUESTION HAS A NEGATIVE SLANT, THEN:

U Resist the desire for freedom; avoid the urge toward independence; don't conceptualize it alone; hold back on starting something that moves fast

R Avoid conceiving of a new self-image; withdraw from the urge toward spirit; oppose the desire for a hidden identity; counteract the possibility of arson

THIS CARD AS A QUESTION:

U If you could be anyone you want, who would you become?
What identity are you imagining?
Do you desire freedom?
Is it possible to wish for heroism?

R Which private self do you feel motivated to express?
How are you planting seeds for a new self-concept?
When did you start to find your personal spirit?
Do you want the option of being alone in nature?

Wands

TWO OF WANDS

GENERAL:

U Choosing a new identity; confirming willingness to take on a particular role; saying yes to independence

R Endorsing new self-image; validating self-esteem; acknowledging personal spirit

AS SOMEONE'S POSITIVE ATTRIBUTE:

U Ability to acknowledge a new role; accept independence; say yes to self-expression; select outdoor activities

R Ability to affirm a healthy self-concept; accept core spirit; prefer a private self; choose to be introspective

AS SOMEONE'S NEGATIVE ATTRIBUTE:

U Tendency to say yes to a dysfunctional role in the world; prefer too much freedom; elect negative forms of self-expression; choose unsound things that move too fast

R Tendency to affirm unhealthy self-concept; endorse a negative sense of soul; validate dysfunctional private self; select despairing loneliness

IF LAYOUT QUESTION HAS A POSITIVE SLANT, THEN:

U Confirm an important role or identity; choose freedom; select individuality; choose a sunny, dry location

R Accept personal spirit; prefer private self; elect hidden identity; acknowledge the hidden flame

IF LAYOUT QUESTION HAS A NEGATIVE SLANT, THEN:

U Don't decide on independence; avoid confirming this role; resist validating this identity; withdraw from endorsing outdoor activities

R Hold back on selecting this self-image; oppose electing a hidden identity; combat the endorsement of this private self; don't select on the basis of private, personal data

THIS CARD AS A QUESTION:

U What part of your personality are you selecting?
Do you select freedom?
How can you validate independence?
How do you acknowledge your anger?

R In what ways do you affirm your self-image?
How can you validate your personal spirit?
Will you say yes to your soul?
When will you elect to be alone?

THREE OF WANDS

GENERAL:

U Planning to express a new identity; promising freedom; intending to declare independence

R Getting ready for self-esteem; contemplating soul; preparing for private self

AS SOMEONE'S POSITIVE ATTRIBUTE:

U Ability to: prepare for a new role; plan for self-expression; make personal promises; symbolize personalized items

R Ability to: study the psyche; identify the key elements of spirit; list the factors that lead to self-esteem; plan a private performance

AS SOMEONE'S NEGATIVE ATTRIBUTE:

U Tendency to plan for negative self-expression; prepare for independence and not act on it ; promise too much autonomy; design destructive outdoor activities

R Tendency to prepare for negative self-image; plan for dysfunctional private self ; compose unsuitable hidden identity; design destructive fires

IF LAYOUT QUESTION HAS A POSITIVE SLANT, THEN:

U Make plans for expressing personality; promise someone else freedom; prepare for independence; study the star performer

R Symbolize personal spirit; promise yourself freedom; identify key elements of self-esteem; design risk-taking activities to do alone

IF LAYOUT QUESTION HAS A NEGATIVE SLANT, THEN:

U Don't plan for independence; avoid preparing for freedom; oppose promising a new role; contest the studying of warriors

R Hold back on developing hidden identity; resist contemplating personal soul; withdraw from studying the psyche; evade identifying key personal data

THIS CARD AS A QUESTION:

U How will you plan for independence?
What are your preparations for self-expression?
When will you identify the key elements of this
  personality?
How will you get ready to be a firefighter?

R How do you contemplate your soul?
What do you promise yourself regarding self-esteem?
What are the key elements of your personal spirit?
What do you do about internalized anger?

Wands

FOUR OF WANDS

GENERAL:

U Manifesting identity; expressing personality; pushing for independence

R Demonstrating self-image; establishing personal spirit; constructing hidden identity

AS SOMEONE'S POSITIVE ATTRIBUTE:

U Ability to: demonstrate persona; act on liberty; do something about new role; take action toward becoming a star

R Ability to: demonstrate personal spirit; manifest core self; reveal private self; establish solitude

AS SOMEONE'S NEGATIVE ATTRIBUTE:

U Tendency to act independently without considering others; manifest a difficult personality; take action toward problematic independence; flaunt aggressive behavior

R Tendency to construct negative self-image; display problematic personal spirit; act out dysfunctional private self; push toward too much isolation

IF LAYOUT QUESTION HAS A POSITIVE SLANT, THEN:

U Demonstrate personality; take independent action; establish freedom; create a warm, sunny location

R Reveal private self; establish personal spirit; act from core self; structure a place where people can be alone

IF LAYOUT QUESTION HAS A NEGATIVE SLANT, THEN:

U Don't create this personality; avoid acting independently; withdraw from displaying individuality; escape from taking outdoor action

R Hold back from revealing core spirit; resist forming private self; oppose establishing this self-image; evade passive-aggressive action

THIS CARD AS A QUESTION:

U How does your behavior reflect your identity?
How do you construct freedom?
In what ways do you act independently?
Would you demonstrate your martial arts skills?

R In what manner do you show your soul?
How can you establish self-esteem?
When will you reveal your core self?
Can you build a hidden fire?

Wands

FIVE OF WANDS

GENERAL:

U Adapting the self; modifying self-expression; overhauling the persona

R Confronting the private self; adjusting self-esteem; altering core self

AS SOMEONE'S POSITIVE ATTRIBUTE:

U Ability to change self-expression; modify personality; confront self; recondition things that move quickly

R Ability to adjust self-image; fine-tune core self; confront the hidden identity; interrupt the isolation

AS SOMEONE'S NEGATIVE ATTRIBUTE:

U Tendency to express a disruptive personality; challenge autonomy too much; create upheaval in this role; behave unpredictably around fuel and fire

R Tendency to behave erratically with regard to the psyche; to create upheaval in personal spirit; disturb the soul; interrupt privacy

IF LAYOUT QUESTION HAS A POSITIVE SLANT, THEN:

U Challenge the self; adapt the persona; change the appearance; interrupt the warrior

R Fine-tune the self-image; modify private sense of self; alter core self; confront loneliness

IF LAYOUT QUESTION HAS A NEGATIVE SLANT, THEN:

U Resist behaving erratically regarding freedom; don't adapt the personality; oppose challenges to the self; escape from disturbing outdoor environments

R Hold back from confronting the core self; avoid disrupting personal spirit; withdraw from overhauling self-image; defy the modifications to privacy

THIS CARD AS A QUESTION:

U What do you need to do to change yourself?
Can you modify your independence?
Will you fine-tune your self-expression?
What happens when you confront self-absorbed people?

R How can you re-model your self-esteem?
What would it take to adapt your core self?
Do you feel like challenging your loneliness?
Do you usually create upheaval with hidden fires?

Wands

SIX OF WANDS

GENERAL:

U Maintaining a predictable self; supporting independence; sustaining individuality

R Reviewing core self; behaving consistently regarding self-esteem; appeasing the soul

AS SOMEONE'S POSITIVE ATTRIBUTE:

U Ability to express self in a predictable manner; stay reliably independent; perpetuate the role; train the star

R Ability to sustain the soul; support the self-image; behave predictably regarding core self; recycle personalized items

AS SOMEONE'S NEGATIVE ATTRIBUTE:

U Tendency to perpetuate a destructive role; maintain dysfunctional independence; support negative identity; repeatedly uphold dangerous or aggressive people

R Tendency to support a negative self-image; appease a problematic psyche too much; repeat problematic private self-expression; sustain unwholesome isolation

IF LAYOUT QUESTION HAS A POSITIVE SLANT, THEN:

U Get into a regular habit of self-expression; uphold the identity; perpetuate liberty; keep the fire burning

R Reincarnate the soul; stabilize the self-esteem; calm the personal spirit; behave reliably with regard to solitude

IF LAYOUT QUESTION HAS A NEGATIVE SLANT, THEN:

U Don't express the predictable personality; avoid supporting freedom; withdraw from training for the role; oppose the maintenance of the sunny place

R Resist appeasing the personal spirit; hold back on sustaining this self-image; don't get into supporting this core self; escape from perpetuating the loneliness

THIS CARD AS A QUESTION:

U What do you need to do in order to maintain your identity?
How do you support your independence?
Can you appease that personality?
Do you train regularly in martial arts?

R How do you stabilize your self-esteem?
When will you calm your personal spirit?
Do you believe that you reincarnate your soul?
How often must you reiterate your need for privacy?

Wands

SEVEN OF WANDS

GENERAL:

U Experimenting with self-expression; stretching the self; amplifying the personality

R Exploring self-image in a variety of ways; behaving open-mindedly regarding soul; extending personal spirit

AS SOMEONE'S POSITIVE ATTRIBUTE:

U Ability to express self in a variety of ways; play with various roles; increase freedom; fan the flames

R Ability to expand the personal spirit; increase self-esteem; explore a private identity; add to private membership

AS SOMEONE'S NEGATIVE ATTRIBUTE:

U Tendency to exaggerate the self; inflate the personality; experiment with too many identities; play with dangerous fire

R Tendency to inflate a negative personal spirit; jump from one questionable self-image to another; play around with problematic private identity; exaggerate loneliness

IF LAYOUT QUESTION HAS A POSITIVE SLANT, THEN:

U Explore and express various parts of self; expand the personality; enlarge the scope of freedom; play with the appearance

R Be curious about the soul; amplify the personal spirit; stretch the self-esteem; be open-minded about solitude

IF LAYOUT QUESTION HAS A NEGATIVE SLANT, THEN:

U Don't expand the role; escape from playing with that kind of personality; oppose expanding the freedom; counteract the elaborate titles

R Resist inflating the self-esteem; hold back on expanding the hidden self; avoid amplifying this self-image; don't get into increasing the self-absorption

THIS CARD AS A QUESTION:

U How do you express yourself when you play?
Will you expand your role?
How have you explored independence?
Do you want to experiment with increased autonomy?

R In what ways have you explored your core self?
Is your personal spirit playful?
Do you tend to exaggerate your loneliness?
Are the passive-aggressive tendencies increasing?

Wands

EIGHT OF WANDS

GENERAL:

U Organizing self-expression; setting limits on parts of the identity; defining personal priorities

R Consolidating the self-image; restructuring the private identity; cutting back to the core self

AS SOMEONE'S POSITIVE ATTRIBUTE:

U Ability to put appearance(s) in order; organize personal direction; handle independence in a systematic way; structure performance opportunities

R Ability to set boundaries for the inner child; restructure self-image; consolidate the core self; put self-confidence in order

AS SOMEONE'S NEGATIVE ATTRIBUTE:

U Tendency to limit the self in a destructive way; set dangerous restrictions regarding independence; withhold self-expression too much; reorganize the role in a problematic way

R Tendency to restrict the core self; diminish the personal spirit; limit self-esteem; set dubious boundaries with inner self

IF LAYOUT QUESTION HAS A POSITIVE SLANT, THEN:

U Get organized about self-expression; set priorities regarding independence; control the self; set boundaries for the aggressive person

R Consolidate the core self; restructure self-image; control the hidden self; put data about private identity in order

IF LAYOUT QUESTION HAS A NEGATIVE SLANT, THEN:

U Shun the tendency to set boundaries for the self; withdraw from organizing the self-expression; don't get into restricting freedom; oppose the organization of the pioneering activities

R Resist narrowing the self-esteem; hold back from diminishing the personal spirit; avoid restricting the inner self; don't limit the private identity

THIS CARD AS A QUESTION:

U How do you reorganize yourself?
Can you control yourself?
What are the boundaries to your expression of freedom?
Can you put this warm, sunny place in order?

R Are you diminishing your self-esteem?
How can you restructure your self-image?
Do you want to put your inner self in order?
Can you control passive-aggressive people?

Wands

NINE OF WANDS

GENERAL:

U Expressing self in a coordinated manner; showing smoothly functioning identity; behaving with graceful independence

R Resonating with core self; unifying the self-image; integrating the inner self

AS SOMEONE'S POSITIVE ATTRIBUTE:

U Ability to integrate the personality; become immersed in freedom; behave with effortless individuality; unify the martial arts efforts

R Ability to becoming immersed in personal spirit; harmonize with core self; synthesize self-image; intermingle with identities from other lifetimes

AS SOMEONE'S NEGATIVE ATTRIBUTE:

U Tendency to appear too faultless; merge into a dysfunctional personality; flow effortlessly toward too much freedom; mingle with self-absorbed people

R Tendency to become immersed in negative self-esteem; coalesce into a destructive psyche; synthesize a problematic self-image; merge with a dangerous inner self

IF LAYOUT QUESTION HAS A POSITIVE SLANT, THEN:

U Integrate the identity; present a unified self-expression; flow into independence; create no boundaries for the fire

R Merge with the inner self; synthesize the personal spirit; become immersed in other lifetimes; unify private identity

IF LAYOUT QUESTION HAS A NEGATIVE SLANT, THEN:

U Withdraw from integrating the personality; don't become immersed in the public role; oppose the flowing movement toward liberty; resist mingling with independent people

R Hold back from integrating this self-image; avoid relaxing with the private identity; don't get into merging with the core self; shun the tendency to flow into other lives

THIS CARD AS A QUESTION:

U When and how is your identity most integrated?
Which role do you harmonize with the most?
Is it possible to orchestrate independence?
Can you move effortlessly through the forest?

R How do you unify your personal spirit?
What would it take to integrate with your inner self?
How is your self-image coalescing?
Can you experience solitude effortlessly?

Wands

TEN OF WANDS

GENERAL:

U Hesitating with regard to self-expression; putting independence "on hold"; stalling with regard to freedom

R Wavering about self-esteem; setting inner self aside for awhile; temporarily separating from personal spirit

AS SOMEONE'S POSITIVE ATTRIBUTE:

U Ability to delay self-expression or self-gratification; take time out from playing the role; defer independence until an appropriate time; look before leaping into the fire

R Ability to buffer the private identity; set aside self-absorption; ignore other self-absorbed people; put off the isolation

AS SOMEONE'S NEGATIVE ATTRIBUTE:

U Tendency to stall with regard to self-expression; falter regarding independence; procrastinate regarding autonomy; delay the firefighters

R Tendency to waver with regard to self-confidence; set aside the core self; avoid the soul; procrastinate too much regarding private self

IF LAYOUT QUESTION HAS A POSITIVE SLANT, THEN:

U Set self aside for awhile; put off independence; suspend the role; avoid self-expression

R Suspend this self-image; set inner self aside for the moment; look before leaping into this private identity; delay isolation

IF LAYOUT QUESTION HAS A NEGATIVE SLANT, THEN:

U Don't get into suspending identity; oppose the hesitation regarding self-expression; resist stalling regarding this role; hold back on waiving independence

R Avoid setting self-esteem aside; don't separate from personal spirit; shun the tendency to falter regarding self-image; withdraw from wavering about the core self

THIS CARD AS A QUESTION:

U When do you hold back and let someone else lead?
How often do you set aside your public persona?
How long will you delay your self-expression?
Will you avoid things that move too fast?

R Are you putting your inner self "on hold"?
Have you temporarily separated from your personal spirit?
Do you hesitate because of your self-image?
How long can you stall regarding your private identity?

Wands

PAGE OF WANDS

GENERAL:

U Taking risks with self-expression; daring to leap into independence; courageously assuming the role

R Betting on self-confidence; undauntedly expressing core self; risking a private identity

AS SOMEONE'S POSITIVE ATTRIBUTE:

U Ability to take risks in self-expression; gamble on independence; leap into the role; dare to use things that move fast

R Ability to speculate on the psyche; adventure into the core self; fearlessly seek the personal spirit; jump into other lifetimes

AS SOMEONE'S NEGATIVE ATTRIBUTE:

U Tendency to: jump into showing-off; gamble on freedom in problematic ways; take dysfunctional leaps regarding autonomy; take too many risks regarding fire

R Tendency to fearlessly, but dangerously, express inner self; boldly operate from dysfunctional self-image; recklessly express core self in problematic ways; dauntlessly continue passive-aggressive behavior;

IF LAYOUT QUESTION HAS A POSITIVE SLANT, THEN:

U Take personal risks; dare to express full personality; leap into independence; courageously pursue martial arts

R Venture boldly into exploring core self; gamble on self-confidence; jump into inner self; bravely create private identity

IF LAYOUT QUESTION HAS A NEGATIVE SLANT, THEN:

U Don't get into risking the self; oppose gambles regarding freedom; counteract fearless self-expression; resist reckless outdoor adventures

R Hold back on leaping into inner self; avoid betting on the self-image; don't leap into private identity; shun the option of speculating on core self

THIS CARD AS A QUESTION:

U Where and how do you want to take risks with self-expression?
How courageous do you feel regarding this role?
What would it take to jump into independence?
Do you act recklessly when angry?

R Can you fearlessly face your inner self?
Do you dare test your self-confidence?
How bold is your personal spirit?
Does it seem adventurous to explore other lifetimes?

Wands

KNIGHT OF WANDS

GENERAL:

U Focusing on independence; paying close attention to self-expression; concentrating on role

R Passionately seeking self-esteem; intensely targeting inner self; dedicated to pursuing the soul

AS SOMEONE'S POSITIVE ATTRIBUTE:

U Ability to concentrate on individuality; target the role; intently pursue self-expression; pay close attention to titles

R Ability to focus on the soul; be passionately self-confident; be dedicated to inner self; express intensity regarding self-image

AS SOMEONE'S NEGATIVE ATTRIBUTE:

U Tendency to become obsessed with self; fixate too much on freedom; zealously show off in dysfunctional ways; be dangerously dedicated to performing as a star

R Tendency to experience dysfunctional passion regarding the inner self; be too devoted to core self; focus on negative self-image too much; obsess on private identity

IF LAYOUT QUESTION HAS A POSITIVE SLANT, THEN:

U Pay intense attention to self; focus on independence; concentrate on the role; ambitiously pursue martial arts

R Pay close attention to personal spirit; devotedly attend to the soul; intently target self-esteem; become passionately dedicated to the inner child

IF LAYOUT QUESTION HAS A NEGATIVE SLANT, THEN:

U Intensely oppose independence; confront the obsession with self; counteract the fixation on self-expression; resist the zealous focus on isolation

R Hold back from single-mindedly pursuing the soul; avoid paying close attention to inner self; don't become obsessed with self-esteem; shun the option to concentrate on loneliness

THIS CARD AS A QUESTION:

U How do you passionately express yourself?
Are you fixating on the role?
Can you pursue independence single-mindedly?
Are you dedicated to pioneering activities?

R Why do you concentrate so hard on your self-image?
Will you become immersed in your inner self?
What happens when you focus on self-esteem?
Are you intensely seeking your soul?

Wands

QUEEN OF WANDS

GENERAL:

U Behaving with maturity; acting the well-versed role; exhibiting a competent personality

R Demonstrating a mellow soul; expressing self-confidence; displaying flawless self-esteem

As Someone's Positive Attribute:

U Ability to express a professional persona; show proficiency in the role; demonstrate mature independence; illustrate full training in martial arts

R Ability to be mature regarding self-image; demonstrate a talented private identity; skillfully experience solitude; explore other lifetimes effectively

As Someone's Negative Attribute:

U Tendency to project a hardened identity; be well-versed in problematic self-expression; pursue an expert quest for dangerous autonomy; skillfully light dangerous fires

R Tendency to demonstrate masterful self-absorption; express full-blown, dysfunctional inner self; exhibit ripened, but unsound, self-esteem; a proficient demonstration of a dangerous self-image

If Layout Question Has a Positive Slant, Then:

U Demonstrate personal maturity; act on individual competence; express veteran persona; exhibit fully trained martial arts skills

R Express mature self-confidence; demonstrate full-grown personal spirit; assert talented core self; exhibit mellowness in solitude

IF LAYOUT QUESTION HAS A NEGATIVE SLANT, THEN:

U Counteract the masterful persona; confront the capable role; resist the competent expression of self; hold back on demonstrating fully trained pioneering activities

R Avoid this full-grown self-image; don't become professional about the soul; shun the opportunity for expressing mature self-esteem; withdraw from hardened isolation

THIS CARD AS A QUESTION:

U How do you experience yourself as a mature person?
Do you like feeling grown-up?
What would cause you to be fully trained?
Are you well-versed in lighting fires?

R Are you fully capable of expressing your soul?
Do you have a competent self-image?
Do you have a professional private identity?
Are you completely qualified to explore the psyche?

Wands

KING OF WANDS

GENERAL:

U Releasing a role; letting go of an identity; moving away from freedom

R Disentangling from a private role; giving of personal spirit; sharing core self

AS SOMEONE'S POSITIVE ATTRIBUTE:

U Ability to let go of independence; release previous personality; give autonomy; share pioneering skills

R Ability to terminate unsound private identity; release personal spirit; untangle inner self; share the soul

AS SOMEONE'S NEGATIVE ATTRIBUTE:

U Tendency to forget or lose the self; terminate healthy self-expression; move away from healthy, high-quality individuals; free dangerous individuals

R Tendency to let go of positive self-esteem; move away from healthy personal spirit; lose the soul; walk away from beneficial solitude

IF LAYOUT QUESTION HAS A POSITIVE SLANT, THEN:

U Let go of independence; share the self; release the role; move away from warm, sunny locations

R Extricate from negative isolation; untangle destructive self-image; disengage from problematic inner self; terminate negative self-absorption

IF LAYOUT QUESTION HAS A NEGATIVE SLANT, THEN:

U Resist the urge to let go of the self; hold back on the desire to end the independence; avoid sharing the identity; don't walk away from the fire

R Shun the opportunity to lose self-esteem; withdraw from losing the soul; don't get into passing on the negative self-image; oppose the chance to let go of solitude

THIS CARD AS A QUESTION:

U What parts of your identity are you ready to release?
Did you release your old name or title?
How will you extricate yourself from the role?
Can you walk away from independence?

R How did you lose your soul?
Why did you let go of self-esteem?
Can you extricate yourself from the isolation?
Can you walk away from the private identity?

Wands

ACE OF CUPS

GENERAL:

U Conceiving of a new emotion; imagining a new intimate relationship; conceptualizing a new friendship

R Sensing the possibility of a new level of intuition; desiring a new, hidden relationship; considering a path toward recovery from addiction

AS SOMEONE'S POSITIVE ATTRIBUTE:

U Ability to stimulate a new relationship; see the possibility of a new level of intimacy; consider a partnership; envision a wet or rainy location

R Ability to tune in to a new type of psychic ability; wish for a hunch; initiate spiritual experience; inspire recovery from co-dependency

AS SOMEONE'S NEGATIVE ATTRIBUTE:

U Tendency to start new relationships without resolving old issues; consider a new problematic relationship; initiate dangerous emotions; experience a desire to be engaged in abuse

R Tendency to desire addiction; provoke depression; initiate co-dependency; wish for destructive psychic experiences

IF LAYOUT QUESTION HAS A POSITIVE SLANT, THEN:

U Begin to think of relating in a new way; imagine that it's possible to have a new feeling; initiate a new friendship or alliance; see the potential of using water

R Tune in to the opportunity for using intuition; wish for a new approach to addictions; sense the possibility of a hidden emotion; consider mental illness

IF LAYOUT QUESTION HAS A NEGATIVE SLANT, THEN:

U Don't initiate the relationship; avoid considering intimacy; resist the potential for an alliance; don't get into starting the plumbing repairs

R Hold back on wishing for psychic awareness; oppose the concept of mental illness; counteract the potential for a hidden relationship; escape from the possibility of addiction

THIS CARD AS A QUESTION:

U What kind of relationship do you wish for?
Have you considered an alliance or partnership?
Can you imagine the emotions?
Do you see the possibility of using imaginative art?

R What would (or did) motivate your recovery?
How did you start down the path of psychic work?
Do you see the possibility of addiction (or co-dependency)?
How did the hidden relationship start?

Cups

TWO OF CUPS

GENERAL:

U Choosing a new feeling; confirming a new relationship; saying yes to a partnership

R Affirming psychic ability; acknowledging addiction or recovery; validating inner feelings

AS SOMEONE'S POSITIVE ATTRIBUTE:

U Ability to choose friendships appropriately; validate emotions; endorse partnerships; select the ocean as a location

R Ability to acknowledge intuition; elect recovery; say yes to inner feelings; accept mental illness

AS SOMEONE'S NEGATIVE ATTRIBUTE:

U Tendency to validate destructive emotions; choose dysfunctional relationships; select emotionally unhealthy friends; decide on a dangerous use of water

R Tendency to prefer destructive psychic experiences; say yes to dysfunctional hidden relationships; endorse addictions; validate unsound hunches

IF LAYOUT QUESTION HAS A POSITIVE SLANT, THEN:

U Choose an important relationship; affirm the feelings; say yes to intimacy; endorse therapy

R Validate intuition; accept the hidden feeling; acknowledge addiction; confirm instincts

IF LAYOUT QUESTION HAS A NEGATIVE SLANT, THEN:

U Resist selecting this friend; hold back on confirming the alliance; avoid endorsing the emotions; don't choose a rainy location

R Shun the option of intuition; withdraw from endorsing addiction; don't get into validating that it's mental illness; oppose the confirmation of a hidden relationship

THIS CARD AS A QUESTION:

U What are you really feeling?
How do you know if a relationship is right for you?
How do you decide on alliances?
What made you choose the watery site?

R How do you elect whether to act on your addiction?
How did you elect recovery as a direction?
Is there a confirmation of mental illness?
When will you say yes to your intuition?

Cups

THREE OF CUPS

GENERAL:

U Planning to express a new emotion; preparing for a relationship; promising intimacy

R Getting ready to utilize intuition; identifying the key elements of mental illness; studying addiction and recovery

AS SOMEONE'S POSITIVE ATTRIBUTE:

U Ability to prepare at the emotional level; make promises to others; identify the key elements of friendship; study the rivers

R Ability to design a plan for recovery; study inner feelings; get ready for psychic experiences; outline the factors leading to addiction

AS SOMEONE'S NEGATIVE ATTRIBUTE:

U Tendency to make doubtful promises; plan for destructive alliances; prepare for relating (without actually relating); make unsound plans for the plumbing

R Tendency to prepare for destructive hidden relationships; make unsound plans for addictive behavior; outline hidden emotions without ever expressing them; study mental illness in doubtful ways

IF LAYOUT QUESTION HAS A POSITIVE SLANT, THEN:

U Make plans for the desired relationship; prepare for a partnership; promise intimacy; identify the key elements of the therapy

R Outline the hidden feelings; list the factors that lead to psychic experience; get ready for spiritual awareness; design a plan for recovery

INAPPROPRIATE ACTION:

U Hold back on the plan for the partnership; avoid getting ready for intimacy; don't outline the emotions; shun the option of medication

R Withdraw from promising psychic awareness; don't get into listing the factors that lead to intuition; oppose the study of addictions; counteract the preparations for co-dependency

THIS CARD AS A QUESTION:

U What do you need to do in order to express the emotion?
How do you prepare for intimacy?
Are you planning for an alliance?
What are the factors that lead to an allergic reaction?

R Are you studying psychic things?
Can you make promises about recovery?
Are you planning for an addictive or binge episode?
Are you getting ready to handle the mental illness?

Cups

FOUR OF CUPS

GENERAL:

U Manifesting a relationship; expressing emotions; constructing an alliance

R Acting on a hidden feeling; demonstrating intuition; building recovery

AS SOMEONE'S POSITIVE ATTRIBUTE:

U Ability to demonstrate the feelings; act cooperatively; build a relationship; display activities in the water

R Ability to take action based on intuition; demonstrate psychic abilities; establish spiritual awareness; build a healing or recovery program

AS SOMEONE'S NEGATIVE ATTRIBUTE:

U Tendency to collaborate too much; build dysfunctional relationships; construct unsound alliances; structure dangerous places near water

R Tendency to manifest problematic psychic experiences; act out dangerous addictions; flaunt dysfunctional hidden relationships; demonstrate destructive co-dependent attitudes

IF LAYOUT QUESTION HAS A POSITIVE SLANT, THEN:

U Demonstrate the feelings; take cooperative action; build the alliance; construct the pond

R Take action on the hunch; reveal psychic abilities; establish spiritual awareness; do something about the mental illness

IF LAYOUT QUESTION HAS A NEGATIVE SLANT, THEN:

U Don't do anything about intimacy; withdraw from constructing a relationship; oppose the creation of an alliance; counteract the establishment of cooperative efforts

R Confront the flaunting of the hidden relationship; resist the display of intuition; hold back on manifesting mental illness; avoid demonstrating co-dependency

THIS CARD AS A QUESTION:

U How does your behavior reflect your emotions?
How do you build alliances?
Do you want to do something about intimacy?
Will you demonstrate your collaborative efforts?

R How are you manifesting your intuition?
When do you act out your addictive behavior?
Will you take steps toward healing or recovery?
Is there a display of mental illness?

Cups

FIVE OF CUPS

GENERAL:

U Challenging the relationship; adapting the partnership; modifying the emotional expression

R Fine-tuning the intuition; altering the private relationship; confronting the addictions

AS SOMEONE'S POSITIVE ATTRIBUTE:

U Ability to change forms of emotional expression; modify relationships; fine-tune the collaborative efforts; overhaul the plumbing system

R Ability to tailor psychic experiences; adapt to spiritual awareness; confront the depression; interrupt the addiction

AS SOMEONE'S NEGATIVE ATTRIBUTE:

U Tendency to behave erratically in relationships; disturb the partnership; disrupt the emotional balance; create upheaval with water

R Tendency to negatively challenge spiritual awareness; behave unpredictably because of addiction; create dysfunctional upheaval in inner feelings; erratically erupt because of mental illness

IF LAYOUT QUESTION HAS A POSITIVE SLANT, THEN:

U Alter the patterns of relating; challenge the alliance; make adjustments in intimacy; fine-tune the plumbing

R Modify the psychic behavior; confront the addictions; shake-up the co-dependency; disrupt the hidden emotions

IF LAYOUT QUESTION HAS A NEGATIVE SLANT, THEN:

U Avoid challenging the relationship; don't modify the partnership; withdraw from emotional upheaval; shun the option of adapting the medication

R Don't get into disruptive psychic behavior; oppose the adaptations to the spiritual activities; counteract the disruptive addictions; resist the upheaval of co-dependency

THIS CARD AS A QUESTION:

U What do you need to do to change your feelings?
How would you like to modify the relationship?
What changes do you foresee for the partnership?
How can we alter the flow of the water?

R Are the addictions disrupting your life?
Does the mental illness create upheaval?
Is there medication that would alter the depression?
How do you fine-tune your intuition?

Cups

SIX OF CUPS

GENERAL:

U Maintaining predictable emotional patterns; stabilizing a reliable relationship; supporting a collaborative effort

R Sustaining the psychic experiences; reliably utilizing intuition; behaving predictably regarding recovery

AS SOMEONE'S POSITIVE ATTRIBUTE:

U Ability to express emotions in a predictable manner; be reliable in a relationship; maintain a partnership; consistently support collaboration

R Ability to use intuition reliably; sustain spiritual awareness; uphold recovery; stabilize the mental illness

AS SOMEONE'S NEGATIVE ATTRIBUTE:

U Tendency to maintain the same old unchanging emotional games; stubbornly hang on to an unhealthy relationship; consistently engage in negative collaborations; perpetuate an unsound or unhealthy water system

R Tendency to sustain the dysfunctional hidden relationship; support destructive psychic experiments; reiterate questionable spiritual dogma; maintain the addiction

IF LAYOUT QUESTION HAS A POSITIVE SLANT, THEN:

U Get into regular emotional expression; sustain the relationship; maintain the alliance; stabilize the medication

R Support intuition; stabilize healing or recovery; habitually practice psychic work; reiterate that there is support for the mental illness

IF LAYOUT QUESTION HAS A NEGATIVE SLANT, THEN:

U Don't behave so predictably in the relationship; shun the option of perpetuating the alliance; withdraw from continuing the partnership; don't get into supporting the water system

R Oppose efforts to sustain psychic work; counteract appeasement of the addict; confront habitual co-dependency; resist the urge to perpetuate the private relationship

THIS CARD AS A QUESTION:

U What do you need to do in order to maintain your relationship?
How can you stabilize your emotions?
What will sustain the collaborative effort?
How can you keep the plumbing going?

R How do you make a habit of spiritual attunement?
What tends to perpetuate your addiction?
What regularly reinforces your recovery?
What habitual behavior is associated with this mental illness?

Cups

SEVEN OF CUPS

GENERAL:

U Experimenting with expressing a variety of emotions; interacting with many different people; expanding the number of people in the alliance

R Exploring psychic dimensions; expressing curiosity about intuition; diversifying recovery treatments

AS SOMEONE'S POSITIVE ATTRIBUTE:

U Ability to express various feelings; interact with a variety of people; play with friends; expand the group

R Ability to experiment with intuition; increase pathways to recovery; explore inner feelings; enlarge the meditative area

AS SOMEONE'S NEGATIVE ATTRIBUTE:

U Tendency to destructively play around with feelings; expand the difficulties in the alliance; compound the problems in intimacy; increase the dangers in the water

R Tendency to exaggerate the psychic ability; jump from one addiction to another; fan the co-dependency; seek diverse, dysfunctional, secret relationships

IF LAYOUT QUESTION HAS A POSITIVE SLANT, THEN:

U Expand your relationships; diversify your liaisons; expand the number of people in the alliance; experiment with expressing more emotions

R Play with psychic experiences; amplify the intuition; open-mindedly explore the mental illness; explore various roads to recovery

IF LAYOUT QUESTION HAS A NEGATIVE SLANT, THEN:

U Shun the option of expanding the group; withdraw from several relationships; don't get into extended collaborative efforts; oppose the expansion of the waterways

R Counteract the experimentation with addiction; resist the various spiritual paths; hold back on amplifying the psychic work; avoid exaggerating about reincarnation

THIS CARD AS A QUESTION:

U What are the many feelings that you are experiencing?
How many different people do you want in your life?
Are you playing with several friends?
Will you expand the water therapy?

R What are your many addictions?
What are the various expressions of the mental illness?
Can you tell me about several different spiritual paths?
Are you exaggerating about your intuition?

Cups

EIGHT OF CUPS

GENERAL:

U Setting boundaries in relationships; defining group priorities; experiencing therapy or counseling

R Putting inner feelings in order; organizing intuitive experiences; creating limits related to addictions

AS SOMEONE'S POSITIVE ATTRIBUTE:

U Ability to put emotions in order; make sense of the feelings; organize the group; create limits around the water

R Ability to set limits on addictions; make psychic boundaries; consolidate recovery efforts; control the medication

AS SOMEONE'S NEGATIVE ATTRIBUTE:

U Tendency to restrict the relationship; withhold emotional expression; diminish the collaborative effort of the group; constrict the flow of the relationship

R Tendency to hold back on recovery; constrict intuitive expression; set problematic boundaries related to co-dependency; dangerously cut back on medication

IF LAYOUT QUESTION HAS A POSITIVE SLANT, THEN:

U Set the boundaries in the relationship; get therapeutic help or counseling; organize the collaborative effort; structure the partnership

R Hold back on addictions; set limits for psychic work; abbreviate the depressive episodes; cut back on spiritual activities

IF LAYOUT QUESTION HAS A NEGATIVE SLANT, THEN:

U Withdraw from the restrictive relationship; don't get into limiting the partnership; oppose the efforts to organize collaborative efforts; counteract the urge to withhold feelings

R Resist the restrictive, hidden relationships; hold back on setting psychic boundaries; avoid intuitive controls; don't diminish the involvement with mental illness

THIS CARD AS A QUESTION:

U How would the relationship benefit from different boundaries?
What are your limits with regard to participating in this alliance?
Do you think therapy would help?
Why are you withholding your emotions?

R How can you use your intuition to structure your life?
How do you limit your addictive behavior?
How do you structure your recovery?
Do you know how to set psychic boundaries?

Cups

NINE OF CUPS

GENERAL:

U Expressing emotions naturally and gracefully; synthesizing the work of the cooperative alliance; harmonizing in the relationship

R Easily integrating intuition into life; effortlessly flowing into psychic experience; relaxing into recovery and healing

AS SOMEONE'S POSITIVE ATTRIBUTE:

U Ability to experience emotions as an integral part of life; effortlessly mingle with others; relax into a unified relationship; gracefully streamline the work around the water

R Ability to easily merge into positive altered states; integrate spirituality into daily life; behave gracefully around the issue of mental illness; become immersed in recovery

AS SOMEONE'S NEGATIVE ATTRIBUTE:

U Tendency to be overly emotional in every part of life; merge into relationships, losing self; flow into problematic collaborations; relax too much on the water

R Tendency to include addictive behavior in every part of life; easily flow into co-dependency; merge problematic mentally ill behavior into activities; become immersed in depression

IF LAYOUT QUESTION HAS A POSITIVE SLANT, THEN:

U Merge the relationship into the fabric of life; harmonize with the group; act in unity with the collaborative effort; gracefully integrate therapy into the relationship

R Effortlessly merge into spiritual awareness; seamlessly include intuition in life; recognize how addiction permeates the whole system; distinguish between effortless co-mingling and co-dependency

IF LAYOUT QUESTION HAS A NEGATIVE SLANT, THEN:

U Don't get into merging with the other person; oppose the undirected flow of feelings; counteract the intermingling of people in this group; resist the effort to blend the groups

R Don't become immersed in psychic realms; avoid relaxing into the intuitive state; hold back from mingling with the addicts; shun the opportunity to slide into mental illness

THIS CARD AS A QUESTION:

U How are important relationships included in your life?
Do these liaisons seem natural and effortless to you?
How can you collaborate so gracefully?
What will happen if the relationship just flows into
    intimacy?

R How do you integrate intuition into your every day life?
How is your recovery a natural part of your life?
Are your co-dependency patterns an integral part of your
    behavior?
Is depressive thinking indistinguishable from normal thinking?

Cups

TEN OF CUPS

GENERAL:

U Hesitating to express emotions; putting a relationship "on hold"; separating from someone for awhile

R Temporarily avoiding psychic activities; looking before you leap into a new level of intuitive awareness; taking time out from a private relationship

AS SOMEONE'S POSITIVE ATTRIBUTE:

U Ability to delay emotional expression; take time out from a relationship; pause before committing to intimacy; look before leaping into the water

R Ability to put psychic activities "on hold"; suspend the mental illness; set aside the addiction for awhile; avoid co-dependency for now

AS SOMEONE'S NEGATIVE ATTRIBUTE:

U Tendency to ignore emotions; avoid important people; pro-crastinate regarding cooperative efforts; waver too long about intimacy

R Tendency to ignore intuition too often; postpone recovery too long; create difficulties by putting off spiritual experi-ence; waffle with regard to addiction

IF LAYOUT QUESTION HAS A POSITIVE SLANT, THEN:

U Set the feelings aside for now; take time out from the rela-tionship; temporarily separate from the group; look before leaping into the partnership

R Take a break from addictions; avoid co-dependency; ignore the intuition for awhile; sidestep the depression

IF LAYOUT QUESTION HAS A NEGATIVE SLANT, THEN:

U Oppose the urge to separate from the partner; counteract the suspension of the group; confront the hesitation regarding the relationship; resist procrastinating about intimacy

R Hold back on avoiding psychic work; avoid putting intuition "on hold"; don't set aside the recovery process; don't get into postponing the topic of depression

THIS CARD AS A QUESTION:

U Why do you hold back on emotional expression?
Why are you wavering with regard to the partnership?
Will you look before you leap into intimacy?
Can you temporarily separate from this person?

R Are you faltering about utilizing your psychic abilities?
Why are you procrastinating in terms of dealing
    with depression?
What helps you ignore the seduction of addiction?
Will you take time out to deal with the mental illness?

Cups

PAGE OF CUPS

GENERAL:

U Taking risks with emotional expression; daring to jump into a relationship; boldly venturing into a partnership

R Daring to believe in intuition; bravely acting according to inner feelings; moving courageously into recovery

AS SOMEONE'S POSITIVE ATTRIBUTE:

U Ability to take risks when revealing emotions; venture boldly into relationship; fearlessly commit to the alliance; bravely leap into the water

R Ability to jump into psychic experiences; take risks with intuition; boldly express hidden feelings; courageously jump into recovery

AS SOMEONE'S NEGATIVE ATTRIBUTE:

U Tendency to take too many risks related to emotional expression; gamble dangerously with intimacy; venture recklessly into dysfunctional partnerships; jump into dangerous waters

R Tendency to make speculations based on doubtful intuitive insights; gamble destructively with secret relationships; undauntedly venture into destructive addictions; take dangerous risks with mental illness

IF LAYOUT QUESTION HAS A POSITIVE SLANT, THEN:

U Leap into the relationship; dare to express emotions; venture boldly into intimacy; gamble on the collaborative efforts

R Speculate based on intuition; bravely jump into psychic experiences; dare to express secret feelings; fearlessly deal with the addiction

IF LAYOUT QUESTION HAS A NEGATIVE SLANT, THEN:

U Counteract the urge to jump into the partnership; confront the risks of intimacy; resist the adventure of the liaison; hold back on leaping into collaboration

R Avoid venturing boldly into psychic arenas; don't take risks based on intuition; shun the option of jumping into addiction; withdraw from the adventure of mental illness

THIS CARD AS A QUESTION:

U Where and how do you want to take more emotional risks?
How do you know when you're ready to leap into a relationship?
Is this group effort worth the gamble?
How do you find the courage to be intimate?

R Do you speculate about spiritual awareness?
Do your addictions lead to reckless behavior?
Can you take the risk of trusting your intuition?
Can you courageously confront the depression?

Cups

KNIGHT OF CUPS

GENERAL:

U Focusing on emotions; paying close attention to others; concentrating on group efforts

R Passionately pursuing psychic growth; purposefully targeting addictions; dedicating energy toward mental illness

AS SOMEONE'S POSITIVE ATTRIBUTE:

U Ability to focus on emotions; commit resources to the relationship; passionately work for the alliance; devotedly attend to the water quality

R Ability to commit resources to psychic work; pay close attention to inner feelings; be passionate in private relationships; concentrate on intuition

AS SOMEONE'S NEGATIVE ATTRIBUTE:

U Tendency to commit too many resources to the group; dysfunctionally obsess on the relationship; fixate on intimacy in an unhealthy way; passionately express too many emotions too often

R Tendency to obsess on doubtful intuitive insights; commit resources to addictions; passionately engage in dangerous, private relationships; cruelly target the mentally ill

IF LAYOUT QUESTION HAS A POSITIVE SLANT, THEN:

U Focus on the feelings; concentrate on this relationship; commit resources to the group; purposefully pursue therapy

R Pursue intuitive goals; pay close attention to inner feelings; become dedicated to recovery; be deeply motivated by spiritual awareness

IF LAYOUT QUESTION HAS A NEGATIVE SLANT, THEN:

U Confront the obsession regarding this relationship; resist the urge to fixate on the feeling; hold back on committing resources to the alliance; avoid focusing on the water damage

R Don't concentrate on psychic work; shun the opportunity to commit resources to the addiction; withdraw from obsessing on co-dependency; don't get into paying close attention to the depression

THIS CARD AS A QUESTION:

U Do you feel passionately about this person?
Will you commit resources to the cooperative effort?
Are you paying close attention to your feelings?
Are you dedicated to being near the water?

R Can you focus your intuition on a specific question?
How will you dedicate yourself to recovery?
Is it important to concentrate on spiritual awareness?
How can I know if I'm obsessed with my addictions?

Cups

QUEEN OF CUPS

GENERAL:

U Expressing emotional maturity; demonstrating a strongly established feeling; showing professionalism with regard to therapy

R Expressing talented intuitive insights; participating in a private, long-term relationship; expressing maturity in recovery

AS SOMEONE'S POSITIVE ATTRIBUTE:

U Ability to express emotions in mature manner; behave effectively in concert with others; interact competently in the collaborative efforts; be professional about the relationship

R Ability to embody recovery in an effective, adult manner; demonstrate proficient psychic ability; show competency in the field of mental illness; expertly illustrate the use of intuition

AS SOMEONE'S NEGATIVE ATTRIBUTE:

U Tendency to be stuck in long-standing, dysfunctional relationship; demonstrate fully hardened, negative emotions; embody dysfunction in professional relationships; show proficiency in undermining the collaboration

R Tendency to persevere in a well-established addictive situation; embody quintessential co-dependency; skillfully, but destructively, express inner feelings; make a profession of being depressed

IF LAYOUT QUESTION HAS A POSITIVE SLANT, THEN:

U Demonstrate emotional maturity; experience an adult relationship; express proficiency in coordinating the collaboration; find mature friends

R Utilize veteran models of recovery; become professional about handling mental illness; embody deep spiritual awareness; demonstrate psychic expertise

IF LAYOUT QUESTION HAS A NEGATIVE SLANT, THEN:

U Resist the mature relationship; hold back on long-term intimacy; avoid well-versed emotional expression; don't participate in the long-standing group

R Shun the opportunity to demonstrate psychic expertise; withdraw from working with addictions at a professional level; don't get into fully familiar co-dependent patterns; oppose the well-versed, practicing addict

THIS CARD AS A QUESTION:

U How do you experience yourself in a mature relationship?
Do you have any expertise in group process?
Can you demonstrate emotions in a mature way?
Are you fully familiar with therapeutic methods?

R Are you fully trained in addictions counseling?
How do you demonstrate your expert intuitive skills?
How long-standing is your depression?
How deeply ingrained are your inner feelings?

Cups

KING OF CUPS

GENERAL:

U Releasing a relationship; letting go of an emotional pattern or issue; ending collaborative efforts

R Grieving a deep, inner loss; walking away from psychic activities; disentangling from addictions

AS SOMEONE'S POSITIVE ATTRIBUTE:

U Ability to let go of negative intimacy; finish the work of alliances; come to emotional completion; give up the water skis

R Ability to end co-dependent patterns; extricate from dysfunctional, secret relationships; pass on psychic skills; terminate addictions

AS SOMEONE'S NEGATIVE ATTRIBUTE:

U Tendency to let go of relationships prematurely; release emotions in dangerous ways; terminate good friendships; pour out too much water

R Tendency to move away from effective psychic insights; lose spiritual awareness; share addictions with others; pass on the depression

IF LAYOUT QUESTION HAS A POSITIVE SLANT, THEN:

U End the relationship; stop using this pattern of emotional expression; finish the cooperative effort; move away from rainy locations

R Let go of addictions; end the co-dependency; pass on intuitive insights; walk away from addicts

IF LAYOUT QUESTION HAS A NEGATIVE SLANT, THEN:

U Hold back on terminating the collaboration; avoid discharging the emotions; don't end the relationship; oppose the termination of the water-related activities

R Counteract the urge to share the intuition; confront the pattern of walking away from mental illness; resist the loss of psychic talents; hold back on the idea of discharging hidden feelings

THIS CARD AS A QUESTION:

U What emotional habits are you ready to release?
Which relationships are passing out of your life?
How can you more effectively share your feelings?
Can you walk away from the alliance?

R Will you share your intuitive skills?
Can you stop the use of addictive substances?
Have you disentangled yourself from the secret relationship?
Have you let go of the depression?

Cups

ACE OF SWORDS

GENERAL:

U Conceiving of a new idea or concept; seeing the potential for a new lifestyle or schedule; stimulating the possibility of communication, education, or travel

R Imagining new beliefs; considering talking to self in a new way; tuning in to private thoughts

AS SOMEONE'S POSITIVE ATTRIBUTE:

U Ability to conceive of a new way of thinking or communicating; approach lifestyle or routine in a new way; be open to travel; envision the possibility of education

R Ability to imagine new psychic dimensions; stimulate intuition; inspire new beliefs; begin talking to self in new ways

AS SOMEONE'S NEGATIVE ATTRIBUTE:

U Tendency to start conversations and not complete them; initiate dangerous travel schemes; originate destructive rumors; provoke negative communication

R Tendency to wish for intuition but never do anything about it; originate dysfunctional beliefs; start talking to self in negative ways; inspire problematic ethics

IF LAYOUT QUESTION HAS A POSITIVE SLANT, THEN:

U Begin to think or communicate in a new way; imagine travel opportunities; see the possibility of new educational directions; consider networking

R Start talking to yourself in positive ways; sense the potential of the new beliefs; imagine private conversations; desire new ethics

IF LAYOUT QUESTION HAS A NEGATIVE SLANT, THEN:

U Don't initiate verbal abuse; shun the possibility of travel; don't get into considering new educational directions; withdraw from initiating the data exchange

R Oppose the thought of new beliefs; counteract negative self-talk, right at the beginning; resist the possibility of private conversations; hold back on conceptualizing a new philosophy

THIS CARD AS A QUESTION:

U How would you like to start communicating?
What learning do you want to initiate?
Which schedule do you want to consider?
Do you want to originate a brand new lifestyle?

R Which new beliefs are you considering?
Have you sensed the possibility of new ethics?
Can you imagine having a private conversation?
Will you consider the underlying principles?

Swords

TWO OF SWORDS

GENERAL:

U Choosing new communication possibilities; saying yes to a travel or educational opportunity; deciding on a lifestyle change

R Affirming the beliefs; acknowledging the self-talk; validating the philosophy

AS SOMEONE'S POSITIVE ATTRIBUTE:

U Ability to claim own ideas; choose to communicate; endorse the travel schedule; say yes to networking

R Ability to confirm personal beliefs; endorse attitudes and ethics; validate the self-talk; elect a private conversation

AS SOMEONE'S NEGATIVE ATTRIBUTE:

U Tendency to claim all the ideas without giving others credit; say yes to educational plans without following through; choose dysfunctional forms of communication; validate verbal abuse

R Tendency to choose dysfunctional beliefs; say yes to dangerous private conversations; talk to self in negative ways; endorse problematic, unsound beliefs

IF LAYOUT QUESTION HAS A POSITIVE SLANT, THEN:

U Choose to communicate; elect education; validate the lifestyle; decide to exchange data

R Select these values; affirm the philosophy; endorse the private thoughts; validate the self-talk

IF LAYOUT QUESTION HAS A NEGATIVE SLANT, THEN:

U Withdraw from acknowledging the communication; don't get into affirming the lifestyle; oppose the educational choice; counteract the validation of the rumors

R Confront the private affirmations; resist the endorsement of this self-talk; hold back on electing these beliefs; avoid validating these ethics

THIS CARD AS A QUESTION:

U What concepts and ideas are you endorsing?
How do you know whether to choose to communicate?
How do you select a network?
Will you validate the rumor?

R What are your personal affirmations?
Can you acknowledge your self-talk?
Will you say yes to a private conversation?
Which ethics have you chosen?

Swords

THREE OF SWORDS

GENERAL:

U Preparing to communicate; planning to act out a new lifestyle; making plans for travel or education

R Preparing to express a new belief; electing a different philosophy; confirming how to talk to self

AS SOMEONE'S POSITIVE ATTRIBUTE:

U Ability to plan and prepare communications; outline travel schedule; list the factors that could lead to an exchange of data; identify the key elements of the logic

R Ability to get ready for new beliefs; promise private conversations; identify the key elements of the philosophy; outline the self-talk

AS SOMEONE'S NEGATIVE ATTRIBUTE:

U Tendency to plan too much before communicating; make unsound plans for important meetings; outline a destructive lifestyle; prepare for travel without following through

R Tendency to outline new beliefs without taking action on them; compose dangerous self-talk; plan dysfunctional private conversations; prepare for instituting negative doctrines

IF LAYOUT QUESTION HAS A POSITIVE SLANT, THEN:

U Plan for communication; prepare for travel; promise a meeting; get ready for an exchange of data

R Outline the philosophy; list the factors that would lead to new beliefs; identify the key elements of the self-talk; study the unwritten codes of conduct

IF LAYOUT QUESTION HAS A NEGATIVE SLANT, THEN:

U Don't get into planning for travel; oppose the outline for the meeting; counteract the plans for communication; avoid preparing rumors

R Resist the urge to outline the beliefs; hold back on planning for a private conversation; avoid listing the factors that form this philosophy; don't identify the key elements of the self-talk

THIS CARD AS A QUESTION:

U How will you prepare the communication?
What is your outline for the discussion?
Can you list the steps that would lead to this lifestyle?
What have you promised to your siblings?

R Will you tell me the key elements of your beliefs?
Are you composing a private conversation?
What values are you studying?
Will you prepare to talk to yourself in this new way?

Swords

FOUR OF SWORDS

GENERAL:

U Manifesting and expressing ideas or thoughts; actively communicating, traveling, or going to school; trying out a schedule or time management plan

R Privately communicating; talking to self; demonstrating personal beliefs or philosophy

AS SOMEONE'S POSITIVE ATTRIBUTE:

U Ability to do something about the communication; establish a schedule; take visible steps toward networking; establish the facts

R Ability to build new beliefs in action; take action on philosophy; establish self-talk; do something about the private conversation

AS SOMEONE'S NEGATIVE ATTRIBUTE:

U Tendency to communicate without considering the consequences; stick to schedule despite its ineffectiveness; communicate in negative ways; take steps to establish a destructive network

R Tendency to demonstrate unsound beliefs; act on unwritten, dubious codes of conduct; reveal private conversations; establish negative self-talk

IF LAYOUT QUESTION HAS A POSITIVE SLANT, THEN:

U Construct the network; travel; go to school; communicate

R Do something about the beliefs; communicate privately; reveal the self-talk; take action on the ethics

IF LAYOUT QUESTION HAS A NEGATIVE SLANT, THEN:

U Oppose the active dialogue; counteract the parade of information; confront the establishment of the network; resist doing something about the communication in any form

R Hold back on manifesting the new beliefs; avoid taking action on the self-talk; don't demonstrate the philosophy; withdraw from revealing the unwritten codes of conduct

THIS CARD AS A QUESTION:

U How does your behavior reflect your ideas?
When will you manifest the lifestyle you want?
Are you doing something about the communication?
Can you establish a network?

R Are you establishing new beliefs?
Will you reveal how you talk to yourself?
Do you take action on the unwritten rules?
Have you constructed a code of ethics?

Swords

FIVE OF SWORDS

GENERAL:

U Adapting ideas or communication; challenging what has been said; changing travel or educational plans

R Adjusting attitudes and beliefs; challenging personal philosophy; changing patterns of self-talk

AS SOMEONE'S POSITIVE ATTRIBUTE:

U Ability to debate or argue fairly; modify the ideas and concepts; adapt the communication style; change the travel plans

R Ability to challenge personal beliefs; modify self-talk; fine-tune ethics; interrupt destructive private conversations

AS SOMEONE'S NEGATIVE ATTRIBUTE:

U Tendency to communicate erratically; disrupt travel experiences; fight and argue in a dysfunctional way; disrupt the network

R Tendency to challenge personal beliefs in a problematic way; create upheaval by abusive private conversations; disturb the positive self-talk; interrupt the private conversations

IF LAYOUT QUESTION HAS A POSITIVE SLANT, THEN:

U Allow the communication to be disruptive; interrupt the verbal abuse; adjust the written rules; modify the data

R Alter the beliefs; interrupt the private communication; modify the self-talk; challenge the unwritten codes of conduct

IF LAYOUT QUESTION HAS A NEGATIVE SLANT, THEN:

U Resist the modifications of the network; hold back on adapting the communication; avoid overhauling the written rules; don't change the travel experience

R Shun the opportunity to challenge the beliefs; withdraw from the disturbing self-talk; don't get into fine-tuning the ethics; oppose the interruption to the private conversation

THIS CARD AS A QUESTION:

U How do you handle verbal conflict?
Why do you behave so erratically with regard to schedules?
Can you edit the book?
Have you changed how you communicate with your
siblings?

R Are you modifying your beliefs?
Will you interrupt the private conversation?
How can you alter your self-talk?
Will you join me in challenging these ethics?

Swords

SIX OF SWORDS

GENERAL:

U Maintaining consistent communication patterns; stabilizing a schedule or routine; expressing predictable ideas in a reliable manner

R Sustaining personal beliefs; repeating the self-talk; maintaining ethical principles

AS SOMEONE'S POSITIVE ATTRIBUTE:

U Ability to communicate in a predictable manner; maintain a regular schedule; support the network; travel repeatedly

R Ability to maintain loyalty to beliefs; talk to self in a calming way; sustain regular private conversations; uphold the unwritten code of conduct

AS SOMEONE'S NEGATIVE ATTRIBUTE:

U Tendency to maintain the same old ineffective communication; stubbornly perpetuate a dysfunctional network; repeat the verbal abuse; keep a problematic schedule

R Tendency to sustain negative beliefs; uphold destructive values; repeat private conversations; consistently talk to self in dysfunctional ways

IF LAYOUT QUESTION HAS A POSITIVE SLANT, THEN:

U Get into a stable pattern of communication; establish a cyclical exchange of ideas and concepts; maintain the schedule or routine; travel on a regular basis

R Sustain the beliefs; perpetuate the private conversations; habitually repeat the self-talk; consistently reiterate the values

IF LAYOUT QUESTION HAS A NEGATIVE SLANT, THEN:

U Hold back on repeating the communication; avoid stabilizing this lifestyle; don't behave predictably with regard to travel; shun the opportunity to support the network

R Withdraw from upholding these beliefs; don't get into supporting the private conversations; oppose the perpetuation of the unwritten code of ethics; counteract the habitual self-talk

THIS CARD AS A QUESTION:

U What do you need to do in order to maintain communication?
How do you handle predictable routines?
What is your regular travel schedule?
Are you repeating the rumors?

R How can you stabilize your beliefs?
Will you maintain your ethics?
What do you reiterate in your self-talk?
Why do you repeatedly seek out private conversations?

Swords

SEVEN OF SWORDS

GENERAL:

U Traveling to various places or learning many things; experiencing a busy schedule or routine; communicating in many languages or styles

R Exploring a variety of beliefs and attitudes; experimenting with different philosophies; talking to self in many ways

AS SOMEONE'S POSITIVE ATTRIBUTE:

U Ability to communicate in various ways or with many people; explore the data; utilize many learning styles; experiment with the schedule

R Ability to play with many different beliefs; experiment with self-talk; enlarge on the principles or philosophy; explore private thoughts

AS SOMEONE'S NEGATIVE ATTRIBUTE:

U Tendency to jump from one idea to another with no closure; engage in scattered thinking; exaggerate the information; enlarge the network too much

R Tendency to play around with destructive beliefs; experiment with dangerous self-talk; exaggerate too much about private conversations; amplify the questionable ethics

IF LAYOUT QUESTION HAS A POSITIVE SLANT, THEN:

U Explore a variety of communication systems; enlarge the network; expand the travel options; experiment with the schedule

R Explore diverse belief systems; talk to self in more than one way; expand the private conversations; elaborate on the philosophy

IF LAYOUT QUESTION HAS A NEGATIVE SLANT, THEN:

U Avoid compounding the communication problems; don't exaggerate the rumors; shun the opportunity to experiment with dialogue; withdraw from attending many meetings

R Don't get into playing around with these beliefs; oppose the urge to elaborate on the unwritten code of ethics; counteract the exaggerated self-talk; confront the increase in private conversations

THIS CARD AS A QUESTION:

U What are the many forms of verbal abuse?
How do you communicate with different kinds of people?
Can you keep your schedule varied and interesting?
What's your attitude toward a hectic lifestyle?

R Do you ever experiment with various belief systems?
Will you enlarge on this philosophy?
Can you increase the positive self-talk?
Are you curious about this person's differing values?

Swords

EIGHT OF SWORDS

GENERAL:

U Defining priorities regarding time management or schedule; structuring travel experiences; setting boundaries for communication

R Restructuring personal beliefs; organizing or limiting self-talk; condensing private thoughts or communications

AS SOMEONE'S POSITIVE ATTRIBUTE:

U Ability to put words, ideas, or opinions in order; set limits regarding communication; organize travel or educational experiences; coordinate the discussion

R Ability to restructure inner beliefs; cut back on the negative private conversations; limit the negative self-talk; restrict the impact of dysfunctional values

AS SOMEONE'S NEGATIVE ATTRIBUTE:

U Tendency to control communication too much; rigidly tighten schedule in a problematic way; restrict beneficial travel or learning experiences; dangerously limit the exchange of data

R Tendency to dangerously limit personal beliefs; destructively restructure philosophy; control self-talk too much; be bigoted

IF LAYOUT QUESTION HAS A POSITIVE SLANT, THEN:

U Organize ideas or communication; set boundaries for conversations; put the lifestyle in order; restrict the exchange of information

R Restructure the beliefs; set boundaries on private thoughts; limit the self-talk; cut back on private conversations

IF LAYOUT QUESTION HAS A NEGATIVE SLANT, THEN:

U Withdraw from controlling the communication; don't get into limiting the travel opportunities; oppose the restrictions in the network; counteract the withholding of information

R Confront the rigidity of personal beliefs; resist the limits on self-talk; avoid diminishing the philosophy; shun the opportunity to constrict private conversation

THIS CARD AS A QUESTION:

U How could your communications include better boundaries?
Do you restrict what you want to say?
How do you organize your written work?
Will you restructure your educational experiences?

R How does your self-talk form an underlying structure
in your life?
Do you control your private thoughts, too?
Do your beliefs limit you?
Will you organize the unwritten rules?

Swords

NINE OF SWORDS

GENERAL:

U Communicating in an integrated way; experiencing a coordinated, easy-going schedule or routine; experiencing traveling or learning as a natural part of life

R Experiencing self-talk as an integral part of life; becoming immersed in private beliefs; effortlessly resonating with the philosophy

AS SOMEONE'S POSITIVE ATTRIBUTE:

U Ability to communicate in a harmonious way; become immersed in wonderful conversation; take it easy when traveling; integrate the data

R Ability to resonate with the beliefs; become immersed in the philosophy; effortlessly integrate the self-talk; streamline private thoughts

AS SOMEONE'S NEGATIVE ATTRIBUTE:

U Tendency to become immersed in dysfunctional communication; resonate with a destructive lifestyle; travel continuously for too long; intermingle the data in a confusing way

R Tendency to become immersed in negative beliefs; flow effortlessly into negative self-talk; continuously slide into dysfunctional values; resonate with destructive secret principles

IF LAYOUT QUESTION HAS A POSITIVE SLANT, THEN:

U Communicate in a continuous, flowing, integrated manner; become immersed in the schedule or routine; travel continuously; share data without any limitations

R Become immersed in personal philosophy; streamline belief system; continuously talk to self; harmonize with these principles

IF LAYOUT QUESTION HAS A NEGATIVE SLANT, THEN:

U Don't get into blending into the conversation; oppose continuous education or travel; counteract the unlimited flow of information; confront the fluent verbal abuse

R Resist the urge to mingle philosophies; hold back on resonating with those beliefs; avoid becoming immersed in these ethics; don't talk to oneself so continuously

THIS CARD AS A QUESTION:

U How could you communicate in a more graceful manner?
Can you harmonize your data with the other information?
Does your schedule or routine flow effortlessly?
Do you like to travel continuously?

R Is your philosophy integrated into your life?
How does your self-talk permeate your consciousness?
Are you immersed in your private thoughts?
Do you integrate your ethics into your daily life?

Swords

TEN OF SWORDS

GENERAL:

U Hesitating in terms of communication; holding back on travel or education; taking time out from the schedule or routine

R Temporarily suspending beliefs; setting self-talk aside for awhile; avoiding the private conversations

AS SOMEONE'S POSITIVE ATTRIBUTE:

U Ability to avoid negative communication; put schedule aside when needed; take time out from travel or learning experiences; suspend the dubious rumor

R Ability to set rigid beliefs aside for awhile; avoid dysfunctional private conversations; temporarily suspend the negative self-talk; ignore unsound philosophies

AS SOMEONE'S NEGATIVE ATTRIBUTE:

U Tendency to postpone positive communication; hesitate regarding healthy lifestyle; set schedule aside too often; avoid getting the real facts

R Tendency to waver in terms of personal beliefs; postpone nourishing private conversations; set aside good values; avoid positive self-talk

IF LAYOUT QUESTION HAS A POSITIVE SLANT, THEN:

U Postpone the communication; set aside the schedule or routine; take time out from traveling; ignore the network

R Set aside the old beliefs and values; waive the opportunity for a private conversation; avoid the negative self-talk; ignore these ethics

IF LAYOUT QUESTION HAS A NEGATIVE SLANT, THEN:

U Oppose the adjournment of the meeting; counteract the delay in communication; confront the stalled community; resist the urge to suspend travel

R Avoid hesitations regarding these beliefs; don't falter about these values; shun the option of setting aside the ethics; don't get into ignoring the self-talk

THIS CARD AS A QUESTION:

U How do you know when it's appropriate to avoid communication?
When do you take time out from your routine or schedule?
Can you set your education aside for awhile?
Will you look before leaping into travel?

R Do you feel hesitant about these beliefs?
Are you ignoring your self-talk?
Will you temporarily suspend these ethics?
Are your private thoughts wavering?

Swords

PAGE OF SWORDS

GENERAL:

U Taking risks with communication; jumping into travel or learning experiences; venturing boldly into the lifestyle

R Daring to believe in a particular philosophy; fearlessly speaking the inner truth; courageously jumping into this kind of self-talk

AS SOMEONE'S POSITIVE ATTRIBUTE:

U Ability to take risks in communication; bravely state the facts; courageously leap into the lifestyle; daringly exchange data

R Ability to courageously honor the inner truth; risk jumping into the beliefs; fearlessly talk to self; courageously face inner thoughts

AS SOMEONE'S NEGATIVE ATTRIBUTE:

U Tendency to take too many risks with communication; recklessly gamble on this lifestyle; leap into destructive learning experiences; boldly step into unsound routine

R Tendency to leap into dangerous beliefs; recklessly gamble on private conversation; jump into destructive self-talk; boldly engage in a problematic philosophy

IF LAYOUT QUESTION HAS A POSITIVE SLANT, THEN:

U Take communication risks; dare to travel; leap into learning; venture boldly into the lifestyle

R Gamble on your beliefs and values; dare to express private thoughts; courageously engage in private conversations; fearlessly pursue the philosophy

IF LAYOUT QUESTION HAS A NEGATIVE SLANT, THEN:

U Counteract the communication risk; confront reckless lifestyle; resist the dangerous travel adventures; hold back on leaping into the schedule

R Avoid taking risks with the beliefs and values; don't jump into this philosophy; shun the option of leaping into private conversations; withdraw from speculative self-talk

THIS CARD AS A QUESTION:

U How do you want to take more risks in communication?
How do you know when you're ready to leap into a routine?
What kinds of travel experiences feel risky or daring to you?
Can you boldly pursue the facts?

R Are you courageous enough to reveal the inner truth?
Do you dare to live by your beliefs?
Can you jump into courageous self-talk?
Are you reckless about ethics?

Swords

KNIGHT OF SWORDS

GENERAL:

U Focusing on communication; paying close attention to education or travel; concentrating on schedule or routine

R Committing resources to beliefs; dedicating energy to philosophy; concentrating single-mindedly on self-talk

AS SOMEONE'S POSITIVE ATTRIBUTE:

U Ability to concentrate on communication; focus on the schedule; pay close attention to learning; intently pursue the travel goals

R Ability to devotedly pay attention to beliefs and values; commit resources to philosophy; concentrate intently on private thoughts; pay close attention to self-talk

AS SOMEONE'S NEGATIVE ATTRIBUTE:

U Tendency to become obsessed with ideas; be fixated on establishing communication; be too zealous about accurate data; commit resources to unsound travel plans

R Tendency to focus on dangerous beliefs; fixate on a dubious philosophy; commit resources to negative inner thoughts; obsess on destructive ethics

IF LAYOUT QUESTION HAS A POSITIVE SLANT, THEN:

U Focus on communication; concentrate on travel; pay close attention to the verbal abuse; commit resources to the network

R Passionately concentrate on beliefs; become dedicated to these values; commit resources to personal philosophy; target the self-talk

IF LAYOUT QUESTION HAS A NEGATIVE SLANT, THEN:

U Don't get into fixating on the lifestyle; oppose the passionate regard for data and facts; counteract committing resources to the network; resist pursuing the travel goals

R Hold back on zealous behavior regarding philosophy; avoid intense self-talk; withdraw from targeting the beliefs and values; don't pay close attention to the unwritten codes of conduct

THIS CARD AS A QUESTION:

U What is your intellectual focus these days?
Do you pay close attention to communication style or content?
Will you concentrate on travel or education?
Can you commit resources to this community?

R Are you concentrating on your beliefs and values?
Are you single-minded about these private thoughts?
Do you pay close attention to your self-talk?
Have you committed resources to this philosophical
    doctrine?

Swords

QUEEN OF SWORDS

GENERAL:

U Expressing competence in communication; embodying the fully developed lifestyle; demonstrating expertise with the data

R Showing effective, mature beliefs; evidencing professional ethics; illustrating proficient self-talk

AS SOMEONE'S POSITIVE ATTRIBUTE:

U Ability to communicate at an expert level; become fully familiar with the data and facts; evidence experience in travel; demonstrate a mellow lifestyle

R Ability to present mature beliefs; demonstrate an adult philosophy; illustrate effective self-talk; be well-versed in private conversations

AS SOMEONE'S NEGATIVE ATTRIBUTE:

U Tendency to be stuck in long-standing, dysfunctional communication; be fully proficient in a destructive lifestyle; present inaccurate data with confident professionalism; demonstrate a well-developed, but ineffective, learning

R Tendency to be an expert at presenting destructive beliefs; demonstrate fully formed, negative values; be fully hardened into dysfunctional ethics; have flawless negative self-talk

IF LAYOUT QUESTION HAS A POSITIVE SLANT, THEN:

U Demonstrate competent communication; show expertise in networking; embody the veteran traveler; evidence an adult lifestyle

R Evidence professional ethics; demonstrate mature self-talk; illustrate fully seasoned beliefs and values; masterfully embody personal philosophy

IF LAYOUT QUESTION HAS A NEGATIVE SLANT, THEN:

U Confront masterful rumors; resist demonstrating fully trained communication skills; hold back on showing expertise about the data; avoid professional travel

R Don't act well-versed in the philosophy; withdraw from evidencing full familiarity with the private talk; don't get into hardened, destructive self-talk; oppose the maturation of these ethics

THIS CARD AS A QUESTION:

U Are you a mature communicator?
Will you demonstrate your talent for scheduling?
Are you a veteran traveler?
Are you well-versed in this lifestyle?

R Will you show us the maturity of your beliefs?
Can you illustrate the full effectiveness of this philosophy?
What are your well-seasoned ethics?
How have you developed effective self-talk?

Swords

KING OF SWORDS

GENERAL:

U Letting go of an old idea or communication pattern; releasing travel or educational plans; moving away from the schedule or routine

R Letting go of a hidden thought; passing on beliefs and values; walking away from this kind of self-talk

AS SOMEONE'S POSITIVE ATTRIBUTE:

U Ability to let go of old ideas; move away from communication; extricate from the network or lifestyle; disentangle the data or information

R Ability to walk away from old beliefs; pass on philosophy; terminate the negative self-talk; conclude the private conversations

AS SOMEONE'S NEGATIVE ATTRIBUTE:

U Tendency to lose important communications or data; pass on rumors; walk away from beneficial communication; let go of a satisfying lifestyle

R Tendency to move away from healthy beliefs and values; release or share private conversations; terminate positive self-talk; lose a sense of ethics

IF LAYOUT QUESTION HAS A POSITIVE SLANT, THEN:

U Stop the verbal abuse; quit traveling; pass on your ideas; move away from the network

R Walk away from that philosophy; grieve for the old beliefs and values; terminate the private conversations; share the self-talk

IF LAYOUT QUESTION HAS A NEGATIVE SLANT, THEN:

U Resist the conclusion of the communication; hold back on terminating this lifestyle; avoid letting go of travel; don't release the network

R Withdraw from sharing the beliefs; don't get into quitting self-talk; oppose the movement away from private conversations; counteract the urge to let go of these ethics

THIS CARD AS A QUESTION:

U What communication patterns are you ready to release?
How can you more effectively share your information?
Have you stopped traveling?
When will you complete school?

R Have you let go of those beliefs?
Can you stop the negative self-talk?
Have you quit having private conversations?
Will you walk away from that philosophy?

Swords

ACE OF PENTACLES

GENERAL:

U Wishing for a new physical experience; experiencing the potential for a new financial direction; sensing the opportunity for new directions in health or healing

R Conceiving of a new possibility in terms of psychological safety; considering long term options for security or commitment; imagining a new form of groundedness

AS SOMEONE'S POSITIVE ATTRIBUTE:

U Ability to begin new practical tasks; consider fresh approaches to health or healing; initiate new directions regarding sexuality; imagine options related to money

R Ability to desire security; wish for groundedness; sense the possibility for long-term security; envision safety

AS SOMEONE'S NEGATIVE ATTRIBUTE:

U Tendency to start projects and not complete them; begin new health regimes without continuing them; experience very brief, unhealthy sexual encounters; initiate violence or abuse

R Tendency to initiate the entrapment of something or someone; instigate a dysfunctional long-term security; desire suicide; start the hidden abuse

IF LAYOUT QUESTION HAS A POSITIVE SLANT, THEN:

U Begin to build or construct in a new way; start new health practices; initiate sex; imagine new financial options

R Conceptualize the options for safety; conceive of the possibility of long-term commitment; wish for groundedness; desire a commitment to staying alive

IF LAYOUT QUESTION HAS A NEGATIVE SLANT, THEN:

U Resist the urge to build or construct; restrict new sexual practices; hold back on imaginative new career options; avoid planting seeds

R Curb the urge to consider safety; oppose the possibility of long-term commitment; counteract the desire for suicide; don't provoke hidden abuse

THIS CARD AS A QUESTION:

U If you could plant any seeds you wanted, what would they be?
If you could start a new job or financial venture what would it be?
Can you consider whether abuse is part of the situation?
Is a new home or location even a possibility?

R How would you initiate safety or security measures?
What makes you start to think about suicide?
Can you imagine luckiness?
Will you tune in to the possibility of commitment?

Pentacles

TWO OF PENTACLES

GENERAL:

U Choosing new health or healing options; saying yes to a job, career, or financial opportunity; deciding on a new direction with regard to sexuality

R Claiming a new kind of safety or groundedness; saying yes to some kind of long-term commitment; reinforcing or acknowledging that a hidden trap exists

AS SOMEONE'S POSITIVE ATTRIBUTE:

U Ability to acknowledge financial needs or decisions; make healthy choices regarding job or career; endorse projects involving construction or land use; say yes to health

R Ability to confirm safety or security measures; prefer staying alive; choose groundedness; acknowledge the hidden abuse

AS SOMEONE'S NEGATIVE ATTRIBUTE:

U Tendency to endorse violence or abuse; elect unhealthy physical activities; choose too many possessions; select inappropriate sexual experiences

R Tendency to say yes to unhealthy commitments; validate unworkable security habits; validate dysfunctional forms of safety; endorse hidden abuse

IF LAYOUT QUESTION HAS A POSITIVE SLANT, THEN:

U Make a choice about job or career; confirm a decision about money; reinforce safe or appropriate sex; say yes to crafts or tactile art

R Decide what's needed regarding security; acknowledge long-term commitments; endorse safety; claim luckiness

IF LAYOUT QUESTION HAS A NEGATIVE SLANT, THEN:

U Resist making choices about practical matters; avoid confirming job, career, or money decisions; curb the urge to affirm a direction involving sex or health; hold back on choices regarding real estate

R Forego a decision about protection; resist a choice about commitment; don't elect long-term security; oppose endorsing the trap

THIS CARD AS A QUESTION:

U What are you choosing regarding health or sex?
What are you affirming about job, money, or career?
How do you reinforce your choices about your craft?
How do you know which item to select?

R What have you decided about safety?
How do you acknowledge commitments?
Will you affirm the need for groundedness?
Did you endorse the suicide attempt?

Pentacles

THREE OF PENTACLES

GENERAL:

U Preparing to take action regarding health or sexuality; making financial, work, or career plans; getting ready to construct something

R Preparing to create security; planning for commitment; promising protection

AS SOMEONE'S POSITIVE ATTRIBUTE:

U Ability to plan for health or healing actions; make financial, work, or career preparations; design homes and buildings; identify the key elements of the practical remedy

R Ability to promise safety; plan for commitment; develop a commitment to the body; list the factors that lead to safety

AS SOMEONE'S NEGATIVE ATTRIBUTE:

U Tendency to over-prepare for sports or other physical activities; make inappropriate promises about work; develop plans for physical abuse; get ready for destructive financial practices

R Tendency to plan for too much long-term safety; promise commitment without following through; outline the security plan without doing anything about it; prepare for cruel traps

IF LAYOUT QUESTION HAS A POSITIVE SLANT, THEN:

U Make plans for building or construction; get ready to work with the boss; study the mountain terrain; develop a financial plan

R Identify the key elements of safety; design a package for long-term security; promise to commit to the body; list the factors that lead to groundedness

IF LAYOUT QUESTION HAS A NEGATIVE SLANT, THEN:

U Resist preparing for construction or building projects; avoid promises regarding sex; restrict financial planning; hold back on studying about farming

R Don't promise long-term commitment; avoid getting ready for suicide; abstain from designing safety measures; forego the preparations for security

THIS CARD AS A QUESTION:

U How do you plan for practical solutions?
What's important in your home or garden design?
How do you prepare for sex?
What are your intentions about competitive sports?

R How do you prepare for safety?
What are the key elements of your commitments?
What are you planning with regard to staying alive?
Can you list the factors that lead to your sense of groundedness?

Pentacles

FOUR OF PENTACLES

GENERAL:

> **U** Constructing or building something on the physical plane; taking action regarding health or healing; doing something about work, money, or career; displaying athletic ability

> **R** Establishing long-term commitments; demonstrating protection; building safety; manifesting security or groundedness

AS SOMEONE'S POSITIVE ATTRIBUTE:

> **U** Ability to take action related to money, job, or business; structure workable health or sexual practices; demonstrate a craft; reveal how abuse is part of the situation

> **R** Ability to create safety or protection; take action regarding long-term commitments; demonstrate a willingness to live or die; construct an effective trap

AS SOMEONE'S NEGATIVE ATTRIBUTE:

> **U** Tendency to flaunt money or professional status; take abusive or violent action; inappropriately display physical talents; act destructively regarding sex

> **R** Tendency to cling inappropriately to perceived safety; be too pushy about forcing commitment; construct unsound security; take steps toward abusing self

IF LAYOUT QUESTION HAS A POSITIVE SLANT, THEN:

> **U** Demonstrate physical talents and strengths; act on health or fitness plans; do something about money, job, or career; go to the mountains

R Establish long-term commitments; demonstrate protection or safety; push for aliveness; reveal luckiness

IF LAYOUT QUESTION HAS A NEGATIVE SLANT, THEN:

U Avoid acting physically; resist financial, career, or business moves; don't establish new health or fitness practices; abstain from taking abusive action

R Restrict demonstrations of long-term commitment; shun active participation in entrapment; avoid revealing the will to live; don't take self-abusive actions

THIS CARD AS A QUESTION:

U What are you doing about your health?
How are you manifesting money in your life?
What action are you taking regarding money, job, or career?
What are you doing about the abuse or violence?

R How do you build a feeling of security?
What do you do to feel safe?
What moves are you making toward long-term
    commitment?
What are you doing about the suicide?

Pentacles

FIVE OF PENTACLES

GENERAL:

U Adapting practical, financial, or business structures; modifying health or healing practices; revising construction or building projects

R Challenging or testing the arrangements for safety or security; adjusting something related to groundedness; adapting the structure of long-term commitment

AS SOMEONE'S POSITIVE ATTRIBUTE:

U Ability to confront a financial or business situation; make changes in the areas of health or fitness; handle upheaval regarding construction or property; recondition the furniture

R Ability to fine-tune the security; challenge commitments that need to be changed; modify factors that lead to psychological safety; confront the self-abuse

AS SOMEONE'S NEGATIVE ATTRIBUTE:

U Tendency to be erratic about attending to safe sex; have unpredictable bouts of ill-health; sudden eruptions of violence, anger, or abuse; create financial upheaval

R Tendency to be unstable regarding the willingness to live; be erratic about commitments; be abusive in confrontations; disturb the safety

IF LAYOUT QUESTION HAS A POSITIVE SLANT, THEN:

U Adapt the health or sexual practices; remodel the home; confront the abuse; challenge the coworkers

R Alter the security system; modify the long-term commitments; confront suicidal urges; disturb the trap

IF LAYOUT QUESTION HAS A NEGATIVE SLANT, THEN:

U Don't shake things up at work; avoid modifying the health or fitness routine; restrict the level of upheaval in the home; resist the urge to change sexual practices

R Resist the temptation to revise the security system; avoid challenging the long-term commitments; don't create upheaval regarding suicide; abstain from altering the traps

THIS CARD AS A QUESTION:

U How do you make changes in your job or career?
How will you modify your health or fitness routines?
How do you confront abuse or violence when it occurs?
What do you want to rearrange in your home?

R What does it take for you to adapt your security habits?
What would force you to change your long-term
   commitments?
How can you fine-tune your sense of groundedness?
How do you interrupt the urge toward suicide?

Pentacles

SIX OF PENTACLES

GENERAL:

U Maintaining consistent financial practices; recycling; behaving predictably regarding sex; sustaining a home

R Behaving reliably about commitment; upholding the will to live; maintaining security and safety; keeping the commitment to the body

AS SOMEONE'S POSITIVE ATTRIBUTE:

U Ability to keep a job; support good health or safe sex habits; be reliable in managing money and resources; consistently practice a craft

R Ability to maintain security; sustain the willingness to stay alive; uphold commitments; perpetuate groundedness

AS SOMEONE'S NEGATIVE ATTRIBUTE:

U Tendency to stay in unsatisfying work; maintain boring sexual habits; perpetuate dysfunctional health habits; support the abuse

R Tendency to maintain problematic forms of security; support unhealthy commitments; get stuck in familiar traps; repeat the cycle of self-abuse

IF LAYOUT QUESTION HAS A POSITIVE SLANT, THEN:

U Maintain the financial system; sustain the job or career; behave predictably regarding sex; train for the sport

R Sustain groundedness; stabilize security measures; uphold commitments; keep staying alive

IF LAYOUT QUESTION HAS A NEGATIVE SLANT, THEN:

U Avoid sticking with the financial plan; don't appease the employer; resist upholding the home situation; don't bother with recycling

R Stay away from old security habits; avoid repeating suicide attempts; resist the temptation to maintain commitments; don't get into repeating old systems of establishing safety

THIS CARD AS A QUESTION:

U What do you need to do in order to maintain financial security?
How do you sustain your health and physical energy?
What helps you keep your job?
What are your regular habits around the house?

R How can you sustain safety?
How do you maintain your commitment to being alive?
How do you stay grounded?
Will you repeat the suicide pattern?

Pentacles

SEVEN OF PENTACLES

GENERAL:

U Experimenting with sports; stretching the money; expanding the job description; exploring sexuality

R Expanding groundedness; exploring commitment; increasing luckiness; amplifying the security system

AS SOMEONE'S POSITIVE ATTRIBUTE:

U Ability to increase the wealth; be curious about sex; expand the job; play athletically

R Ability to extend safety; expand the willingness to stay alive; be increasingly curious about commitment; amplify groundedness

AS SOMEONE'S NEGATIVE ATTRIBUTE:

U Tendency to jump from one job to another with no permanency; experiment destructively with sex; play around with violence; exaggerate athletic ability

R Tendency to play with suicide; create elaborate traps; exaggerate the degree of commitment; falsely inflate a sense of luckiness

IF LAYOUT QUESTION HAS A POSITIVE SLANT, THEN:

U Explore the job options; experiment with sex; expand the home; diversify in sports

R Experiment with various forms of groundedness; be open to luckiness; expand the commitment to being alive; increase stability

IF LAYOUT QUESTION HAS A NEGATIVE SLANT, THEN:

U Don't experiment with sex; avoid adding to your financial responsibilities; resist additional jobs; don't bother to diversify in business

R Deny the urge to play with suicide; stay away from elaborate security systems; don't jump from one spot of perceived safety to another; avoid exaggerating about luck

THIS CARD AS A QUESTION:

U How diverse are your investments?
How do you experiment with sex?
How curious are you about alternative health-care systems?
How many different jobs have you tried?

R Do you ever play with the idea of suicide?
How can you expand your sense of groundedness?
How much security do you need?
Can you explore the concept of commitment?

Pentacles

EIGHT OF PENTACLES

GENERAL:

U Setting boundaries related to health or sex; cutting back on spending; setting limits about abuse; restricting sports activities

R Coordinating safety systems; controlling the urge toward suicide or self-abuse; putting commitments in order; limiting the entrapment

AS SOMEONE'S POSITIVE ATTRIBUTE:

U Ability to put practical tasks in order; organize financial affairs; set good boundaries related to sex; structure appropriate health or fitness routines

R Ability to organize the security; set boundaries related to safety; control the suicidal urges; restrict the inappropriate commitments

AS SOMEONE'S NEGATIVE ATTRIBUTE:

U Tendency to unnecessarily restrict the cash flow; withhold healthy physical contact; negatively control the home; cut back on good health-related habits

R Tendency to inappropriately limit the willingness to stay alive; cut back on necessary security measures; constrict luckiness; restrict healthy commitment

IF LAYOUT QUESTION HAS A POSITIVE SLANT, THEN:

U Restrict sex; reorganize the home; set boundaries regarding money; set limits about abuse

R Structure the security system; hold back on commitments; limit suicidal behavior; control the safety in the situation

IF LAYOUT QUESTION HAS A NEGATIVE SLANT, THEN:

U Avoid controlling things at work; resist the need to coordinate the tasks; abstain from withholding sex; don't bother to restrict sports or physical activities

R Resist the tendency to limit commitment; don't try to control the retirement plans; avoid restricting the willingness to live; don't limit the luck

THIS CARD AS A QUESTION:

U How could you reorganize things at work?
Which boundaries do you need to set regarding health or sex?
How will you structure your financial situation?
Why are you cutting back on your involvement with your craft?

R What restricts your sense of security?
Why are you holding back on commitment?
What diminishes your groundedness?
How can you organize your safety?

Pentacles

NINE OF PENTACLES

GENERAL:

U Blending systems of healing; unifying the home; being immersed in sex

R Effortlessly creating security; resonating with safety; going along with commitment

AS SOMEONE'S POSITIVE ATTRIBUTE:

U Ability to move in a graceful manner; mend or heal and make whole again; integrate financial considerations into daily life; harmonize at work

R Ability to integrate safety into the flow of things; stay effortlessly grounded; become immersed in healthy commitments; streamline long-term security measures

AS SOMEONE'S NEGATIVE ATTRIBUTE:

U Tendency to be overly relaxed about health issues; integrate financial worries into all parts of life; participate in ongoing abuse; become immersed in unsound business practices

R Tendency to ceaseless and pervasive worry about safety; remain too easy-going about commitments; merge or flow into suicidal behavior; become too immersed in other lifetimes

IF LAYOUT QUESTION HAS A POSITIVE SLANT, THEN:

U Harmonize regarding money; be easy-going about health; merge sexually; mingle with employers

R Unify the security; integrate the desire to stay alive; flow into luckiness; become grounded in a harmonious way

IF LAYOUT QUESTION HAS A NEGATIVE SLANT, THEN:

U Avoid merging money; don't integrate business concerns into rest of life; hold back from harmonizing at a sexual level; resist integrating the health programs

R Don't go along with safety concerns; avoid merging into commitment; resist integrating this form of security into your life; don't get into seductive traps

THIS CARD AS A QUESTION:

U How do you go about merging money?
How do you blend health consciousness into everyday life?
With whom do you mingle at work?
Do you express your sexuality effortlessly?

R Are you easy-going about safety?
Are you at peace with your sense of security?
How is luck intermingled in your life?
Do you like to become immersed in other lifetimes?

Pentacles

TEN OF PENTACLES

GENERAL:

U Hesitating about financial decisions; experiencing lay-offs at work; procrastinating about health

R Putting security concerns "on hold"; setting commitments aside; faltering about suicide

AS SOMEONE'S POSITIVE ATTRIBUTE:

U Ability to set work aside when necessary; take time out from stressful physical activities; avoid violence; look before leaping into business decisions

R Ability to wait before making commitments; avoid traps; temporarily put security worries "on hold"; limit suicidal thoughts

AS SOMEONE'S NEGATIVE ATTRIBUTE:

U Tendency to avoid financial issues; stall regarding practical matters; lay off employees; ignore the abuse

R Tendency to procrastinate about safety issues; falter with regard to commitment; delay too long with regard to security; suspend the willingness to stay alive

IF LAYOUT QUESTION HAS A POSITIVE SLANT, THEN:

U Set money matters aside for awhile; take time out from sexual activity; put off business decisions; avoid buying or selling the home

R Hold off on commitments; hesitate regarding self-abuse; postpone safety decisions; delay with regard to decisions about long-term security

IF LAYOUT QUESTION HAS A NEGATIVE SLANT, THEN:

U Don't hold back on money matters; avoid procrastinating about property decisions; restrict the tendency to waver about sex; counteract the temptation to separate

R Forego the urge to hesitate about safety decisions; restrict the tendency to procrastinate with regard to commitments; don't put security "on hold"; don't postpone the exploration of other lifetimes

THIS CARD AS A QUESTION:

U How do you know when to hesitate about sex?
How often do you take time off from work?
Can you postpone this decision about health?
Will you temporarily be leaving home?

R Why are you waffling about commitment?
Are you looking before you leap toward security?
Can you set aside your suicidal urges?
When do you avoid safety?

Pentacles

PAGE OF PENTACLES

GENERAL:

U Speculating with money; jumping into a job; behaving courageously with regard to health

R Daring to make commitments; behaving fearlessly regarding security; taking risks regarding groundedness

AS SOMEONE'S POSITIVE ATTRIBUTE:

U Ability to take financial risks; behave boldly in business; be physically adventuresome; be daring about making a residence change

R Ability to leap into commitment; to take appropriate risks with security; courageously explore other lifetimes; fearlessly face self-abuse

AS SOMEONE'S NEGATIVE ATTRIBUTE:

U Tendency to speculate too much in business or financial affairs; engage in high-risk sexual activity; use resources in a hazardous way; gamble recklessly

R Tendency to behave hazardously regarding safety; take risks with suicide; gamble dangerously regarding long-term security; leap into traps without thinking

IF LAYOUT QUESTION HAS A POSITIVE SLANT, THEN:

U Speculate with money; take career risks; behave boldly regarding sexual activity; leap into fitness or sports activities

R Take some risks with long-term security; dare to explore other lifetimes; behave fearlessly regarding commitment; courageously seek groundedness

IF LAYOUT QUESTION HAS A NEGATIVE SLANT, THEN:

U Avoid jumping into business decisions; don't leap into sex; resist the urge to speculate with money; hold back on hazardous healing practices

R Don't take risks regarding safety; avoid reckless self-abuse; abstain from leaping into suicide; forego the brave jump into commitment

THIS CARD AS A QUESTION:

U What kinds of risks do you take at work?
Do you gamble?
How are you physically adventurous?
Are you willing to bravely relocate your home?

R Would you ever take risks with your security?
How bold are you regarding commitment?
Will you bet on life?
Do you dare to consider yourself lucky?

Pentacles

KNIGHT OF PENTACLES

GENERAL:

U Focusing on work; paying close attention to money; committing resources to health

R Concentrating on safety; dedicating attention to groundedness; intensely committing to staying alive

AS SOMEONE'S POSITIVE ATTRIBUTE:

U Ability to concentrate on work or profession; focus on violence; pursue financial goals; be dedicated to healing

R Ability to pay close attention to safety; passionately pursue the feeling of groundedness; be fully dedicated to commitments; commit resources to long-term security

AS SOMEONE'S NEGATIVE ATTRIBUTE:

U Tendency to become obsessed with money; be fixated on sex; be overly ambitious regarding career; focus too intensely on health

R Tendency to perseverate about safety; fixate on long-term security; be compulsive about suicide; be obsessed with the issue of luck

IF LAYOUT QUESTION HAS A POSITIVE SLANT, THEN:

U Pay close attention to money; concentrate on work or business; be purposeful in taking action regarding property; focus on sex

R Concentrate on safety; focus on commitment; pay close attention to the potential for suicide; commit resources to becoming grounded

IF LAYOUT QUESTION HAS A NEGATIVE SLANT, THEN:

U Avoid focusing on sex; don't fixate on money; resist concentrating on career ambitions; restrict zealousness about health

R Curb the urge to obsess on safety; oppose the fixation with suicide; counteract the concentration on commitment; abstain from committing resources to security

THIS CARD AS A QUESTION:

U How much do you focus on work?
What happens when you really concentrate on sex?
Do you pay close attention to your health?
Are you passionate about your career goals?

R Are you paying close attention to safety?
What makes you concentrate on commitment?
Are you intensely on track with regard to your security?
Do you commit your resources to stability?

Pentacles

QUEEN OF PENTACLES

GENERAL:

U Expressing maturity regarding health or fitness; behaving in a professional way with respect to career or business; embodying mastery of money or resource management

R Symbolizing adult commitments; representing grounded-ness that is well-seasoned; embodying mellowed stability

AS SOMEONE'S POSITIVE ATTRIBUTE:

U Ability to demonstrate expertise concerning finance or business; exemplify fully trained fitness; convey proficiency regarding home related issues; represent professionalism with respect to career

R Ability to convey fully seasoned stability; represent maturity with respect to groundedness; be adult about committing to the body; embody professionalism regarding safety

AS SOMEONE'S NEGATIVE ATTRIBUTE:

U Tendency to continue long-standing financial problems; stay in a well-established but inappropriate job; convey a hardened aspect regarding business; symbolize proficient abusiveness

R Tendency to exemplify dysfunctional security habits; typify inappropriate rigidity regarding safety; demonstrate veteran skill at unhealthy entrapment; evidence expert self-abuse

IF LAYOUT QUESTION HAS A POSITIVE SLANT, THEN:

U Demonstrate maturity regarding work or money; illustrate expertise concerning health or fitness; convey experience with respect to abuse issues; demonstrate proficiency in gardening

R Impart mature sense of stability; convey well-established security; exemplify proficiency regarding staying alive; illustrate effective groundedness

IF LAYOUT QUESTION HAS A NEGATIVE SLANT, THEN:

U Avoid illustrating financial proficiency; don't symbolize business success; hold back on exemplifying well-trained athleticism; restrict well-versed violence

R Forego mature demonstrations of stability or security; withhold demonstrations of a talent for long-term commitments; don't represent a capability for staying alive

THIS CARD AS A QUESTION:

U How do you experience yourself as a mature business person?
What are your well-established physical or athletic talents?
How do you typify financial success?
How hardened are you with regard to abuse or violence?

R What is your professional opinion concerning a sense
of safety?
How do you demonstrate maturity regarding commitment?
Do you fully embody the desire to stay alive?
Are you fully qualified to create long-term security?

Pentacles

KING OF PENTACLES

GENERAL:

U Releasing outworn or unnecessary possessions; moving away from a pattern of sexual expression; completing work on a home or construction project; quitting a job

R Letting go of commitments; terminating a pattern regarding suicide; sharing a sense of groundedness

AS SOMEONE'S POSITIVE ATTRIBUTE:

U Ability to let go of old work habits; move away from a business deal; release abuse patterns; share money or possessions

R Ability to give up old security habits; release worn-out commitments; walk away from old patterns of security; disengage from suicidal tendencies

AS SOMEONE'S NEGATIVE ATTRIBUTE:

U Tendency to lose or spend money; quit jobs; terminate healthy fitness or healing plans; discharge violence

R Tendency to drop useful safety measures; walk away from needed security; let go of important commitments; give up on the will to live

IF LAYOUT QUESTION HAS A POSITIVE SLANT, THEN:

U Let go of the money or possessions; quit the job; share practical skills; disengage from sex

R Release the security; extricate from the commitment; surrender to stability; give up on suicide

IF LAYOUT QUESTION HAS A NEGATIVE SLANT, THEN:

U Don't surrender the financial control; avoid letting go of health or fitness routines; hold back on the option to complete the structure; resist the temptation to quit the job

R Don't let go of the will to live; resist the temptation to walk away from groundedness; avoid releasing security or safety habits; hold back from ending the commitment

THIS CARD AS A QUESTION:

U What work habits are you ready to release?
When will you quit your job?
Can you disengage from your sexual issues?
Why are you relocating?

R What has to happen in order for you to let go of your old security?
Can you release your commitments?
What happened to make you lose your groundedness?
Is there anything that would make you give up on life?

Pentacles

10

The Major Arcana

The following pages contain interpretations for the Major Arcana—with particular emphasis on the theme of relating. Remember that the Major cards represent large life issues, big themes and lessons that can be experienced many ways, even within the context of relating.

Therefore, in addition to the regular upright and reversed interpretations, I've included ways in which each card can represent people, places, things, activities, information, or feelings. These applications make sense depending on the specific questions you ask. For example, if you ask, "Who am I likely to meet at the conference?" and the card you choose in The Magician, it probably means that you'll meet someone who is analytical and discerning. If, on the other hand, you ask what to buy for a friend's birthday and you select The Magician, it shows that an appropriate gift could be something that will help her solve problems. Based on your knowledge of her, you would then decide whether a calculator or a self-help book would be most appropriate! As always, we need to use creativity and common sense when working with the insights of the tarot.

THE FOOL: 0 OR XXII OR 22

FAITH

People: Who are trusting, faith-filled, optimistic, or naive
Places: Where trust is demonstrated, where people of similar faith gather
Things: That symbolize trust, "good faith," or the spirit of belief
Activities: That demonstrate trust, faith, hope
Information: About whether you or others are trustworthy
Feelings: Of believing, having faith, trusting

GENERAL:

U Having faith in the world; experiencing trust or confidence in others; believing that circumstances will ultimately work out positively

R Having faith or confidence in self; trusting in the cosmic scheme of things; having confidence that self can handle everything that arises

AS SOMEONE'S POSITIVE ATTRIBUTE:

U Ability to have faith, confidence, or trust in others; maintain a positive attitude about life or about others; believe in the "goodness" of others

R Ability to have faith, confidence, or trust in self; maintain a positive attitude about self or spirit; believe in the "goodness" of self

AS SOMEONE'S NEGATIVE ATTRIBUTE:

U Tendency to have too much faith, confidence, or trust in others; fantasize that something "out there" will fix things;

R naively assume that everything will turn out okay

Tendency to have too much faith, confidence, or trust in self; imagine self to be super-human or super-hero; believe that own inappropriate behavior is divine will

IF LAYOUT QUESTION HAS A POSITIVE SLANT, THEN:

U Have faith or trust in this person or this situation; believe in the practical possibilities; assume that the worldly details will work out fine

R Have faith, confidence, or trust in self; believe in the psychological possibilities; believe in the divine plan

IF LAYOUT QUESTION HAS A NEGATIVE SLANT, THEN:

U Withdraw from trusting this person; don't get caught up in the fantasy; don't believe that everything will work out okay

R Resist your current instincts; hold back on thinking that this is part of the divine plan; abstain from self-confidence

THIS CARD AS A QUESTION:

U Whom do you trust?

Do you think these circumstances will come out okay?

How do you keep your positive attitude toward life?

R Do you trust yourself?

Do you believe in the positive power of the universe?

How do you maintain your self-confidence?

The Fool

THE MAGICIAN: I OR 1

DISCERNMENT

People: Who are analytical, problem-solvers, discriminating, discerning

Places: Where problems are solved, facts are found, analysis happens

Things: That help solve problems, find answers, contribute to the solution

Activities: That are oriented to logic, analysis, and problem-solving

Information: That is factual, that dispels illusion, that gives answers

Feelings: Of wanting an answer, desiring to clear the illusions

GENERAL:

U Having discernment about other people; utilizing analytical or problem-solving skills in the world; figuring out if something external is based in reality or illusion

R Having discernment about self; analyzing or solving personal problems; figuring out if something internal is based in reality or illusion

AS SOMEONE'S POSITIVE ATTRIBUTE:

U Ability to analyze worldly events; solve the external problem or puzzle; do a "reality-check" to discover what's true

R Ability to analyze self; solve own problems; discern whether inner experience is reality or illusion

AS SOMEONE'S NEGATIVE ATTRIBUTE:

U Tendency to be hypercritical or blameful of others; be overly analytical about others or external events; obsess on practical problem-solving

R Tendency to criticize or blame self too much; overly analyze self; experience self as "the problem" to be solved

IF LAYOUT QUESTION HAS A POSITIVE SLANT, THEN:

U Figure out what's real and what's the illusion in the situation; logically analyze what's going on; solve the problem; look at the facts

R Look at own issues; solve own problems; notice true feelings or experiences, not illusions

IF LAYOUT QUESTION HAS A NEGATIVE SLANT, THEN:

U Avoid being too analytical about others or the situation; stay away from problem-solving; permit the fantasy or illusion to exist in this situation

R Resist analyzing self too much; abstain from blaming self; maintain personal imagination; approach it from the heart

THIS CARD AS A QUESTION:

U What are the facts of the situation?
What's true and what's just an illusion?
How do you evaluate people and circumstances?

R How are you self-analytical?
How do you know when you're trapped in illusion about yourself?
How realistic are you?

The Magician

THE HIGH PRIESTESS: II OR 2

SPIRITUALITY

People: Who are spiritual, intuitive, psychic, spacey, ungrounded

Places: Where spiritual, psychic, or healing activities occur

Things: That aid in spiritual or intuitive insights

Activities: That are spiritual or intuitive in nature

Information: About spirituality or psychic phenomena

Feelings: That are intuitive, sensitive, cosmic, spacey, altered state

GENERAL:

U Meditating in an observable way; publicly assuming the role of psychic, intuitive, or spiritual guide; physically removing self from others or from the world at large

R Privately turning inward; following a personal spiritual path; taking a mental time-out without physically going anywhere

AS SOMEONE'S POSITIVE ATTRIBUTE:

U Ability to be psychically or intuitively sensitive to others; meditate or tune-in; physically remove self from others or from the world

R Ability to rely on inner truth, higher power, spiritual sources; follow own intuition, instincts, hunches; psychologically distance self from others as needed

AS SOMEONE'S NEGATIVE ATTRIBUTE:

U Tendency to invade other people's emotional space; behave in a spacey or vague manner; inappropriately leave or withdraw from the situation

R Tendency to appear to be present while mentally being far away; avoid personal responsibilities; lose track of inner self; drift away

IF LAYOUT QUESTION HAS A POSITIVE SLANT, THEN:

U Open up to intuitions about others and about the world; actively meditate or tune in; physically withdraw from the situation

R Psychologically or mentally withdraw from the situation; discover and embrace personal spirituality; utilize intuition and psychic awareness about self

IF LAYOUT QUESTION HAS A NEGATIVE SLANT, THEN:

U Avoid discussing or displaying your spiritual interests; stay away from demonstrating psychic skills; don't leave the situation

R Avoid spacing out; abstain from getting lost in psychic or intuitive pursuits; curb the urge to get lost in inner space

THIS CARD AS A QUESTION:

U What can you tell me about your active spiritual experiences? Are you interested in psychic or intuitive experiences? Where do you go when you leave?

R Are you curious about my intuitive insights? When do you tend to space out? How can you disassociate while staying physically present?

The High Priestess

THE EMPRESS: III OR 3

NURTURANCE

People: Who are nurturing, caring, supportive, parental
Places: That are comforting, safe, nurturing
Things: That symbolize nurturance, comfort, and support
Activities: That feel safe, supportive, embracing, caring
Information: About safety, comfort, caregiving
Feelings: Of comfort, nurturance, safety, support

GENERAL:

U Nurturing or comforting others; parenting or taking care of others; contributing resources or support to another person or situation

R Nurturing or comforting the self; parenting or taking care of the self; contributing resources or support to self

AS SOMEONE'S POSITIVE ATTRIBUTE:

U Ability to be nurturing or comforting to others; parent or take care of others; contribute resources and support to others

R Ability to nurture or comfort self; parent or take care of self; contribute resources or support to self

AS SOMEONE'S NEGATIVE ATTRIBUTE:

U Tendency to smother others or give unwanted support; drain self in taking care of others; give too much to others

R Tendency to take too much; focus too much on receiving support; be clingy and needy

IF LAYOUT QUESTION HAS A POSITIVE SLANT, THEN:

U Take care of someone or something; be more nurturing or comforting; assume parental responsibility

R Take care of yourself; nurture and comfort yourself; return some of own resources and strength to self

IF LAYOUT QUESTION HAS A NEGATIVE SLANT, THEN:

U Don't get involved in someone else's neediness; abstain from nurturing or taking care of this person; resist the urge to be comforting, supportive, or parental

R Avoid getting lost in your own needs; stay away from self-pity; don't spend all energy or resources on self

THIS CARD AS A QUESTION:

U In what ways do you nurture and care for others?
How do you create an atmosphere of comfort?
What is your parenting style?

R In what ways do you take care of yourself?
What's most comforting or nurturing for you?
How do you like to be parented?

The Empress

THE EMPEROR: IV OR 4

POWER

People: Who are powerful, controlling, forceful, managerial
Places: Where power is found or demonstrated
Things: That symbolize power and authority
Activities: That demonstrate power or organizational influences
Information: About power structure, about influence, authority, empowerment
Feelings: Of power or control

GENERAL:

U Experiencing worldly power, authority, and success; orienting to big business, government, or large organizations; wielding institutionalized power

R Experiencing personal power, inner authority, self-defined success; having inner empowerment or hidden power; being involved with entrepreneurial or small business activities

AS SOMEONE'S POSITIVE ATTRIBUTE:

U Ability to hold and wield position, power, and authority; climb the ladder of worldly success; rise high in big organizations

R Ability to demonstrate personal power or hidden power; achieve personally defined success; run a small business or entrepreneurial venture

AS SOMEONE'S NEGATIVE ATTRIBUTE:

U Tendency to "power-trip" and be controlling of others; obsess on work, career, or material success; hurt others in the climb to success

R Tendency to exert obsessive control on own behavior; take on too much hidden personal responsibility; inappropriately step into small business

IF LAYOUT QUESTION HAS A POSITIVE SLANT, THEN:

U Take control; assume the power; align with the big organization

R Empower yourself; manage your own work; stick with the smaller business or entrepreneurial effort

IF LAYOUT QUESTION HAS A NEGATIVE SLANT, THEN:

U Avoid big business, government, or large organizations; resist the urge to take control or assume power; abstain from focusing on worldly success

R Stay away from small business or entrepreneurial ventures; don't focus so much on empowerment or personal power; forego the urge to wield power behind the scenes

THIS CARD AS A QUESTION:

U How do you assume power within large organizations?
What has power in your life?
What's your status or position in the world?

R How do you empower yourself?
How do you express your personal power?
Do you like working in a small business?

The Emperor

THE HIEROPHANT: V OR 5

MORALITY

People: Who are teachers, preachers, or speakers of philosophy

Places: Where people demonstrate their religious/philosophical preferences

Things: Symbols of specific religious, ethical, or moral systems of belief

Activities: That are oriented to religion, philosophy, ethics, teaching

Information: About religion, philosophy, ethics, morals, or someone's "truth"

Feelings: Of "rightness" about particular beliefs or ethics

GENERAL:

U Expressing external ethical, moral, or religious principles/authority; studying, preaching, teaching, or sharing "the truth"; publicly acting or living according to a deeply held philosophy

R Adhering to personal ethics or principles; teaching self or independently studying a particular philosophy; preaching or teaching, quietly or privately

AS SOMEONE'S POSITIVE ATTRIBUTE:

U Ability to teach, preach, and share "the truth" with others; demonstrate a set of teachings or ethical principles; adhere to moral or philosophical viewpoint

U Ability to live quietly, according to personal philosophy; teach self; teach others in a quiet or unassuming way

AS SOMEONE'S NEGATIVE ATTRIBUTE:

U Tendency to be preachy or pontifical; publicly obsess on a philosophy or religion; loudly proclaim "the truth"

R Tendency to inappropriately restrict self based on morals/beliefs; privately obsess on a particular set of teachings; quietly influence others in negative ways

IF LAYOUT QUESTION HAS A POSITIVE SLANT, THEN:

U Profess and demonstrate philosophy, religion, or ethics; teach, preach, or speak "the truth"; publish information about beliefs

R Privately commit to personal ethics or principles; quietly share beliefs; live "the truth"

IF LAYOUT QUESTION HAS A NEGATIVE SLANT, THEN:

U Don't tell others about "the truth"; hold back on teaching, preaching, or sharing philosophy; resist the urge to publish information about beliefs

R Resist committing to a system of ethics or principles; avoid adhering to a particular moral perspective; don't live according to these standards

THIS CARD AS A QUESTION:

U Do you have religious affiliations? Which ones?
What "truths" do you preach, teach, and share with others?
What do you think is ethical in this situation?

R What are your deepest held beliefs?
By which principles and ethics do you personally live?
How do you share your "truth" with your intimates?

The Hierophant

THE LOVERS: VI OR 6

COOPERATION

People: Who like to cooperate, network, or bring others
              together
Places: Where people can come together on neutral ground
Things: That symbolize collaboration or teamwork
Activities: That reinforce cooperation; teambuilding
Information: Related to partners, cooperative efforts, joint ventures
Feelings: Of being drawn to work or play cooperatively with
              others

GENERAL:

U Experiencing cooperation, collaboration, joining forces;
coming together for the sake of a larger, joint purpose; being
brought together through the intervention of others

R Finding ways that two or more parts of the self can work
together; discovering how two parts of own life can coexist;
cooperating—behind the scenes

AS SOMEONE'S POSITIVE ATTRIBUTE:

U Ability to cooperate and collaborate without losing individuality; work together for highest good of all concerned;
combine forces

R Ability to combine two or more distinct parts of self; work
cooperatively, behind the scenes; use several personal skills

AS SOMEONE'S NEGATIVE ATTRIBUTE:

U Tendency to try to combine two forces that can't mix; inappropriately bring people together; attempt to create cooperation where no cohesion exists

R Tendency to use two or more personal talents that are incompatible; inappropriately force two parts of self to work together; cooperate secretly, to the detriment of all concerned

IF LAYOUT QUESTION HAS A POSITIVE SLANT, THEN:

U Collaborate or cooperate with others; bring others together; join forces for the common good or goal

R Combine own skills into a working whole; find points of agreement between parts of self; cooperate, behind the scenes

IF LAYOUT QUESTION HAS A NEGATIVE SLANT, THEN:

U Avoid collaborating or cooperating with others; don't get into bringing others together; stay away from joining forces with others

R Oppose the attempt to combine various parts of the self into one; resist the urge to collaborate behind the scenes; separate own skills

THIS CARD AS A QUESTION:

U How do you cooperate or collaborate with others?
Do you want to join forces for a common good?
Who could connect us with the others?

R How do you combine your various talents and skills?
How do you bring the parts of your self together?
Do you ever quietly collaborate, behind the scenes?

The Lovers

THE CHARIOT: VII OR 7

CONTROL

People: Who hold the reins or control, facilitate, and direct the change

Places: Where rapid change occurs in controlled circumstances

Things: That help people to lead, direct, and manage during changes

Activities: Related to controlling, directing, or facilitating the change

Information: About who holds the reins; about how to manage the rapid growth

Feelings: Of things moving so quickly that they are just barely in control

GENERAL:

U Holding the reins or guiding the behavior of others; directing or controlling the fast-moving action; facilitating, guiding, or coordinating the project

R Facilitating own inner process; directing or controlling rapid personal change or growth; staying in charge of own behavior

AS SOMEONE'S POSITIVE ATTRIBUTE:

U Ability to stay in control when everything is moving very quickly; direct or coordinate others in a complex project; facilitate the group process

R Ability to manage own, multifaceted and rapid, growth; direct own behavior; facilitate ongoing personal growth

AS SOMEONE'S NEGATIVE ATTRIBUTE:

U Tendency to try to manage the unmanageable; coordinate something that can't be externally controlled; inappropriately facilitate the group process

R Tendency to inappropriately direct own rapid growth or change; unsuccessfully try to control self; pull in the reins on self too much

IF LAYOUT QUESTION HAS A POSITIVE SLANT, THEN:

U Seize the reins; become the director; facilitate the rapid changes of others

R Manage your own multilevel growth; be your own director; coordinate own progress

IF LAYOUT QUESTION HAS A NEGATIVE SLANT, THEN:

U Avoid trying to manage the chaos; don't step in as the facilitator of the rapid growth and change; abstain from directing others

R Step away from trying to control own growth and change; resist the urge to coordinate own process; don't guide the fast-moving personal changes

THIS CARD AS A QUESTION:

U How do you facilitate the changes of others?
In what manner do you lead, guide, and direct others?
How do you steer a straight course through the chaos?

R Are you in charge of your own growth and development?
How do you manage your personal evolution?
Can you control your own rapid growth?

The Chariot

STRENGTH: VIII OR 8; XI OR 11

SURVIVAL

People: Who are survivors of physical or psychological hardships

Places: Where people build strength or come together to celebrate survival

Things: That help people become stronger; that symbolize survival

Activities: That strengthen people either physically, financially, or emotionally

Information: Regarding physical or emotional survival or strength

Feelings: Of strength, determination, survival, coping

GENERAL:

U Experiencing physical or economic survival; demonstrating physical strength; acting out "animal" nature or behavior

R Experiencing emotional or psychological survival; demonstrating emotional strength; utilizing gut instincts

AS SOMEONE'S POSITIVE ATTRIBUTE:

U Ability to survive physically or financially; act according to animal nature; demonstrate physical strength

R Ability to survive at an emotional or psychological level; demonstrate emotional strength; utilize gut instincts

AS SOMEONE'S NEGATIVE ATTRIBUTE:

U Tendency to experience life as a fight or a struggle to survive; inappropriately contribute to survival of something; get lost in animalistic behavior

R Tendency to struggle unnecessarily for emotional survival; use outworn, compulsive, survival mechanisms; inappropriately utilize gut instincts

IF LAYOUT QUESTION HAS A POSITIVE SLANT, THEN:

U Hang on, fight the fight; keep it physically or financially alive; get in touch with animal nature

R Ensure emotional survival; take care of psychological well-being at any cost; follow gut instincts

IF LAYOUT QUESTION HAS A NEGATIVE SLANT, THEN:

U Don't fight so hard; let go of the struggle; avoid seeing the world as a survival mission; stay away from animal behavior

R Don't get into the emotional struggle; resist the thought that psychological survival is at stake; restrict gut instincts

THIS CARD AS A QUESTION:

U How did you survive physically or financially?
What do you do when times get tough?
How do you relate to animals?

R How did you survive emotionally or psychologically?
What's your inner coping strategy in difficult situations?
Are you in touch with your gut instincts?

Strength

THE HERMIT: IX OR 9

KNOWLEDGE

People: Who know the answer, lend perspective, think things through

Places: Where people can go on retreat or get some distance on things

Things: That help people get perspective, that reveal the truth

Activities: That encourage people to get a new perspective or find information

Information: About what really happened; related to retreat experiences

Feelings: Of needing to withdraw, sort out the truth, get perspective

GENERAL:

U Having awareness, information, or facts about others; holding or representing the knowledge or wisdom of the group; stepping back to gain perspective on the situation

R Having self-awareness or self-knowledge; knowing or reflecting the truth about self; gaining perspective or wisdom about self

AS SOMEONE'S POSITIVE ATTRIBUTE:

U Ability to know or understand the facts about the situation; physically withdraw in order to gain perspective; hold or represent the wisdom of the group

R Ability to turn inward for self-knowledge; psychologically withdraw to gain perspective; hold or reflect own wisdom

AS SOMEONE'S NEGATIVE ATTRIBUTE:

U Tendency to carry and remember useless information or facts; withdraw in order to gain perspective—and not return; reflect the dubious knowledge of a dysfunctional group

R Tendency to be completely withdrawn into own point of view; be egotistical about knowing or holding information; obsess about personal awareness

IF LAYOUT QUESTION HAS A POSITIVE SLANT, THEN:

U Get more knowledge or facts about people or events; take some time to think things over and gain some perspective; shine the light of wisdom on the situation

R Turn inward for knowledge or awareness about self; psychologically withdraw in order to think about self; accept own wisdom

IF LAYOUT QUESTION HAS A NEGATIVE SLANT, THEN:

U Avoid finding the truth; don't step back and get perspective on this; resist the urge to withdraw physically from the situation

R Counteract personal knowledge and awareness; restrict the urge to withdraw emotionally; don't try to gain perspective on yourself

THIS CARD AS A QUESTION:

U How do you get perspective on things?
What happens when you take time out to think things over?
How can we find the facts, information, or the truth?

R How do you get perspective on yourself?
How will I know if you've withdrawn emotionally?
Are you able to gain perspective on yourself?

The Hermit

THE WHEEL OF FORTUNE: X OR 10

CAUSE/EFFECT

People: Who are able to do their part and then detach

Places: Where people set things in motion and then wait for responses

Things: That support people to initiate action and then wait

Activities: Involved with starting something and then waiting for reactions

Information: About taking personal responsibility and practicing detachment

Feelings: Willingness to do one's part and leave the rest for others

GENERAL:

U Setting something tangible in motion and waiting for a response; initiating a practical action and seeing what happens; doing all that can be done and noticing the outcome

R Getting things going psychically and letting the universe respond; taking emotional action and sensing the reactions; initiating hidden or private action and observing the result

AS SOMEONE'S POSITIVE ATTRIBUTE:

U Ability to set something tangible in motion and notice the effect; initiate practical action and wait for the payoff; do what needs to be done and watch for consequences

R Ability to initiate movement psychically and wait for a reply; set things in motion emotionally and notice responses; start a hidden or private action and observe results

AS SOMEONE'S NEGATIVE ATTRIBUTE:

U Tendency to initiate action and inappropriately drop responsibility; start something destructive and ignore the consequences; set problematic things in motion, disregarding the effect

R Tendency to expect the universe to "fix" it while taking no action; set emotional "games" in motion to watch the effect; start unsound, covert activity and avoid responsibility

IF LAYOUT QUESTION HAS A POSITIVE SLANT, THEN:

U Do your share at a practical level, then wait for a response; set it in motion tangibly and be curious about what might happen; start something in the real world and observe the reactions

R Set it in motion intuitively, then notice the universe's feedback; begin things in a private way, then notice the consequences; initiate emotional action and sense the response

IF LAYOUT QUESTION HAS A NEGATIVE SLANT, THEN:

U Take practical action without releasing control; don't set it in motion if you're expecting a response; avoid starting things in the real world and waiting for a reaction

R Abstain from initiating things psychically if expecting results; don't set private things in motion in order to watch the reactions; curb the urge to take emotional actions for the sake of a response

THIS CARD AS A QUESTION:

U How do you know when you've done enough at a
    practical level?
Can you take action, and detach yourself from the outcome?
If you set something in motion, do you notice the responses?

R Do you trust the universe to respond to your psychic pleas?
How do you initiate emotional actions and observe reactions?
If you start things privately, do you consider the
    consequences?

The Wheel of Fortune

JUSTICE: XI OR 11; VIII OR 8

EQUILIBRIUM

People: Who are able to create peace, maintain balance and harmony

Places: That are peaceful; that are conducive to maintaining balance

Things: That support the establishment of peace and harmony

Activities: That are oriented to creating harmony, balance, and equilibrium

Information: About ways to make peace, establish equilibrium

Feelings: Of harmony, equilibrium, and balance

GENERAL:

U Establishing balance in a real-world situation; experiencing equilibrium within the practical circumstances; creating harmony among the people

R Experiencing internal equilibrium; establishing personal balance; sensing inner harmony

AS SOMEONE'S POSITIVE ATTRIBUTE:

U Ability to be the peacemaker for others; establish practical equilibrium; create tangible harmony

R Ability to maintain personal equilibrium; stay in balance, internally; experience harmony

AS SOMEONE'S NEGATIVE ATTRIBUTE:

U Tendency to attempt to create harmony when it's impossible; ignore real issues while trying to be the peacemaker; try to reach equilibrium in a totally unstable situation

R Tendency to stay calm at great cost to self; reach for inner harmony to escape or avoid problems; search for personal equilibrium at great cost to others

IF LAYOUT QUESTION HAS A POSITIVE SLANT, THEN:

U Create harmony in the situation; establish practical equilibrium; be the peacemaker among these people

R Find inner balance; establish personal equilibrium; search for individual harmony

IF LAYOUT QUESTION HAS A NEGATIVE SLANT, THEN:

U Don't try to establish balance in this situation; avoid making peace among these people; counteract the attempt to create harmony here

R Don't rush into finding personal equilibrium; allow things to be out of balance for awhile; abstain from seeking individual harmony

THIS CARD AS A QUESTION:

U How do you make peace with others?
How do you help people get along and stay in harmony?
Can you establish a practical equilibrium in this situation?

R How do you maintain your inner equilibrium?
How do you find personal harmony and a sense of balance?
How do you stay centered?

Justice

THE HANGED MAN: XII OR 12

WAITING

People: Who are able to wait patiently until the time is right to act

Places: In which people wait for the appropriate time or circumstances

Things: That symbolize waiting for the right time or situation

Activities: That involve waiting for the appropriate circumstances

Information: About the best time, place, and situation in which to take action

Feelings: Of feeling ready, of knowing when it's time to act

GENERAL:

U Waiting for the right outer circumstances in which to act; hanging around until the time is right; observing outer events, and moving forward at the correct time

R Waiting to feel ready internally, before acting; patiently accepting personal lack of preparedness; letting self hesitate until inner self is motivated to act

AS SOMEONE'S POSITIVE ATTRIBUTE:

U Ability to wait for the appropriate circumstances before acting; consider the practical timing of events; move forward only when it's appropriate

R Ability to wait until internally ready before taking action; pause while inner self prepares for next step; allow self to remain in limbo until the time is right

AS SOMEONE'S NEGATIVE ATTRIBUTE:

U Tendency to wait too long (forever?) for better circumstances; avoid needed action by saying the timing is not right; procrastinate by thinking a better opportunity will arise

R Tendency to avoid taking necessary action by feeling "unready"; indefinitely maintain inner lack of preparedness; stay in personal limbo too long

IF LAYOUT QUESTION HAS A POSITIVE SLANT, THEN:

U Wait for better timing; act according to the outer indicators; be patient until the circumstances are right

R Wait until self is internally ready to act; consider personal timing; move forward; be patient with own pace and progress

IF LAYOUT QUESTION HAS A NEGATIVE SLANT, THEN:

U Avoid thinking that better opportunities will come along; counteract the notion that the timing is wrong; resist the urge to wait for improved circumstances

R Avoid the assumption that self will be more prepared later; don't procrastinate at a personal level; withdraw from the inner limbo

THIS CARD AS A QUESTION:

U How do you know when the situation is right for action?
When will the outer circumstances be right for you?
What is the appropriate timing for this action?

R How will you know when you're ready to make the next step?
Can you tell the difference between procrastination and patience?
How long will it take you to become prepared?

The Hanged Man

DEATH: XIII OR 13

TRANSFORMATION

People: Who are going through transformation; who are
                agents of transition

Places: Where transformation, transition, death, or birth
                occur

Things: That symbolize or create transformation, transition,
                death, or birth

Activities: Related to letting go, releasing, transition, or trans-
                formation

Information: About transformation, transition, death, or birth

Feelings: Of transformation, death and rebirth, complete and
                total transition

GENERAL:

U Experiencing tangible transformation; participating in
birth, death, or near-death situations; making complete
change at visible level

R Going through complete inner transformation; experiencing
major psychological transition; undergoing emotional birth,
death, or rebirth

AS SOMEONE'S POSITIVE ATTRIBUTE:

U Ability to completely transform things or people; participate
in situations involving birth or death; cause or experience
total, tangible change

R Ability to engage in major psychological change; experience
deep emotional transition; step into personal spiritual transformation

AS SOMEONE'S NEGATIVE ATTRIBUTE:

U Tendency to destroy or harm people or things; express the potential for violence; dangerously transform the circumstances

R Tendency to engage in emotional abuse; be addicted to emotional trauma and upheaval; undergo unhealthy inner transformation

IF LAYOUT QUESTION HAS A POSITIVE SLANT, THEN:

U Transform it at a tangible level; take the people through a complete transition; totally release it and start over

R Step into emotional transformation; engage in deep spiritual work; quietly make a major change, behind the scenes

IF LAYOUT QUESTION HAS A NEGATIVE SLANT, THEN:

U Don't throw it away; resist the urge to transform it completely; avoid destroying or abusing it

R Don't get into inner transformation; abstain from psychological transitions and upheavals; curb the urge toward personal death/rebirth experiences

THIS CARD AS A QUESTION:

U What kinds of transformative experiences have you had?
How do you know when it's time to let go and start over?
How comfortable are you, with regard to death (or birth)?

R What has been your deepest emotional transition?
How has spirituality touched you at the core?
Have you privately transformed things?

Death

TEMPERANCE: XIV OR 14

CREATIVITY

People: Who are artistic or creative; who combine others into groups

Places: Where art and creativity happen; where people join forces in unity

Things: That symbolize the arts; that bind people together

Activities: That are creative or artistic; that demonstrate wholeness or unity

Information: About creativity; about wholeness and integration

Feelings: Of creative expression; of wholeness, unity, integration

GENERAL:

U Uniting individuals or groups into new groups; merging ideas into larger, new concepts; creatively combining things into new wholes

R Experiencing a sense of personal wholeness; integrating parts of self into a cohesive whole; having an inner sense of creativity

AS SOMEONE'S POSITIVE ATTRIBUTE:

U Ability to create or make art; blend things or ideas into new wholes; bring people together and unify them

R Ability to sense internal wholeness; see self as a work of art; integrate various aspects of personality

AS SOMEONE'S NEGATIVE ATTRIBUTE:

U Tendency to inappropriately force people to come together; try to blend ideas or things that are incompatible; create dubious or destructive art

R Tendency to submerge creativity under other parts of the self; inappropriately integrate parts of personal life; completely lose self in the pursuit of art

IF LAYOUT QUESTION HAS A POSITIVE SLANT, THEN:

U Bring people together; make art; be creative; combine these ideas or things

R Make yourself whole; experience personal integration; combine different parts of you into one organic experience

IF LAYOUT QUESTION HAS A NEGATIVE SLANT, THEN:

U Resist the temptation to bring these people together; avoid combining these ideas or things; don't focus on art or creative expression right now

R Abstain from losing part of self in the other parts of life; curb the urge to blend one part of your life into another part; don't hide your art

THIS CARD AS A QUESTION:

U How are you artistic or creative?
When and how do you bring people together?
Can you merge or combine these ideas or things?

R What do you do to feel personally whole?
How do you integrate the various parts of your life?
Do you have a secret desire to be an artist?

Temperance

THE DEVIL: XV OR 15

STRUCTURE

People: Who set boundaries and limits; who take responsibility
Places: Where limits are set; where responsibility is taken
Things: That symbolize boundaries, limits, or responsibility
Activities: That involve setting limits, creating boundaries, being responsible
Information: About who's responsible; about boundaries and limits
Feelings: Of being responsible; dealing with limits or boundaries

GENERAL:

U Building or valuing structure; setting or utilizing boundaries and limits with others; participating in responsible, orderly action

R Setting boundaries for self; engaging in self-limiting behavior; exerting psychological control, mental orderliness; experiencing inner foundations or structure

AS SOMEONE'S POSITIVE ATTRIBUTE:

U Ability to set or adhere to practical boundaries or limits; create basic structure; behave in a responsible manner

R Ability to set limits for own behavior; create or experience solid inner structures; control own psyche or mind

AS SOMEONE'S NEGATIVE ATTRIBUTE:

U Tendency to rigidly adhere to inappropriate boundaries in the system; construct limiting or unsafe structures; become responsible for destructive behavior

R Tendency to limit self too much; construct inner, constricting, walls; rigidly or cruelly control the mind

IF LAYOUT QUESTION HAS A POSITIVE SLANT, THEN:

U Set external boundaries and limits; create basic structure; be responsible for the behavior or actions

R Set limits for self; respect personal boundaries; be responsible for the feelings or thoughts

IF LAYOUT QUESTION HAS A NEGATIVE SLANT, THEN:

U Resist taking responsibility for the people or situation; curb the urge to set or honor boundaries with others; oppose the creation of basic structure

R Abstain from setting boundaries for self; counteract the inner walls; avoid taking personal responsibility

THIS CARD AS A QUESTION:

U How do you create structure for people or organizations?
How do you set or honor boundaries with others?
Will you assume responsibility in the situation?

R How and when do you set limits and boundaries for yourself?
When do you restrict yourself?
In what circumstances do you take responsibility for yourself?

The Devil

THE TOWER: XVI OR 16

CATALYST

People: Who shatter or reform the status quo; who change existing beliefs

Places: Where changes and reforms occur; where beliefs are changed

Things: That shatter the existing structure; that are agents of change

Activities: That change the system or shatter the status quo; reform movements

Information: About if and how to challenge the existing structure or beliefs

Feelings: Of being shattered; of reformist zeal; of breakthrough

GENERAL:

U Being a catalyst or agent of change; experiencing a shake-up in the system or shattering of structure; changing beliefs about other people or the world

R Challenging or catalyzing the self to change; changing beliefs about self; exploding the inner structure

AS SOMEONE'S POSITIVE ATTRIBUTE:

U Ability to be an agent of change or reform; achieve breakthroughs in the system or structure; change beliefs about other people or the world

R Ability to commit self to change or reform; experience personal breakthroughs; change beliefs about self

AS SOMEONE'S NEGATIVE ATTRIBUTE:

U Tendency to inappropriately shatter existing structures; challenge healthy beliefs about people or the world; rebel in a destructive manner

R Tendency to challenge the self in a dysfunctional way; shatter own fragile structures; change healthy beliefs about self

IF LAYOUT QUESTION HAS A POSITIVE SLANT, THEN:

U Change beliefs and attitudes about people or the world; reform or challenge the existing structures; move toward breakthroughs

R Change beliefs or attitudes about the self; reform self; have a personal breakthrough

IF LAYOUT QUESTION HAS A NEGATIVE SLANT, THEN:

U Resist the urge to challenge or shatter the existing structure; don't change your beliefs or opinions about people or the world; abstain from reforming the system

R Counteract the challenge to change self; avoid reforming beliefs about self; don't get into secret destruction of the system

THIS CARD AS A QUESTION:

U How do you challenge other people to change?
What attitudes about others have you had to change?
When will you shatter the existing structure?

R How do you know when it's time for you to hatch?
What beliefs about yourself have you had to change?
Can you reform yourself?

The Tower

THE STAR: XVII OR 17

RESOURCES

People: Who are able to channel the flow of money, skills, or resources

Places: Where money, resources, or energy are moved and directed

Things: That symbolize the flow of energy, money, or other resources

Activities: That result in the movement of money, energy, or resources

Information: About the movement of money, energy, or resources

Feelings: Of abundance; of plenty

GENERAL:

U Directing resources, money, or abundance to others; channeling energy or things to people; bringing needed supplies into the situation

R Directing resources, money, or abundance to self; channeling the energy or emotional resources to self; receiving needed supplies

AS SOMEONE'S POSITIVE ATTRIBUTE:

U Ability to direct the flow of resources to people; move money, skills, or things to appropriate places; bring energy or support to situation

R Ability to draw or attract energy, money, or resources to self; receive abundance or supplies; call in emotional resources

AS SOMEONE'S NEGATIVE ATTRIBUTE:

U Tendency to negatively manipulate the flow of money or resources; direct the energy to inappropriate people or places; support a dysfunctional system

R Tendency to inappropriately pull money or resources to the self; be greedy; drain the resources of others

IF LAYOUT QUESTION HAS A POSITIVE SLANT, THEN:

U Direct the flow of money or application of skills; channel the resources and energy to others; bring energy or support into the situation

R Allow self to receive abundance; draw energy, money, or resources to self; receive support

IF LAYOUT QUESTION HAS A NEGATIVE SLANT, THEN:

U Don't manipulate the flow of money or resources; abstain from sending the energy to others; withdraw the support in this situation

R Restrict the flow of resources or money to self; avoid directing the feelings to the self; stay away from getting support

THIS CARD AS A QUESTION:

U How do you create or handle abundance?
How do you direct the flow of money to others?
Can you support this person or situation?

R How do you attract abundance to you?
How do you allow yourself to receive money?
Can you take in emotional support?

The Star

THE MOON: XVIII OR 18

GUIDANCE

People: Who tend to give feedback, insight, or guidance
Places: Where feedback, insight, or guidance is given
Things: That symbolize or strengthen the reception of
                guidance or insight
Activities: That involve giving or receiving feedback or guidance
Information: About how to get feedback; that is useful as guidance
                or insight
Feelings: Of ah-hah!; of insight; of flashes of guidance or
                inspiration

GENERAL:

U Receiving guidance, messages, or indicators from others; noticing omens and portents, signs and signals; getting feedback from outside sources

R Receiving inner guidance; tuning in to intuition or hunches; experiencing guidance through dreams or visions

AS SOMEONE'S POSITIVE ATTRIBUTE:

U Ability to receive guidance or feedback from others; pay attention to outer signs and signals; watch for external indicators

R Ability to pay attention to inner guidance or intuition; listening to the messages of dreams or hunches; receive subtle signals

AS SOMEONE'S NEGATIVE ATTRIBUTE:

U Tendency to watch obsessively for omens and signals; depend too much on others for guidance or direction; overly rely on outside feedback

R Tendency to be obsessed with the messages of dreams; confuse emotional dysfunction with intuition; disguise own desires as inner signals or hunches

IF LAYOUT QUESTION HAS A POSITIVE SLANT, THEN:

U Listen to others; pay attention to external guidance; get feedback

R Pay attention to inner voice; listen to intuition or hunches; attend to the guidance in personal dreams or visions

IF LAYOUT QUESTION HAS A NEGATIVE SLANT, THEN:

U Don't utilize the guidance from others; resist the outside messages; oppose this feedback

R Don't pay attention to your inner voice(s); ignore the messages in these dreams; avoid the hunches or intuitive signals

THIS CARD AS A QUESTION:

U How do you seek guidance from others?
Can you take external feedback?
Can you listen to what they have to say?

R Do you pay attention to your own inner guidance?
How do you utilize the insight from your dreams or intuition?
What's your hunch about this?

The Moon

THE SUN: XIX OR 19

REBIRTH

People: Who are able to re-energize or revitalize people, projects, or things

Places: Where rebirth, revitalization, or repair occur

Things: That have been revitalized or repaired; that aid the rebirth process

Activities: That involve re-energizing, rebirthing, or renewing people or things

Information: About how or whether to renew or re-inspire some thing or someone

Feelings: Of renewal, revitalization, rebirth

GENERAL:

U Renewing the energy in the situation; revitalizing others; repeating past actions in a slightly altered way

R Revitalizing the self; re-energizing or recharging the self; repeating past feelings, with a few adjustments

AS SOMEONE'S POSITIVE ATTRIBUTE:

U Ability to renew the enthusiasm or energy for a project; revitalize and re-inspire people; redo it with a few adjustments

R Ability to renew personal energy; recharge self and start over; revisit old feelings with new perspective

AS SOMEONE'S NEGATIVE ATTRIBUTE:

U Tendency to inappropriately re-inspire others; do only a superficial or "cosmetic" adjustment; repeat same dysfunctional behavior in a new disguise

R Tendency to renew dysfunctional attitudes; make minor changes without solving inner problems; disguise same old emotional games in new language

IF LAYOUT QUESTION HAS A POSITIVE SLANT, THEN:

U Revitalize or renew this project; give people new inspiration; re-energize the relationship with slight alterations

R Revitalize the self; renew personal commitment in slightly adapted form; rebirth the self without losing what was valuable from before

IF LAYOUT QUESTION HAS A NEGATIVE SLANT, THEN:

U Don't keep resurrecting this old interpersonal game; curb the urge to revitalize this project; avoid redoing the same old behavior in a new disguise

R Don't put a "cosmetic fix" on the self; avoid re-engaging in a particular emotional state; restrict the urge to engage in same old feelings

THIS CARD AS A QUESTION:

U How can you revitalize or re-energize this relationship?
How do you breathe new life into something?
In what ways are you adapting, yet repeating, past behavior?

R How can you re-energize or rebirth yourself?
Can you make a few inner changes but keep the core intact?
Are you repeating the same emotional cycle in new forms?

The Sun

JUDGEMENT: XX OR 20

GRADUATION

People: Who have graduated, retired, or been promoted
Places: Where graduation, evolution, retirements, or promotions occur
Things: That symbolize graduation, promotion, or moving on
Activities: That relate to graduation, promotion, retirement, or moving on
Information: Regarding graduation, retirement, promotion, or maturation
Feelings: Of moving on, evolving to new levels, aging

GENERAL:

U Graduating or retiring; experiencing a promotion or upgrade; reaching puberty, menopause; experiencing cues regarding aging

R Experiencing an inner sense of emotional "graduation"; engaging in personal evolution; becoming aware of inner growth or subtle aging cues

AS SOMEONE'S POSITIVE ATTRIBUTE:

U Ability to grow in skills and be promoted; embrace puberty, menopause, retirement; upgrade or improve the system

R Ability to personally evolve or grow up; become subtly aware of inner aging cues; "graduate" from past emotional games

AS SOMEONE'S NEGATIVE ATTRIBUTE:

U Tendency to move on, graduate, or retire inappropriately; age prematurely; obsessively (or expensively) upgrade the system

R Tendency to be overly involved with inner evolution; "leave behind" emotions that could be useful signals; obsessively examine subtle aging cues

IF LAYOUT QUESTION HAS A POSITIVE SLANT, THEN:

U Graduate, retire, take the promotion, step into the next phase; embrace puberty, menopause, or other phases of aging; upgrade or improve it

R Grow up internally and emotionally; evolve the self into new phases; allow the self to reach a new level of awareness or maturity

IF LAYOUT QUESTION HAS A NEGATIVE SLANT, THEN:

U Don't graduate, move on, take the promotion, or retire; combat the aging process; avoid upgrading, improving, or getting a bigger or better one

R Restrict obsessive personal growth; don't leave these emotional patterns behind; resist the feeling of inner maturity

THIS CARD AS A QUESTION:

U How will you graduate, seek a promotion, or retire?
What would it take to upgrade it?
Can you embrace this natural phase of life?

R How do you evolve or mature yourself?
Which of your emotions emerge from the aging process?
Do you really think you're internally mature enough?

Judgement

THE WORLD: XXI OR 21

CHOICE

People: Who are multidimensional; who explore options and possibilities

Places: Where many choices are available

Things: That symbolize choices, opportunities, or a "world" of options

Activities: That involve choices, options, and alternatives

Information: About the many choices and possibilities that are available

Feelings: Of open-endedness, multidimensionalness, opportunity

GENERAL:

U Experiencing choices, options, and alternatives; noticing the open doors and possibilities; knowing that the whole world is, literally, available to you

R Experiencing inner choices and personal possibilities; noticing the psychological or emotional alternatives; knowing that the self is multidimensional; inner worlds are open

AS SOMEONE'S POSITIVE ATTRIBUTE:

U Ability to generate or embrace lots of options and alternatives; notice and consider many choices; view the world as full of possibilities

R Ability to experience multidimensional aspects of self; notice many different emotional options; operate from a choice-centered perspective

AS SOMEONE'S NEGATIVE ATTRIBUTE:

U Tendency to juggle too many alternatives and possibilities; keep all options open, avoiding decisions; escape into the world

R Tendency to feel fractured into various parts of self; become emotionally paralyzed by too many options; pursue inner worlds at great cost to the self or others

IF LAYOUT QUESTION HAS A POSITIVE SLANT, THEN:

U Embrace the real possibilities; hold open the options; consider many practical choices

R Explore all the parts of self; consider the ways in which self is multidimensional; explore inner worlds

IF LAYOUT QUESTION HAS A NEGATIVE SLANT, THEN:

U Don't keep juggling all the practical options and choices; abstain from creating more alternatives; resist the urge to travel the world

R Don't get into multidimensional realities; avoid exploring the inner world; curb the urge to explore emotional options

THIS CARD AS A QUESTION:

U How do you handle all the choices and opportunities?
Have you considered all the possibilities?
Can you think at the international level?

R How do you experience your multidimensionalness?
How do you explore your inner world?
What's the range of your personal emotions?

The World

Author's Afterword

There you have it. This is what I know, to date, about using the tarot to elucidate the process of choice-centered relating. If at least one comment or sample layout or interpretation has helped you to broaden your understanding of relating, I'm satisfied. I know that your ways of interacting with others will continue to evolve over time, just as mine continue to evolve. Furthermore, your experience of the tarot will deepen over time, just as mine continues to deepen. What I hope you've gained from this book is an expanded sense of yourself as a person who makes creative, effective choices within the context of relating. I'd love to hear your comments and feedback. Contact me at the following address:

Gail Fairfield
P. O. Box 8
Smithville, IN 47458
phone: USA (812) 331-0501
e-mail: gailfair@kiva.net

www.gailfairfield.com

Please give me time to answer! I may be traveling when you e-mail or write.

Brief Bibliography

Arrien, Angeles. *The Tarot Handbook: Practical Applications of Ancient Visual Symbols*. Sonoma, CA: Arcus, 1987.

Bridges, Carol. *The Medicine Woman Inner Guidebook: A Woman's Guide to Her Unique Powers*. Stamford, CT: U. S. Games Systems, Inc., 1990.

Butler, Bill. *Dictionary of the Tarot*. New York: Schocken Books, 1977.

Eakins, Pamela. *Tarot of the Spirit*. York Beach, ME: Samuel Weiser, 1992.

Fairfield, Gail. *Choice Centered Tarot*. York Beach, ME: Samuel Weiser, 1984, 1997.

Greer, Mary. *Tarot for Yourself*. North Hollywood, CA: Newcastle, 1984.

Noble, Vicki. *Motherpeace: A Way to the Goddess through Myth, Art, and Tarot*. San Francisco: HarperSanFrancisco, 1983.

Riley, Jana. *Tarot Dictionary and Compendium*. York Beach, ME: Samuel Weiser, 1995.

Wanless, James. *Voyager Tarot: Way of the Great Oracle*. Carmel, CA: Merrill-West, 1989.

Index

Gail Fairfield was born in China and raised in Japan by missionary parents who encouraged her to discover her own answers to life's questions. After college studies in psychology and education, she was intuitively drawn to the tarot in 1973. Since then, she has been teaching classes and workshops, doing business and personal consultations, and has developed her choice-centered orientation to the tarot and to life. She is the author of the best-selling *Choice Centered Tarot* (Weiser) and *Choice Centered Astrology* (Weiser).